Virtual Private Networks

Addison-Wesley Professional Computing Series

Brian W. Kernighan, Consulting Editor

Please see our web site (http://www.awl.com/cseng/series/professionalcomputing) for more information on these titles.

Virtual Private Networks

Technologies and Solutions

Ruixi Yuan
W. Timothy Strayer

Addison-Wesley

Boston • San Francisco • New York • Toronto • Montreal
London • Munich • Paris • Madrid
Capetown • Sydney • Tokyo • Singapore • Mexico City

The publisher offers discounts on this book when ordered in quantity for special sales. For more information, please contact:

Pearson Education Corporate Sales Division
One Lake Street
Upper Saddle River, NJ 07458
(800) 382-3419
corpsales@pearsontechgroup.com

Visit AW on the Web: www.awl.com/cseng/

Library of Congress Cataloging-in-Publication Data

Yuan, Ruixi.
    Virtual private networks : technologies and solutions / Ruixi Yuan, W. Timothy Strayer.
       p. cm.
    Includes bibliographical references and index.
    ISBN 0-201-70209-6
       1. Extranets (Computer networks) I. Strayer, W. Timothy. II. Title

    TK5105.875.E87 Y93 2001
    004.6--dc21

                                                                    2001018848

The Chinese characters on the front of this book are pronounced "Xu Ni Zhuan Wang" and literally mean "virtually simulated dedicated network."

ISBN 0-201-70209-6
Text printed on recycled paper
1 2 3 4 5 6 7 8 9 10—MA—0504030201
First printing, April 2001

To my parents.
    —Ruixi Yuan

*To my family, extended and immediate,
especially Carmen, Ellie, and Abby.*
    —Tim Strayer

Contents

Part II VPN Technologies   55

Chapter 4 Tunnels   57

Chapter 5 IPsec   75

Chapter 6 Authentication   103

Preface

The Internet has been around in one form or another for more than three decades now, but it really has been since the middle of the 1990s that the use of the Internet became a daily part of people's lives. Connectivity to the Internet is now imperative for almost all companies, regardless of what their business really is. Individuals can find Internet access at school, work, and home, in cafés and kiosks, and in cell phones and PDAs. Staying connected has become an obsession.

The focus has shifted from being connected to being *securely* connected. It is one thing to have Internet access, but without security, the usefulness of the connectivity is rather limited. People want to have the reach of the Internet, but they should not have to compromise their privacy or expose proprietary resources.

Fortunately, all of the ingredients are present for constructing a private network on top of a public one. The challenge comes in putting the technologies together so that the result is a viable and secure *virtual private network*.

This book provides a comprehensive guide to the technologies used to enable VPNs, the VPN products built from these technologies, and the combinations of various components to provide practical VPN solutions.

VPN technologies and solutions are still rapidly evolving. This book describes the current state of the art in this field. But things change quickly, so when appropriate, we have attempted to point out the continued effort in the industry to develop new technologies and solutions.

Audience

This book is intended for a broad range of readers interested in virtual private networks.

For network engineers and managers, this book serves as a practical guide to the technologies and solutions. It discusses issues to be considered in designing and implementing a VPN.

For VPN software and hardware developers, it provides the necessary background material to understand the functions to be developed and the rationale behind them.

For IT managers and executives, this book sets the overall context of VPNs and provides the means for assessing various implementations from equipment vendors and service offerings from service providers.

For students and educators, this book can be used as a reference text for a course in network security or electronic commerce.

Book Organization

This book is organized in three parts. Part I—VPN Fundamentals—consists of three chapters: *Introduction*, *Basic Concepts*, and *VPN Architectures*. Chapter 1 introduces the concept of VPN and how it permits flexibility in facilitating private communication in a public network. We also classify the relevant technologies into four distinct categories. Chapter 2 sets VPNs in context by briefly reviewing the development of the Internet and how security has been thrust to the forefront. It also reviews the basic IP networking and cryptography concepts that pertain to VPNs. Chapter 3 presents VPN architectures in two ways. The first approach is based on designing VPN around practical networking solutions: site-to-site intranet, extranet, and remote access. The second approach focuses on the different traffic aggregation points where security services are applied.

Part II—VPN Technologies—consists of five chapters: *Tunnels, IPsec, Authentication, Public Key Infrastructure,* and *Access Control*. Chapter 4 is concerned with the most important technology category—tunneling. We investigate the many different tunneling technologies that are important in VPN solutions. Chapter 5 concentrates on IPsec, the security protocol for IP standardized by the IETF and, in our opinion, the VPN tunneling technology that will be most prevalent going forward. Chapter 6 describes authentication in a broad context first and then describes the various two-party and three-party schemes that widely applied in networking. The most important three-party scheme—PKI—is then presented in

Chapter 7. In Chapter 8, we look at access control technologies, an often over-looked but vital aspect of VPNs. We describe how access policies can be presented, managed, and enforced in a networked environment.

Part III—VPN Solutions—consists of four chapters: *VPN Gateways, VPN Clients, VPN Network and Service Management,* and *VPN Directions: Beyond Connectivity.* This part describes how the various technology components can be assembled to create practical VPN solutions. Chapter 9 starts with the roles played by a VPN gateway, then derives the requirements imposed on the gateway, and finally describes the various functions that should be implemented. It also presents a concrete design example. Chapter 10 details the many issues of VPN clients, some similar to VPN gateways and some different. Chapter 11 presents the needs and approaches for performing continued management of VPNs from the viewpoints of both a network and a service. Finally, we discuss the future directions of VPNs in Chapter 12 and how important it is to realize that networking is the means, not the goal, and to look beyond simple connectivity in the networking arena.

How to Read the Book

There are two ways to read this book. For novices, we recommend completing Part I before proceeding to either Part II or Part III. For readers already knowledgeable in networking and security, each chapter is self-contained and can be read separately.

Readers are encouraged to read Chapters 4 and 5 together to obtain a fuller grasp on the concept of tunneling and IPsec as a layer-three tunneling technology. Similarly, Chapters 6 and 7 deal with authentication, with Chapter 7 exploring public key infrastructures in detail. It is also a good idea to review how a certain technology is introduced in Part II before seeing how it is applied to a VPN solution in Part III.

Acknowledgments

This book would not have been possible without the help and contribution of many people. We would like to thank our excellent technical reviewers: Kimberly Claffy, Scott G. Kelly, David Kensiski, Brian Kernighan, Gregory Minshall, Adam Moskowitz, Joyjeet Pakrasi, Ravi Prakash, Craig Partridge, Vernon Schryver, Lori

Sylvia, and Wray West. Their comments and suggestions improved this book a great deal. We also owe much appreciation to our colleagues who provided insightful discussions and helpful feedback: Chengli Cao, Ralph Dement, Benjamin Doe, Darren Dukes, Rich Kennelly, Steve Kent, Gary Kessler, Donna Woznicki Murphy, Alex Snoeren, James Sterbenz, John Summers, Jesse Walker, and John Zao. We would like to thank Craig Partridge in particular for giving indispensable advice throughout the writing of this book.

We are indebted to the staff at Addison-Wesley, especially our editor, Karen Gettman, Mary Hart, Emily Frey, Elizabeth Ryan, and Jason Jones.

Finally, we would like to thank our families—Ruixi's wife Li Xiong and his son, David, and Tim's wife Carmen Pancerella and his daughters, Ellie and Abby—for their understanding, encouragement, sacrifice, and support during the course of writing this book.

Ruixi Yuan
Tim Strayer

Boston, Massachusetts
March 2001

 **Part I**

VPN
Fundamentals

Introduction

To learn something new, and review it
from time to time, is quite joyful.
—CONFUCIUS

As long as human beings have had the ability to communicate, we have had the need to keep certain conversations private. No matter the medium, one technology or another has been invented to hide content from unwanted listeners: from whispering to enciphering to scrambling pay TV channels. Private conversations discriminate between the intended audience and all others.

There are, in general, two ways to make a conversation private: *physical separation*, where only the intended audience can access the signal, and *obfuscation*, where—even though many might detect the signal—only the intended audience can understand the message. When the communication happens in a public medium, obfuscation is the only solution.

In a historical sense, the Internet is a recent phenomenon, yet it has had such a profound impact on the way people communicate that it ranks among the greatest hallmarks in the evolution of communication. The Internet has fundamentally changed both social and commercial interactions. For businesses in particular, the Internet is rapidly becoming *the* communications medium of choice. Yet conducting business requires private communications, and the Internet is a public medium. In a *virtual private network* (VPN), various networking technologies are applied toward the goal of providing private communications within the public Internet infrastructure.

A VPN is a concept composed of two parts: a *virtual network* overlaid on top of the ubiquitous interconnection of the Internet[1] and a *private network* for confidential communications and exclusive usage.

In VPNs, "virtual" implies that there is no physical network infrastructure dedicated to the private network. Instead, a single physical network infrastructure is shared among various logical networks. For example, you can use the same network access circuit to access the Internet, to connect different corporate sites, and to connect to another business's network. This virtual network allows the construction of additional logical networks by changing device configuration only. This approach is faster to deploy and is less costly than employing dedicated physical infrastructures.

Perhaps even more important is the "private" aspect of the VPN. The very purpose of a private network is to keep the data—and sometimes even the act of communicating the data—confidential so that it can be received only by the intended audience. This privacy ensures that advantages you gain by using a public infrastructure do not come at the expense of data security.

Therefore, a VPN is defined as a logical network that is created within a shared infrastructure while retaining the properties of a private network; the communication across this logical network is kept private, and the quality of the communication channel is maintained. The aim of VPNs is to use the public Internet to enable private communication to be conducted securely and reliably across the globe.

VPNs are applicable to a wide variety of users—anyone requiring private communication over a public medium. Although there is certainly much motivation outside the corporate world, business communication offers a particularly compelling case for the application of VPNs.

1.1 Business Communication

There are many types of business communication. Broadly speaking, business communication can be classified into three categories:

---

1. VPN has several other meanings, such as software-defined telephone network and frame relay networks. Unless otherwise noted, we use VPN to mean an Internet-based VPN.

- **Internal communication** The message is limited to selected internal audiences. For example, a corporation may periodically distribute an updated company employee directory to all its employees. Confidentiality is essential.
- **Selected external communication** The message is intended for selected external audiences. For example, a retail store may want to order a product from its supplier. Although not all communications of this type are considered proprietary, one company's business with another is generally confidential.
- **Communication with public and other external audiences** The message is intended for general public consumption. Sometimes, the wider audience the message reaches, the better. For example, a company may place a 30-second commercial during a sporting event to reach a large audience. At other times, a targeted message is designed to cater to a specific audience to maximize its impact. This type of communication is generally not confidential.

Businesses have traditionally used specialized technologies for these different types of communication and have managed them separately.

The Convergence of Business Communication

Although businesses have a variety of communication types—and hence the need for different modes of communication—the digitization of information, and the creation of computer networks to deliver it, has been a unifying factor. Internal memos are now emails, and employee directories are kept in databases. Orders can be placed online. The World Wide Web provides a means for publishing sophisticated product brochures. Although there will always be the need for traditional forms of information dissemination, much business communication is converging on a digital network.

The computer networking technologies are also converging. There used to be many types and formats of computer networks, each developed by a different vendor. IBM offered Systems Networking Architecture (SNA) for its mainframe and minicomputers. Digital had DECNET, used in the once-popular VAX computing environment. In the PC environment, Novell's Netware was dominant and still is fairly widely used for PC interconnections. Nonetheless, with the development of the Internet, most computer networks have migrated to an IP-based infrastructure.

IP—the Internet Protocol—serves as the common format for all connected network devices on the Internet.

Private Networks

To meet their information infrastructure needs, corporations have invested heavily in internal networks called *intranets*. Intranets serve the employees at the corporate site, but not employees on the road or telecommuting from home. To accommodate the remote access needs of "road warriors" and telecommuters, companies have set up remote access servers to extend intranets into the field. Usually, a bank of modems allows these users to dial in through public switched telephone networks (PSTNs). Furthermore, employees at branch offices require access to the same information and the same resources, so private lines are used to interconnect the various sites to make one corporatewide intranet.

Special arrangements are sometimes made to allow business partners to have limited access to some part of the corporate intranet.[2] These networks, usually called *extranets*, provide the means to improve the efficiency of business information flow.

Each form of access to the intranet, as shown in Figure 1-1, is a separate private networking solution. This is true even when some aspects of each solution, such as the underlying networking protocols used, are the same. Each form of access also has its own requirements for privacy—requirements that are met by keeping data transmission on separate dedicated channels.

Public Networks

It is also imperative for a corporation to exchange information outside the established private networks. This requires access to a public networking infrastructure such as the Internet.

In addition, the public network opens a new avenue of commerce. It is now unthinkable for a corporation not to have a presence in the World Wide Web. For

2. Here and elsewhere, we use the term *business partner* to mean external corporate organizations—such as vendors of parts or supplies—that work closely with your business and to which you give limited access to certain records.

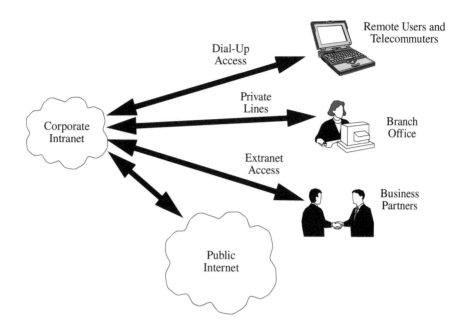

Figure 1-1 Separate private networks

many companies, such as Amazon.com, there is no "brick and mortar" storefront. The only place where they face customers is in cyberspace.

Virtual Private Networks

Protection of private corporate information is of utmost importance when designing an information infrastructure. However, the separate private networking solutions are expensive and cannot be updated quickly to adapt to changes in business requirements. The Internet, on the other hand, is inexpensive but does not by itself ensure privacy. Virtual private networking, as shown in Figure 1-2, is the collection of technologies applied to a public network—the Internet—to provide solutions for private networking needs. VPNs use obfuscation through secure tunnels, rather than physical separation, to keep communications private.

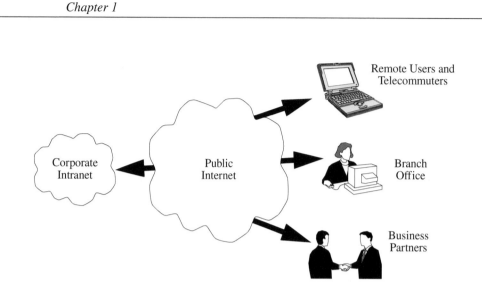

Figure 1-2 Virtual private networking

1.2 VPN Motivation

Why is it useful to employ virtual private networks for business communication? After all, separate private networks have been set up to serve the specific communication needs of many businesses. What advantages do you gain by converting the existing separate private networks to an Internet-based VPN?

Ubiquitous Coverage

The Internet offers far wider coverage compared with the private data network infrastructures offered by telecommunication providers. Adding new destinations to a private network means adding new circuits. Unlike the Internet, which has public and private peering points all over the world, few interconnection agreements exist between the service providers. Thus, the coverage of a private network is limited.

The Internet, on the other hand, is a vast interconnection of heterogeneous networks. Any host connected to a network that is connected to the Internet is in turn connected to any other host connected to a network connected to the Internet.

Cost Reduction

Another advantage gained by using an Internet-based VPN is cost reduction based on the system's economy of scale. Simply put, it eliminates the need to purchase and maintain several special-purpose infrastructures to serve the different types of communication needs within a corporation.

Security

VPNs use cryptographic technology to provide data confidentiality and integrity for the data in transit. Authentication and access control restrict access to corporate network resources and services.

In traditional private networks, the security of the data during transit relies on the telecommunication service provider's physical security practices for data confidentiality. For example, frame relay networks have no built-in provision for encrypting data frames. Consequently, data frames, if intercepted, can be easily decoded. In VPNs, you need not trust the perceived physical security of the telecommunication service provider. Instead, data is protected by cryptography.

E-Commerce

More and more business is being conducted using the Internet. Electronic commerce is not only a major new method of retailing merchandise (called "B2C" for business-to-consumer e-commerce), but it is also a way for businesses to trade goods and services among themselves (called "B2B" for business-to-business e-commerce). Interconnectivity of businesses is essential, and the Internet is the logical choice for the interconnection technology.

E-commerce must be secure. Private networks use physical separation for security, but it is impractical to have a separate infrastructure for each customer or B2B partner. Therefore, a closed, inflexible private network is not well suited for supporting e-commerce. A public infrastructure is more flexible but lacks security. VPNs provide both interconnectivity and security.

1.3 The VPN Market

VPNs, in one form or another, are becoming a crucial component of corporate networking solutions. Corporate networks use the Internet for various forms of business communication, and, for many organizations, VPN technologies are used to conduct private and commercial activities. Indeed, the trend is to migrate existing private corporate networks to Internet-based VPNs, and newly created corporate networks are increasingly using the Internet as their shared infrastructure.

To meet these needs, there has been tremendous growth in VPN offerings, which we separate into two categories: VPN products and VPN services. We will also discuss barriers to the development and deployment of VPN products and services.

VPN Products

VPN products are the hardware and software that make VPNs possible. One way to classify VPN products is based on how the product protects corporate resources. A *VPN gateway* is a stand-alone device that enables authorized access to the protected network resources. The resources are not located on the same physical device with the VPN gateway. A *VPN client*, on the other hand, is installed on the same network device it is supposed to protect. Usually, the client is a software package installed on the host computer.

VPNs require at least two cooperating devices. The communication path between these devices can be viewed as a secure tunnel across an insecure Internet infrastructure. Wrapped around this tunnel is a series of functions, including authentication, access control, and data confidentiality and encryption.

Depending on how these functions are implemented, VPN products can also be separated into two categories:

- **Software-based** Special software is added on top of a general computing platform, such as a UNIX or Windows operating system, to enable the use of VPN functions.
- **Hardware-based** Special hardware augmented with software is used to provide VPN functions. Sometimes, VPN functions are added to a hardware-based network device such as a router or a firewall. In other cases, VPN

functions are built from the ground up, and routing and firewall capabilities are added.

Many vendors network equipment are adding VPN products to their product lines. Some vendors add VPN functions to their existing products, and others build specialized VPN devices from the ground up.

VPN Services

A corporation can either create and manage the VPN itself or purchase VPN services from a service provider. When a corporation creates its own VPN, it obtains only IP connectivity from the service provider. All other functions pertaining to the virtual private network service are managed by the corporation. These functions include the purchase and installation of equipment, network monitoring, and configuration management.

In the case of a contracted VPN service, the service provider attempts to mask the complexity of the VPN service. The idea is that the service provider, by virtue of being in the network service business, has the expertise to manage the Internet-based VPN. Because the service provider may operate networks for many different corporations, it has the advantage of economy of scale and can run a network operations center with 24×7 availability. This may not be economically feasible for a small company with limited resources. Additionally, Internet service providers (ISPs) control the network infrastructure, so they are better equipped to deal with problems that arise within the network infrastructure.

When you purchase a VPN service, one issue is who retains control of the network. The data being sent through the VPN is critical. Putting such critical data in the control of a service provider can be sensitive for the corporation. A trust relationship must exist between the service provider and the corporation.

Another issue is the quality of the service. Specific performance guarantees, called *service level agreements* (SLAs), are negotiated between the service provider and the customer. Various measures can be taken when the SLAs are not met.

VPN Barriers

There are several barriers to widespread deployment of VPNs. First is the lack of interoperability of IPsec implementations. IPsec is the Internet Engineering Task Force's (IETF) security standard for IP. Although IPsec was standardized in November 1998, many vendors' implementations of these complex protocols have not yet achieved full interoperability with each other, even if they claim to be IPsec-compliant. Also, the Public Key Infrastructure for the Internet (PKIX) standard—X.509 authentication adapted for use in the Internet—is still moving slowly in the IETF working group. (For more on X.509, see Chapter 6.) This important standard provides a strong certificate-based authentication mechanism, but it is not expected to be widely available in the Internet in the near term.

Second, the lack of widely used quality of service (QoS) standards, as well as the sparse deployment of QoS-capable infrastructures, has made it very difficult to guarantee the quality of Internet connectivity, especially when traffic traverses the infrastructures of multiple ISPs. Many time-sensitive applications require certain guarantees to function correctly. This is not a new problem, and several proposals are on the table, but none has established itself as a clear winner.

Third, the Internet infrastructure is still largely focused on providing connectivity and does not yet offer services beyond connectivity. Security services in support of VPNs must be constructed from additional hardware and software components. Furthermore, computer operating systems in general, and Microsoft Windows in particular, do not yet contain mature built-in security functionality.

1.4 VPN Technologies

Several key technologies are employed by VPNs, as illustrated in Figure 1-3. A virtual or overlay network relies on *tunneling*, a concept discussed in great detail in this book. With tunneling, a network looks as if there is a set of simple links between the several sites when, in reality, the links may be a set of complex routes through the Internet. *Authentication* is the process whereby the identities of the VPN users and devices are verified. *Access control* provides ways to ensure authorized use of private corporate resources. The data transmitted over the VPN must

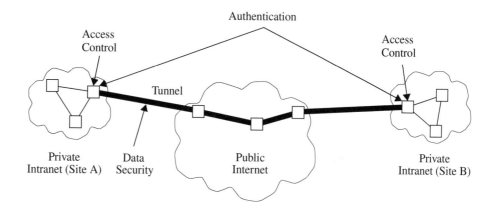

Figure 1-3 Key technologies of VPNs

be obscured from all but the intended recipient: cryptographic technologies pro-vide *data security* for VPNs.

The technologies that form the building blocks of VPNs are the topics for chap-ters in Part II of this book.

Tunneling

Tunneling is defined as the *encapsulation* of a certain data packet (the original, or *inner* packet) into another data packet (the encapsulating, or *outer* packet) so that the inner packet is opaque to the network over which the outer packet is routed. The encapsulation is done in such a way that one or more protocol layers are repeated. For example, when an IP packet is put into a User Datagram Protocol (UDP) packet (which is itself put into an IP packet), we say that UDP is tunneling IP.

The need for tunneling arises when it is not appropriate for the inner packet to travel directly across the network for various reasons. For example, tunneling can be used to transport multiple protocols over a network based on some other proto-col, or it can be used to hide source and destination addresses of the original packet. When tunneling is used for security services, an unsecure packet is put into a secure, usually encrypted, packet.

Two components can uniquely determine a network tunnel: the endpoints of the tunnel and the encapsulation protocol used to transport the original data packet within the tunnel. In most cases, a tunnel has two endpoints: one where the tunnel starts (encapsulation) and one where the tunnel ends (decapsulation). In the multicast case, a tunnel can have one starting point and multiple ending points, but we do not consider those tunnels in this book. In a VPN, authentication and access control decisions are made, and security services are negotiated and rendered, at these endpoints. Depending on the required services, different encapsulation protocols can be chosen.

Chapter 4 discusses details regarding tunneling technologies and the various standard tunneling protocols. One of the more important protocol suites, IPsec, is addressed in Chapter 5.

Authentication

Before any communication can be called private, each party must know the identity of the other. The same holds true for secure network communication: One network system must make sure that the other network system is the intended correspondent. The process of such identity verification is called *authentication*.

Authentication ensures that the data is indeed coming from the source it claims to be. In the traditional circuit-switched network, authentication is carried out only during the circuit provision phase. Verification of identities is implicit because the circuit is provisioned by the administrators, who presumably know the communicants. After the establishment of the circuit, the circuit, and thus the assumption of identity, remains in place indefinitely until it is explicitly torn down through another provisioning action.

When a secure VPN tunnel is established, the two endpoints (where the security service is negotiated and rendered) must authenticate each other.

Authentication methods can be broadly categorized into two kinds: two-party authentication and trusted third-party authentication. These methods are discussed in Chapter 6; Chapter 7 focuses on PKI, or public key infrastructure, the most important trusted third-party method.

Access Control

When the authentication process is completed, the communication entities can decide whether to allow the communication session to continue or to reject the session. In the case of VPNs, one purpose of secure communication is to allow authorized access to resources. When an access request is presented, the resource (or the security proxy responsible for safeguarding that resource) makes a decision as to whether to allow the access request to proceed. Usually, this *access control* procedure is performed at the endpoints of the tunnel.

An access control process has two aspects. The first aspect is the information on which the access control decision is made. Usually, this information includes the identity of the entity that is requesting access, the resources to be accessed, and rules governing the access. The complete identity information of the requester and resources can be presented at the time of the request, or it can be derived from stored information using data or credentials provided at the time of the request, such as username or IP address or both.

The second aspect is how the access control decision is made based on the information available. For example, the decision-making process can be carried out entirely at the location where the security service is negotiated and rendered, or the system can query a separate policy server for such decision. Having all the policies administered at a centralized server can make it easier to manage.

Chapter 8 addresses access control and explains how it can be performed in a VPN scenario.

Data Security

Data security touches on all VPN technology building blocks. Overall security is only as secure as its weakest link. If one link in the sequence that leads to the delivery of data is not secure, the entire process is not secure.

Because VPNs use a shared infrastructure to transport private traffic, it is possible for the data to be intercepted and even altered by others during its transit over the public infrastructure. Thus, strong encryption and data integrity should be applied to every data packet to make it opaque to interceptors. In addition, the packet delivery system should also be able to guard against replay attacks. In a *replay* attack, the attacker simply retransmits a previously captured packet. Because the original packet was authentic, it can pass all the cryptographic checks. If the receiver inserts a replayed packet into the received data stream, the entire message becomes incorrect, thus denying normal service.

Having strong encryption algorithms and well-conceived keys helps to ensure that the integrity of the data cannot be compromised by the interceptor without knowledge of the cryptographic keys. Changing the encryption in the middle of a communication session—a technique sometimes called *over the air rekeying* (OTAR)—helps to further the guard against attacks on the keys.

The basic concepts of cryptography are discussed in Chapter 2. Chapter 5 discusses the IPsec protocol suite, in which data security techniques are employed for IP-based networks.

1.5 VPN Solutions

In building a house, simply having the right materials does not mean that the house is built well. Similarly merely having the relevant technological building blocks is not enough to construct a virtual private network. A correct solution requires the right materials, and they must be put together in the right way.

Determining which kind of functions to provide at the tunnel endpoints, and how to implement these functions, is central to creating a VPN solution. When the VPN functions are implemented and integrated into an Internet device (e.g., a gateway), that device becomes a VPN device.

A VPN solution consists of multiple, appropriately configured VPN devices that are placed in the appropriate locations within the network. As with any network, after all the VPN devices are installed and configured, the network should be continually monitored and managed.

These aspects of an overall VPN solution are the topics of the chapters in Part III of this book.

VPN Gateways

The most common VPN device is the VPN gateway, which acts as the gatekeeper for network traffic to and from protected resources. Tunnels are established from the VPN gateway to other appropriate VPN devices serving as tunnel endpoints.

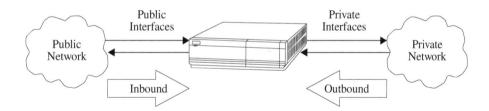

Figure 1-4 VPN gateway interfaces

A VPN gateway is usually located at the corporate network perimeter, and it acts on behalf of the protected network resources within the corporate intranet to negotiate and render security services. The gateway assembles the tunneling, authentication, access control, and data security functions into a single device. The details of how these functions are integrated within a VPN gateway are specific to a vendor's implementation. Sometimes these functions can be integrated into existing router or firewall products. Sometimes a VPN gateway can be a stand-alone device that performs pure VPN functions, without firewall or dynamic routing exchange capabilities.

In general, a VPN gateway has two or more network interfaces (see Figure 1-4). At least one network interface connects to the unsecure network; interfaces of this type are usually referred to as the public, or external, interfaces of the VPN gateway. The VPN gateway also has one or more network interfaces connecting to the secure corporate intranet, usually referred to as private, or trusted, interfaces.

The data traffic coming from the public interfaces is termed *inbound* traffic. Because the inbound traffic is from the unsecure network, it is thoroughly examined according to the security policies. Usually, only the traffic from the established secure tunnels should be processed by the VPN gateway. If no secure tunnel is found, the traffic should be dropped immediately. Depending on the implementation, an alert or alarm can be generated to notify the network management station.

At least one exception exists. The gateway must process traffic whose purpose is to negotiate and establish these tunnels according to the negotiation protocols. Other exceptions may apply, as in responding to certain diagnostic requests. In general, however, the fewer exceptions there are, the more secure a gateway can be.

The data traffic coming from the private interfaces and exiting to the public interface is termed *outbound* traffic. Because the outbound traffic is from the private network, it is deemed secure a priori, even though many network attacks are generated within a corporate network. The outbound traffic is examined according to a set of policies on the gateway. If secure tunneling is required for the traffic, the VPN gateway first determines whether such a tunnel is already in place. If it is not, the gateway attempts to establish a new tunnel with the intended device—either another VPN gateway or simply some other device with secure tunneling capabilities. After the tunnel is established, the traffic is processed according to the tunnel rules and is sent into the tunnel. The traffic from the private interface can also be dropped if a policy cannot be found. Depending on how quickly a secure tunnel can be established, the VPN gateway may buffer the outbound packet before the secure tunnel is in place.

A VPN gateway implements some or all of the VPN technologies mentioned in the preceding section. Which functions are selected and how they are implemented is largely the choice of the device implementor. Chapter 9 is devoted to the details of issues surrounding the design, implementation, and evaluation of VPN gateways.

VPN Clients

The VPN client is software used for remote VPN access for a single computer or user. Unlike the VPN gateway—which is a specialized device and can protect multiple network resources at the same time—the VPN client software is usually installed on an individual computer and serves that computer only.

Generally, VPN client software creates a secure path from the client computer to a designated VPN gateway. The secure tunnel enables the client computer to obtain IP connectivity to access the network resources protected by that particular VPN gateway.

VPN client software also must implement the same functions as VPN gateways—tunneling, authentication, access control, and data security—although these implementations may be simpler or have fewer options. For example, the VPN software usually implements only one of the tunneling protocols. Because the remote computer does not act on behalf of any other users or resources, the access control can also be less complex.

Unlike the VPN gateway, in which all of the gateway's hardware and software is geared toward the VPN functionality, VPN client software is usually just an application running on a general-purpose operating system on the remote computer. Consequently, the client software should carefully consider its interactions with the operating system.

Today, most remote access is achieved through telephone dial-up. As broadband access (e.g., cable modems and digital subscriber lines, or DSL) deployment becomes more common, dedicated high-speed remote access will be popular. In many dial-up cases, the modem speed is relatively slow, so the VPN client software must perform IP data compression before encryption to increase the bandwidth performance.

One of the important concerns regarding VPN client software is the simplicity of installation and operation. Because client software is expected to be deployed widely on end users' machines, it must be easily installed and easily operated by regular computer users who may not know much about the operating system, software compatibility, remote access, or VPNs. A VPN gateway, on the other hand, is usually deployed on the company's corporate network site and is managed by information technology professionals.

Authentication on the client software can take several different approaches. The VPN software may have its own authentication mechanism, or it may inherit the authentication scheme from the operating system. It is often desirable to have a single sign-on for all the services on the desktop. Either digital certificates or some type of shared secret authentication scheme can be used.

In some cases, VPN client software can be designed to allow only specific application access to a server—for example, secure shell applications or a program working within a browser session. These types of clients are sometimes referred to as *thin* VPN clients.

Chapter 10 discusses the many details regarding the implementation and deployment of VPN client software.

VPN Network and Service Management

All networks require management to remain in good working condition; occasionally, the network topology and configuration must be changed according to business and application requirements. This management is especially important in the VPN scenario. Owing to the dynamic nature of VPNs, the networks require continuous network and service management.

We specifically use the term *service management* because, in many cases, a VPN is a service offered from telecommunication carriers or ISPs to their customers. The customers of the VPN service do not directly manage the VPN but rather view it as just another network service.

It is important for the service provider to guarantee a certain level of service quality according to its SLA. SLAs provide a factor that differentiates service providers. In the VPN space, SLAs are usually related to infrastructure availability and performance metrics. For example, in dedicated site-to-site intranet VPN, a certain level of availability (e.g., 99.9%) can be applied to the VPN gateways, and a certain amount of average latency between the VPN gateways can also be provided. In a remote access VPN, the modem availability and connection speed are the subjects of performance monitoring and guarantee.

Because a VPN is a secure network service, it is paramount for the network to be managed in a secure fashion. A network cannot be secure if its configuration can be altered without security checks and strong authentication mechanisms.

Traditionally, network management relies on the management information base (MIB) and the Simple Network Management Protocol (SNMP). Standard MIBs are geared toward device-specific information management. A VPN, on the other hand, by its nature, relates to more than one device. Therefore, new MIBs need to be developed (some are already under development) to address the VPN management problem.

A good VPN service management solution should take into consideration (but not be limited to) all the aspects we have mentioned. Chapter 11 addresses the many issues regarding VPN network and service management.

VPN Directions

VPN technology is still emerging, and, as with any new technology, it will experience continued developments. The performance of VPN devices will certainly improve dramatically with advances in component technology. Innovative ways to design and implement VPN functions will also be invented. Although it is impossible to predict the future, we can certainly make some observations on business and technology trends.

One such trend is the integration of VPN and firewall functions into a single device. In this way, you can manage security in a unified way rather than having separate policies and interfaces for the two devices. Additionally, incorporating routing and quality of service features into the VPN device will make it even more versatile.

Another important trend is the move toward adding intelligence to the network. In the telephone network, intelligence resides mostly within the switched telephone network; the telephone itself is a simple device. Currently in the Internet, the connected devices are computers that have substantial processing power. The routers and switches merely forward the packets without knowing what is inside them or how to process them accordingly. Having intelligence in the network enables service providers to offer value-added services to customers. We anticipate that VPNs will be among the first services to be supported by these more intelligent networks.

These and other trends in the VPN arena are discussed in Chapter 12.

Basic Concepts

A thousand-mile journey starts
from the ground under the feet.
— CHINESE PROVERB

To place VPNs in context, it is useful to briefly review the basic concepts of networking and describe how the world's most successful public data network, the Internet, was created. We also review some fundamentals of cryptography, an essential component for performing authentication and data security in the Internet.

2.1 A Brief History of the Internet

The Internet we know today has changed and evolved in many significant ways since the early days of packet data communication, but perhaps more interesting is how little the fundamental concepts have changed. Whether by luck or amazing foresight, the Internet today uses the same structures and basically the same protocols that it did decades ago. This consistency stems partly from inertia, but the network works in ways and has scaled to sizes that the original designers could only have dreamed about. To appreciate where the Internet is now, it is instructive to see from whence it came.

The ARPANET

In the late 1960s, the Advanced Research Projects Agency (ARPA) of the U.S. Department of Defense (DoD) commissioned the building of an interconnection network to link ARPA-funded research centers to specialized computing facilities scattered around the country. This was the fabled ARPANET [ARPA68], the forerunner of the Internet.

The ARPANET used 50 kbps leased lines between sites. Interface Message Processors, or IMPs [BBN69], took the data received from the computer host, converted them into 1 Kbyte packets, and transmitted the packets over the leased lines. The term *packet switching* refers to networks in which packets are the atomic entity routed through the network. In 1969, the first message was transmitted from UCLA to Stanford, and by 1972, the first electronic mail (email) message was sent over the ARPANET.

In the early days of the ARPANET, several protocols were used to ensure the proper transmission of data through the network and to the intended recipient. It was not clear at that time which protocol or protocols would become the standard. NCP (Network Control Program) [RFC714] was implemented as the first end-to-end protocol. Transmission Control Protocol (TCP) was defined in 1974 [CERF74] and was split into two protocols—TCP and IP, the Internet Protocol—in 1978. The advantages of separating these two protocols into a *transport layer* and a *network layer* became apparent as the ARPANET deployment continued, and by 1983, the ARPANET was completely cut over to the TCP/IP protocol suite [RFC801].

Internetworking with IP

IP [RFC791] had features that made it conducive to join many otherwise autonomous networks into one large "internetwork." One of the most important aspects of IP was the notion of a globally unique IP address, thus enabling cross-network communication. By the early 1980s, the ARPANET had become what is called a *backbone network*, and many regional and campus networks were connected to the backbone via gateway computers (now called *routers*). A packet originating from a computer on a campus network leaves that campus network by a gateway to another network. That network, in turn, forwards the packet through to perhaps yet another network, until eventually the packet finds its way onto its destination network and finally into the destination computer. Forwarding happens because each router along the way knows the next hop to which to send the packet and because each IP address is globally unique and describes both the network and the individual computer on the network.

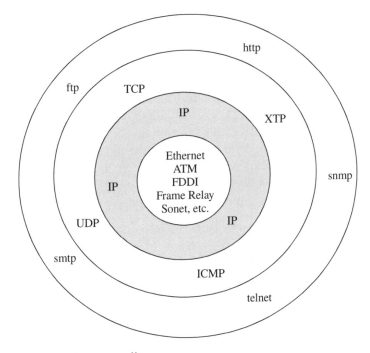

Figure 2-1 IP as the layer of commonality

The simplicity of IP, and the fact that its implementations were freely available (e.g., in BSD UNIX) contributed to the success of IP deployment. The wide deployment that resulted in the ubiquity of IP in turn contributed to the success of the IP-based Internet.

For the many interconnected networks, IP is the point of commonality: Individual networks run any link layer protocol and use whatever physical media they desire as long as IP packets can be transmitted over those media. Furthermore, IP does not care which end-to-end protocol the hosts are using—TCP [RFC793], UDP [RFC768], or other research or experimental protocol—as long as the end-to-end protocols can be transported over an IP network. Figure 2-1 illustrates how IP carries many different higher-layer protocols and can run over many varieties of link layer protocols and physical media.

The Growth and Commercialization of Internet

Although successful, the ARPANET was not open to everyone who wanted access. Other networks were formed to serve various communities, including USENET (1979), BITNET (1981), CSNET (1981), EUnet (1982), and many others. These networks provided the means for like-minded individuals to communicate with each other—not only about research ideas, but about anything. At first, discussions were conducted over email lists; then news groups (especially via USENET) provided electronic bulletin boards for discussions about topics ranging from television shows to religion. In 1986, the National Science Foundation (NSF) built a large backbone, called the NSFNET, and even more universities and commercial companies came online.

Then, in 1989, Tim Berners-Lee at CERN—the Center for European Nuclear Research in Geneva—invented a system to allow nuclear scientists around the world to exchange experimental data via a single interface using hypertext [BERN89]. He called this system the World Wide Web.[1] The idea really caught on in the Internet community when a graphical browser, MOSAIC, was introduced in the National Center for Supercomputer Applications (NCSA) at the University of Illinois in 1993.

It is worth noting the significance of combining a graphical browser with the intrinsic hypertext-linking capability of the World Wide Web. This easy-to-use interface enabled the majority of the population, not being computer-savvy, to use an intuitive tool to tap into the vast resources available on the Internet.

In the early 1990s, it became clear that the Internet had outgrown its previously intended charter as a research and education network and was evolving into a commercial entity. In 1995, the NSFNET backbone was privatized.

The year 1995 also marked a watershed on Wall Street with the initial public offering (IPO) of Netscape Communications, a technology company exclusively focused on the World Wide Web infrastructure. Netscape's vision lay in its ability to see the huge potential of the Internet beyond simple curiosity browsing.

Web servers quickly sprouted across the globe. Anyone with a computer and access to the Internet now had a powerful means of mass communication at a fraction of the cost of traditional print or broadcast media methods. The increase in

---

1. For more insight into the Web, see *Weaving the Web: The Original Design and Ultimate Destiny of the World Wide Web by Its Inventor*, by Tim Berners-Lee and Mark Fischetti, Harper Collins, 1999.

Web content availability gave rise to other opportunities, such as directory and search services. This trend was marked in 1996 with Yahoo!'s IPO. The subsequent dot-com phenomenon has shown the result of a positive feedback loop between Wall Street and Main Street.

The Internet has now become a daily part of private and public life. Television and print advertisements regularly include the dotted phrase beginning with *www*. The letter *e* has become a favorite prefix, as in e-commerce and e-government.

2.2 Network Architecture

Constructing data communication systems is a complex task involving a large number of hardware and software components. A common approach to network architecture design has been to divide the functionality needed for system interconnection into separate modules. The International Organization for Standardization (ISO) formalized this approach as the Open Systems Interconnection (OSI) Reference Model [ISO7498].

2.2.1 ISO OSI Reference Model

The OSI Reference Model is a seven-layer architecture[2] for data communication protocol suites, as shown in Figure 2-2. When used as a generalized network architecture, the OSI Reference Model facilitates the task of defining standards for linking heterogeneous computers by providing a canonical division of protocol functionality. The model has proved valuable in its role as a conceptual and functional framework for coordinating the development of protocol standards. The actual protocols specified by ISO have been less effective.

The OSI Reference Model defines a set of communication functions within each layer, as summarized in Table 2-1. Each layer provides a set of services to the next higher layer and requests a set of services from the next lower layer. Layer interaction takes place on well-defined boundaries through small numbers of service primitives. These primitives abstract the details of the more primitive tasks being performed in the service-providing layer.

---

2. Although the OSI Reference Model does not number the seven layers, conventionally the layers are numbered from bottom (layer 1) to top (layer 7).

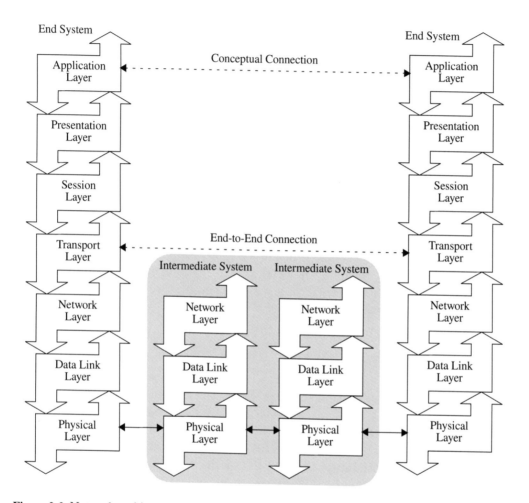

Figure 2-2 Network architecture: the OSI Reference Model

The *physical* layer, layer 1, is primarily concerned with the electrical and mechanical characteristics of the signaling medium used to transform binary information into signals that the medium propagates. Layer 2, the *data link* layer (often simply called the link layer) is concerned with using the serial bit stream services of the physical layer to provide data communication services along a single network link. The data link layer demarcates the serial bit stream into data units, called *frames,*

Table 2-1 The functions of the protocol layers

Layer	Layer Function
7 — Application	Application-specific services (e.g., FTP, Telnet)
6 — Presentation	Data compatibility between heterogeneous systems (e.g., ASN.1, XDR)
5 — Session	Dialog maintenance (e.g., SSL, TLS)
4 — Transport	End-to-end data transfer (e.g., TCP, UDP)
3 — Network	Routing between networks (e.g., IP, IPX)
2 — Data Link	Basic framing and multiplexing (e.g., PPP, Frame Relay)
1 — Physical	Signaling on medium for transmission (e.g., Ethernet, SONET)

containing address and error-detection fields. This layer also multiplexes several logical links onto the one physical network.

The *network* layer, layer 3, provides the routing and relaying of network layer data units, called *packets*, across multiple network segments and multiple networks. Network layer entities reside both at end systems and at intermediate systems (called *gateways* or *routers*) internal to the network. Network layer design issues include the functions related to routing and relaying packets within a network and between different networks (called *internetworking*).

The fundamental duty of a router in a packet-switched network is, naturally, to route packets. A router examines a packet's network address to determine whether its destination is on the local segment or on a remote segment of the network. If the destination is remote, the packet is forwarded to the next router along the path. By transparently performing routing and relaying, the network layer protects the transport layer from the details of the network topology. Instead, the transport layer can use the abstraction of a unified network in which any peer user can be reached by knowing its global address.

The fourth layer, *transport,* enhances the network layer delivery service by providing a message transfer service between end systems. The transport layer masks the details of the network layer service from the transport user and thus provides end-to-end services that are entirely independent of the underlying interconnection architecture. This service can be reliable, as in TCP, or best effort, as in UDP.

The lower four layers of the OSI Reference Model shield the upper layers from the details of the communication infrastructure. The focus in the upper layers is on user requirements for data exchange services and specific application needs.

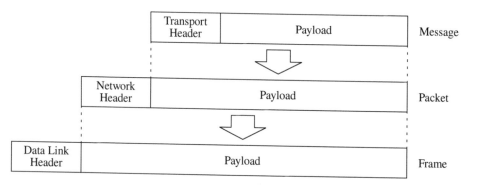

Figure 2-3 Layer-wise encapsulation

Using the data delivery services of the transport layer, the *session* layer provides the means for organizing, synchronizing, and managing dialogs between end systems. The *presentation* layer is responsible for ensuring that end systems can communicate successfully, regardless of their internal representations of data. The *application* layer provides general and application-specific services at the boundary between the open systems communication environment and the application processes that use it.

Generally, the session and presentation layers are tightly coupled with the application layer, and sometimes they do not have well-defined header formats. Typically, application data, together with its presentation and session layer overhead, is placed into a transport layer message as its payload. This transport layer message then becomes the payload for a network layer packet, which, in turn, is the payload for a link layer frame. We say that a layer *encapsulates* the layer above it when the protocol data unit (the header and payload) from the layer above becomes the payload for that layer (see Figure 2-3).

2.2.2 IP

IP—the fundamental protocol of the Internet—is a layer 3 protocol. The format of the IP header, shown in Figure 2-4, is of particular interest in several chapters of this book, so we give a brief overview of it here. (The numbers in parentheses are the field sizes in bits.) The fields of the IP header are as follows:

Version (4)	HdrLen (4)	Type of Service (8)	Total Length (16)	
Identification (16)			Flags (3)	Fragment Offset (13)
Time to Live (8)		Protocol (8)	Header Checksum (16)	
Source Address (32)				
Destination Address (32)				
Options (variable)				Padding (variable)

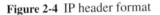
← ——————————————— **32 bits** ——————————————— →

Figure 2-4 IP header format

- **Version** The *version* field indicates the format of the IP header. Version 4 is run over the vast majority of networks. Version 6 is anticipated to be the successor to version 4, but it has yet to see widespread deployment.
- **HdrLen** The *header length* field gives the length of the IP header in 32-bit words. This length is normally 5, for the 20 bytes of a header without options present.
- **Type of Service** The *type of service* (TOS) field provides a way for the IP packet to carry a notion of the quality of service desired. The values of the TOS field are used as a guide for the selection of the actual service parameters when the packet is transmitted through a particular network.
- **Total Length** The *total length* field indicates the total length of the IP packet, including the header, measured in octets (bytes). An IP packet can have a maximum length of 65,535 octets, since there are a total of 16 bits in this field.
- **Identification** The *identification* field is a value assigned by the sender to aid in assembling fragments of an IP packet. If an IP packet is too large for a particular router to handle, it may be divided into several smaller IP packets called *fragments*. The identification field helps to identify the various fragments.
- **Flags** The *flags* field indicates whether this IP packet is allowed to be fragmented and, if so, that there are more fragments to follow. If the packet has the *don't fragment* flag set, the router will drop the IP packet before fragmentation can occur. If a packet is indeed fragmented, the *more fragments* flag indicates that this IP packet is a fragment—but not the last fragment—of a once larger IP packet.

- **Fragment Offset** The *fragment offset* field indicates where in the original IP packet this fragment fits.
- **Time to Live** The *time to live* (TTL) field indicates the maximum amount of time this IP packet is allowed to remain in the network. Each router is required to decrement this value as it routes the packet. The packet is dropped if this value ever reaches 0.
- **Protocol** The *protocol* field indicates what the payload is. Typically, the payload of an IP packet is a packet for a higher-layer protocol such as TCP or UDP. All transport layer protocols are assigned a unique number called the *protocol number*.
- **Header Checksum** The *header checksum* field is the value calculated by running a checksum function over the IP header only. Each router must check the integrity of the IP packet by verifying the checksum. Some fields, such as the TTL field, change as the packet traverses the network, so a new checksum value is calculated and inserted at each router.
- **Source Address** The *source address* field is the IP address of the sender of this IP packet.
- **Destination Address** The *destination address* field is the IP address of the destination of this IP packet.
- **Options and Padding** The *options* field carries any other information relating to how this IP packet is processed. If the options field does not end on a 32-bit boundary, the *padding* field fills it out.

2.3 Network Topology

Another way to view a network is topologically. Packet-switched networks, such as those based on IP, use routers to steer packets from the source computer to the destination. Each router along a packet's path receives the packet, discovers its destination, and forwards it to the next router along the path, as illustrated in Figure 2-5. An IP packet from host 1 with destination address host 2 is routed through the network on a hop-by-hop basis. Host 1 knows to send outgoing traffic to router A. Router A looks up host 2 in its forwarding table and finds that router B is the next hop. Router B likewise forwards the packet to router C, and router C to router D. At this point, router D, knowing that host 2 is attached to its network, forwards the packet to host 2.

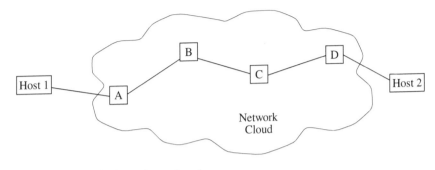

Figure 2-5 A packet's path through a network

In this example, the topology of the network is a series of routers and links that forms a path from the source to the destination. These routers reside somewhere in the network; if the location or the reason for the existence of these routers is of no concern, then the network can be abstracted as a *cloud* into which packets are sent and from which packets are received. Inside the cloud, it turns out, there is actually a collection of networks, linked together using routers called *border gateways*. Figure 2-6 shows this network of networks.

2.4 The Need for Security

Although security was certainly an issue in the early days of the ARPANET development (as evidenced by the required "Security Considerations" section customarily found at the end of the text in most Requests for Comments, or RFCs), security was not necessarily the top concern of the developers (as evidenced again by the statement "Security issues are not addressed" in the "Security Considerations" sections of many RFCs).

Some people in the military and intelligence communities, however, could see the potential for espionage or attack.[3] The Private Line Interface (PLI) [BBN75], built by BBN for the U.S. Navy and the National Security Agency (NSA), was the first packet network encryption device and the first one approved by NSA for protec-

---

3. An interesting account of a real-life search for a computer spy is given in *The Cuckoo's Egg: Tracking a Spy Through the Maze of Computer Espionage*, by Clifford Stoll, Doubleday, New York, 1989.

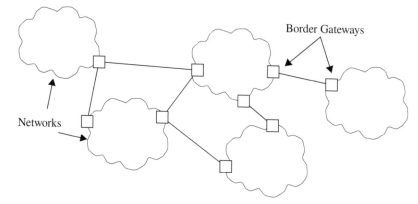

Figure 2-6 A network of networks interconnected via gateways

tion of classified traffic. Some people may consider the PLI to be the first VPN device.

On November 2, 1988, a computer program called a "worm" worked its way through vast parts of the Internet [SPAF89]. This worm—a program that replicated itself and sent itself to other sites to continue replicating—took advantage of the weaknesses in two programs: *fingerd* and *sendmail*. This incident greatly increased the awareness of the need for computer network security.

Network security becomes even more important when the Internet is used for business communications, where the data being transported are sensitive and can carry monetary implications. For example, when a person purchases an item online using a credit card, the card number and expiration date can be intercepted and used by others if its transmission from the person to the online vendor is not encrypted. This is why most Web sites offering secure transactions use Secure Sockets Layer (SSL).

Putting corporate networks on the Internet has also made them subject to network-based attacks. If a corporate network is not protected, an external user can enter the internal corporate network and obtain valuable information about the company and, perhaps more common, alter internal information such as the company's public Web site. Even if company information is not exposed or altered, company networks can be rendered almost useless by denial-of-service attacks.

The need for network security has given rise to a segment of Internet devices whose sole purpose is to address network security concerns. Firewalls, intrusion detection systems, and VPN gateways are examples of such devices. A *firewall* is used to provide a layer of isolation between the internal network and the external network. Usually, internal users can access the external network, but external users can have only limited access to the internal network (such as to a mail server). *Intrusion detection systems* are systems that monitor network traffic, host activities, or both to detect attempts to break into or misuse system resources. Elaborate protection schemes can have several layers of firewalls and intrusion detection systems, each layer with its own purpose.[4]

Whereas the main purpose of a firewall and intrusion detection system is to screen out unwanted network access from external networks, a VPN gateway's main purpose is to allow authorized network access from the external networks. Chapter 9 provides a complete description of the VPN gateway.

2.5 Cryptography

Cryptography is the science of obfuscating data to the point where it cannot be understood by anyone except those specifically intended to have access. It is a fundamental technology for private communication when physical isolation is not possible. Data is subjected to a function that transforms it from *cleartext* or *plaintext* data into encrypted data, called *ciphertext*. The function, called an *encryption algorithm*, generally takes one or more parameters called *cryptographic keys*. *Decryption* converts the ciphertext back into cleartext form.[5]

The standardized cryptographic algorithms are publicly known, having been published and scrutinized for vulnerabilities. (Some cryptographic schemes rely on secret algorithms, popular in the past but generally not used today.) The strength of an encryption algorithm does not depend on how well the algorithm itself is guarded. Rather, its strength is measured by how easily the encrypted data can be transformed back into cleartext without prior knowledge of the keys. Therefore, the safety of the keys is the critical component of the overall effectiveness of cryp-

---

4. The book *Firewalls and Internet Security: Repelling the Wily Hacker*, by William R. Cheswick and Steven M. Bellovin [CHES94], offers a useful guide on this subject.
5. Bruce Schneier's book *Applied Cryptography* [Schn96] and RSA Security's FAQ [RSA00c] provide excellent and detailed descriptions of how cryptography works and why it is useful.

tography. The generation, transmission, and storage of keys is called *key management*.

Converting a message into a form that only a selected recipient can read—encrypting it—provides *confidentiality*, that is, the assurance that the message remains private between the two communicants. *Authentication* ensures that the entity claiming to have sent the message is the entity that actually sent the message. Confidentiality and authentication are basic concepts in providing the private aspect of a virtual private network.

In addition, sometimes there is a need to ensure that the message communicated has not been altered during transit. This is called *data integrity*. Often, a short digest of the message is used for this purpose.

There are two basic types of cryptographic algorithms: *symmetric* algorithms, in which the same shared key(s) are used for both encryption and decryption, and *asymmetric* algorithms, in which different keys are used for encryption and decryption. Symmetric key cryptography has been around for a very long time, but asymmetric key cryptography, also known as *public key* cryptography, really started in 1976 with the publication of "New Directions in Cryptography" by Whitfield Diffie and Martin Hellman [DIFF76].

2.5.1 Shared Key Cryptography

A *shared key* cryptographic system is a symmetric system in which both the encryptor and the decryptor use the same value for the cryptographic key, as shown in Figure 2-7. The cryptographic algorithm consists of two mathematically related functions: an encrypt function E and a decrypt function D.

$$E(k, m) = c$$
$$D(k, c) = m$$
$$D(k, E(k, m)) = m$$

where k is the shared key, m is the message, and c is the ciphertext. The encrypt function takes the key and the message as input and produces ciphertext. The decrypt function takes the key and the ciphertext and returns the plaintext message.

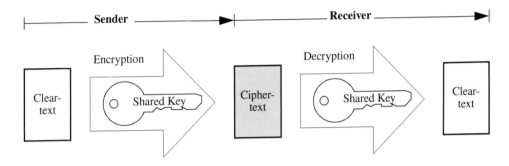

Figure 2-7 Shared key cryptography

Some shared key algorithms, such as the Data Encryption Standard (DES), use the same function for both encryption and decryption.

Shared key cryptography provides both confidentiality and authentication as long as the shared key remains a secret known only by the sender and the receiver. This implies that the method used to distribute the key must be at least as strong as the key itself. If the shared key is ever learned by someone other than the intended receivers, the encryption scheme is compromised, and a new key must be generated and used.

DES [NBS77] is the most widely used shared key cryptographic algorithm and is both a U.S. and an international standard. DES was developed by IBM and deemed "secure enough" by NSA. DES is a 64-bit block cipher (that is, it works on chunks of data at a time, as opposed to a stream) using a 56-bit key. Although DES remains popular and has been shown to guard against cryptanalysis, the rapid growth in computer power has made it feasible to break the encryption using brute force—that is, trying each of the 2^{56} possible key values one at a time.[6]

AES, the Advanced Encryption Standard, is the effort led by the National Institute of Standards and Technology (NIST) to replace DES. The Rijndael algorithm was chosen from the five final candidates under evaluation [NIST00]. Until AES makes its way into common products, NIST recommends using the so-called

---

6. July 15, 1998, the Electronic Frontier Foundation cracked DES using unclassified special-purpose hardware. An account of this is given in *Cracking DES: Secrets of Encryption Research, Wiretap Politics & Chip Design* by Electronic Frontier Foundation, O'Reilly and Associates, 1998.

3DES (pronounced "triple DES," running DES three times and variations on that) as a more secure version of DES.

Of course, there are now many other shared key cryptography systems, including IDEA [LAI91], Blowfish [SCHN94], and Skipjack. The latter is used in the Clipper [NIST93a] and Capstone [NIST93b] chips.

2.5.2 Public Key Cryptography

An asymmetric *public key* cryptographic system has two different but related keys: Data encrypted by one key can be decrypted only by the other. To be useful, one key must not be derivable from the other. Again, the cryptographic algorithm consists of two mathematically related functions: an encrypt function E and a decrypt function D.

$$E(p, m) = c$$
$$D(q, c) = m$$
$$D(q, E(p, m)) = m$$

where p and q are the keys, m is the message, and c is the ciphertext.

One key is deemed *public* and is made available to anyone. The other key is deemed *private* and is not disclosed to any other party.

A useful public key cryptographic system is one in which either the public key or the private key can be used to encrypt the data, and the other to decrypt the data. Figure 2-8 shows how such a system works in the two situations. In the first, the sender wants to communicate privately with the receiver. The sender encrypts the cleartext message with the receiver's public key. Because the matching private key is a tightly held secret and only the private key can decrypt the message, the message contents are kept confidential between the sender and the receiver, the holder of the private key. However, the receiver cannot tell with certainty who sent the message because the public key is widely known and anyone with the public key could have sent the message.

The second situation in Figure 2-8 shows how the sender can be authenticated to the receiver. Here, the sender uses its private key to encrypt the message. Anyone with the sender's public key can decrypt the message, so it is not useful for confidentiality, but the fact that a message can be decrypted with a particular public

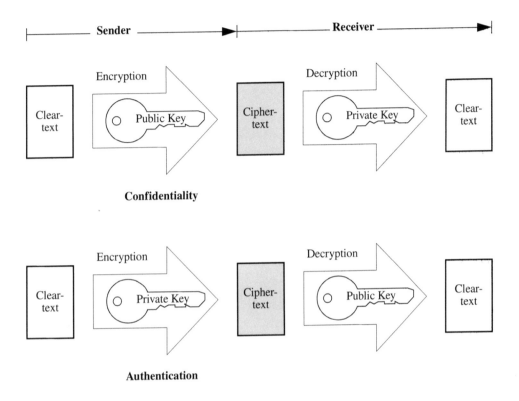

Figure 2-8 Public key cryptography

key proves that it was generated by the matching private key. As long as the private key is protected from disclosure, the sender is authenticated.

One big advantage of public key cryptographic systems is the simplicity of key management. Suppose there are N parties that need to securely communicate with each other. In a shared key situation, each party must have $N-1$ secret keys to communicate with other $N-1$ parties, so $N(N-1)/2$ total keys are needed. Secure distribution and management of these keys is difficult when N is large. In a public key situation, only $2N$ keys are needed. Furthermore, a secure communications channel to distribute the public keys is not needed.

Another advantage of public key cryptography is the possibility of *nonrepudiation*. Because the private key is not shared, the owner of the private key cannot *repudiate*, or dispute the authenticity of, data encrypted with the private key; only the owner of the private key can possibly create encrypted data using the private key. When secure timestamping is used, a recognized timing authority can vouch for the time of the use of the private key, so even if the key is later compromised, its use while valid cannot be repudiated.

One major disadvantage, however, is the complexity of the algorithms; shared key algorithms are usually significantly faster than public key algorithms.

Although there have been many proposed public key algorithms, RSA [RIVE78] (named for Ronald Rivest, Adi Shamir, and Leonard Adleman, its inventors) is by far the most popular. It is based on the difficulty of factoring very large numbers—the product of two very large prime numbers (e.g., 1024 bits in length). In spite of patent encumbrances, RSA has become the de facto standard throughout much of the world. The RSA patent expired in September 2000, and the RSA algorithm is now in the public domain.

Two other schemes are Rabin [RABI79], based on the difficulty of finding square roots modulo a composite number, and ElGamal [ELGA85], whose security is based on the difficulty of calculating discrete logarithms in a finite field. The nice thing about ElGamal is that it was one of the first public key cryptography algorithms suitable for both encryption and digital signatures unencumbered by patents. In fact, it is included in an open source implementation of Pretty Good Privacy (PGP) called GnuPG [GPG].

2.5.3 Digital Signatures

It is important, both legally and socially, to be able to prove the authorship of a document and to prove that the document has not been altered since it was authored. A handwritten signature does this, although it has technical flaws. A *digital signature* is the electronic analogy to a handwritten signature, and in many ways it is an even stronger device.

A signature, digital or otherwise, should have five properties: it is authentic, it cannot be forged, it cannot be reused, it attests to the unaltered contents of the document, and its validity cannot be rejected (nonrepudiation). Encrypting a document using a shared key does not meet this standard because, by definition, the key is shared by at least one other party. You may trust the person you share your key with, but others may not, so there is no way to tell whether it was you or your partner who really signed the document. Furthermore, only the person or persons who share the key can verify the signature. One way to use shared keys for signatures is to employ a third party whose integrity is trusted by all. The trusted third party becomes a digital version of a notary public.

Public key cryptography, when appropriately applied, can meet all five properties. A document decrypted by the use of a person's public key can have been encrypted only by the use of that person's private key, so it can be said that the owner of the private key signed the document by encrypting it with the private key. Because the public key is known by all, anyone can verify the signature. The signature is authentic by virtue of the fact that the private key is associated with only one person. If the private key is indeed kept private, the signature cannot be forged. Because the encrypted document is the signature, it cannot be reused. Because the document is encrypted, it cannot be altered without spoiling the decryption. Finally, because a document decrypted by the use of a particular public key can have been encrypted by the corresponding private key, the signer cannot later claim he or she did not sign it (as long as the private key has not been compromised).

Encrypting the whole message, however, is not strictly necessary, because privacy is not the issue. A better way is to encrypt a short representation of the message. A special type of function—a *hash function*—takes a variable-length input (the message) and produces a fixed-length value (the hash value). If the hash value has certain properties (elaborated next), encrypting the hash value is sufficient to preserve the properties of a signature.

Hash functions are often used in computer science—in databases and other storage and retrieval data structures—to provide an efficient way to aid in finding the much larger and more cumbersome data. Hash functions interesting to cryptography have the property that it is easy to compute the hash value but impossible to reverse the process. These are called *one-way hash functions* [DAVI80].

Another essential property of hash functions used for digital signatures is that they be *collision resistant*. A hash function reduces a large amount of data to a small hash value (say, 128 bits). Consequently, there will always be multiple inputs that hash to the same hash value. A collision-resistant hash function satisfies the requirement that, given a known message and its hash value, it is extremely difficult to find another message that will hash to the same hash value.

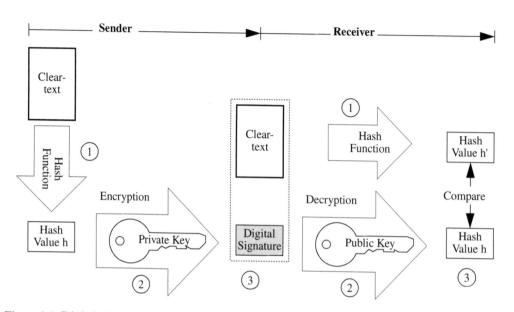

Figure 2-9 Digital signature authentication

Figure 2-9 illustrates the steps required for creating a digital signature using a one-way hash function:

1. Calculate the hash value h of message m, using a hash function H: $H(m) = h$

2. Encrypt the hash value using the private key p to create the digital signature s: $E(p, h) = s$

3. Send the message with the digital signature appended.

The receiver verifies the authenticity and integrity of the message by doing the following:

1. Calculate the hash value h' over the received message: $H(m) = h'$

2. Decrypt the digital signature s using the public key q to recover the sent hash value: $D(q, s) = h$

3. Compare h with h'. If they are identical, then the contents of the message have not been changed, and only the encryptor could have generated the message.

In general, a hash function is much less computationally intensive than an encryption function, so running a message through a hash function and then encrypting the hash value is a more efficient means of authenticating the message than is encrypting the whole message. Furthermore, the process of authenticating is decoupled from the processing of the message and the digital signature can be kept separate from the original message.

The two most common one-way hash functions are MD5 and SHA-1. The MD5 function [RFC1321] was designed by Ronald Rivest, an RSA designer, and produces a 128-bit hash value. The SHA-1 (Secure Hash Algorithm 1) function [NIST95], designed by NIST and NSA, is 160 bits in length.

In 1991, NIST proposed the Digital Signature Algorithm (DSA) [NIST94b] using SHA-1 as its one-way hash function. DSA is used only for digital signatures; it is not appropriate for encryption. DSA was intended to be a royalty-free, worldwide digital signature standard. It was officially released as a standard in 1994.

RSA is also often used as a digital signature algorithm, but until recently it was encumbered by patent rights.

2.5.4 Message Authentication Codes

Another way to provide authenticity without secrecy is by using a *message authentication code* (MAC). A MAC is an authentication tag derived by applying a keyed authentication scheme to a message. When the authentication scheme is a one-way hash function, the result is termed an HMAC, for hash function–based MAC. Only someone with an identical key can verify the hash. Keyed MD5 [KALI95] is a good example of an HMAC. Unlike in the digital signature scheme, in which the private key is used to encrypt the hashed value, the HMAC's secret key is a shared key between the sender and the receiver.

An HMAC is used for authentication of UNIX passwords. The user and the computer share a secret: the user's password. Actually, when the user enters the password for the first time, the password is used as the key in an HMAC to hash a phrase known by the computer. The result is placed in the password file, and the password is forgotten. When the user logs in, the prompt asks for the password. The computer then calculates the HMAC value and compares it with the value stored in the password file. If they are the same, the user is authenticated.

3

VPN Architectures

*Without compasses and rulers
you cannot draw squares and circles.*
—CHINESE PROVERB

The essence of creating a VPN is to assemble the technological components according to a cohesive architecture in order to create practical solutions for organizational communication needs and to be able to manage these solutions after the VPN is created. These components make possible both the "virtual" and the "private" aspects of VPN. We classify them into four categories: tunneling, authentication, access control, and data security.

The technological components are implemented in VPN devices (or in software), and then these devices are positioned at the various points of the network to perform designated functions. Although the methods of constructing the solution can differ depending on the various VPN application scenarios, there is some degree of commonality among the various VPN solutions.

Broadly speaking, VPN architectures can be separated into three common scenarios: the site-to-site intranet VPN, the remote access VPN, and the extranet VPN.

- **Site-to-site intranet VPN** In this case, multiple network sites located at different geographical locations within the same organization are connected using a VPN. Each site can have multiple IP subnetworks that form a corporate intranet. A VPN is used to interconnect these sites to form a single larger corporate intranet.
- **Remote access VPN** In this case, a VPN is used to connect a single remote network device to the corporate intranet. This single network device can be a

portable computer accessing the network via the telephone network or a tele-commuting computer accessing the network via cable modem, DSL, or some other form of connectivity. Except for that single network device, the accessing network is not under the control of the corporation.

- **Extranet VPN** In this case, network resources within one corporation are opened for access to other corporations for various purposes, such as business transactions. Such access differs from the intranet case in that it spans multiple administrative trust domains, and different types of resources are opened for outside access.

Traditionally, these three network scenarios are solved using three different kinds of networks. In an Internet-based VPN, these three scenarios can be consolidated, with the Internet as the common infrastructure. The ways that VPN solutions are constructed for these scenarios illustrate the different architectural approaches.

3.1 Site-to-Site Intranet VPNs

Traditionally, connecting two branch offices of the same company required leasing a dedicated private circuit or a frame relay permanent virtual circuit (PVC) between the two locations.

When many corporate sites must be interconnected, you can use either fully or partially meshed dedicated circuits or a hub-and-spoke–style connectivity. Provisioning a private circuit or a frame relay line can take a long time. For example, connecting two sites with a frame relay PVC typically involves ordering a local loop from a local telecommunications carrier to a frame relay port on a switch located at the service provider's point of presence (POP) for each site; a PVC with a designated committed information rate (CIR) connects the two ports. Completing this process can take 30 to 90 days. In many cases, especially when meshed connectivity is needed among a large number of sites, the frame relay approach is expensive because dedicated PVCs must be set up between each pair.

The traditional private networking approach is supposed to guarantee the availability and security of the network. However, dedicated circuits do not provide any form of guaranteed redundancy and reliability. A single private circuit can go down, making the network unavailable. Because the data traveling over the network is not encrypted, it is only as secure as the lines and switches along the data transit route.

Furthermore, data traffic is particularly bursty at various times of day. Dedicated circuit bandwidth is not in use when the traffic is light. Underprovisioned circuits experience congestion and packet loss when the traffic is heavy. There is no efficient way to set a static bandwidth for dynamic data traffic.

Internet access has become ubiquitous in the United States and is increasing across the globe. It is common for different corporate sites to have Internet connectivity. In addition, most business applications have migrated from other proprietary protocols (such as Novell's IPX) to IP. It makes sense, therefore, to leverage Internet connectivity to carry private network data traffic between different locations.

Because IP itself makes no provision for data security, data traffic carried in IP packets travels over the Internet in the clear. Consequently, these packets are subject to network-based attacks.[1] To prevent private corporate data from being compromised while transiting the shared network infrastructure, it is important to apply encryption and authentication services to the data before it enters the shared public network.

Figure 3-1 shows a typical network architecture for a site-to-site intranet VPN. A VPN gateway located at the boundary between a private corporate network and the shared public Internet encrypts the data traffic and sends it through the Internet to another VPN gateway. After receiving the encrypted traffic from the Internet, the destination VPN gateway decrypts the traffic and sends the data to the private corporate network. In this way, the traffic between the locations is encrypted when it travels across the Internet. Because the cryptographic keys used for the encryption are known only to the VPN gateway devices, no third party can compromise the data. The secure communication link between two sites is referred to as a *VPN tunnel*.

As shown in Figure 3-1, one VPN gateway device located at a site can handle traffic going to and coming from two other sites. In the three-site scenario depicted, three VPN tunnels are created—one for each site-to-site pair. No dedicated physical circuit is required between the sites, so creating and deleting the VPN tunnels is simply a matter of changing the device configuration. This makes the VPN flexible and dynamic.

---

1. Although there is a common perception that layer 2 transports such as ATM (Asynchronous Transfer Mode) or frame relay are secure, this is not entirely correct because these networks are also subject to network-based attacks such as eavesdropping.

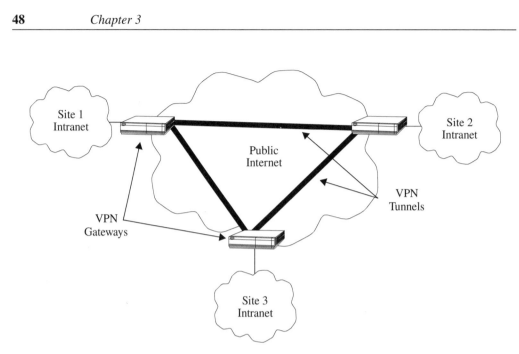

Figure 3-1 Architecture of a site-to-site intranet VPN

Although VPN gateways protect private data sent across the Internet, not all traffic sent from a site requires this much protection. Nonetheless, the traffic must obey the rules of the firewall located at the network perimeter or the rules of the firewall functions within the VPN gateway itself. Chapter 9 describes the detailed interaction between the VPN gateway and other network devices at the boundary of the corporate network.

VPNs are intended to provide the means for a corporation to rapidly add branch office sites to its intranet simply by installing VPN gateway devices at the new sites and changing the configuration of the other VPN gateways to establish the appropriate VPN tunnels. In this way, no additional long distance private circuit or frame relay PVC is needed.

The Internet offers the implicit redundancy and reliability not available in a dedicated private circuit. Because the Internet is a dynamic, packet-switched network, it can reroute traffic in case links along the path fail.

However, because the Internet is a shared public network, the resources are not dedicated for any particular organization. In many ways, the Internet is still a best-effort service network, so explicit quality of service (QoS) guarantees are not available. In spite of this, service providers are beginning to offer explicit QoS guarantees if the traffic path stays within the service provider's network—the so-called *on-net* traffic. This value-added service is possible because a single service provider has control of the entire infrastructure.

3.2 Remote Access VPNs

With today's workforce becoming more mobile and the demand for telecommuting on the rise, providing employee access to the corporate network from remote locations becomes increasingly important. This gives rise to the remote access VPN scenario, also referred to as *virtual private dial network* (VPDN).

The traditional way to enable remote access securely is to construct a *remote access server* (RAS) at the corporate location. Users then dial through the telephone network to reach the RAS and hence the corporate network. This option suffers two major disadvantages. First, toll charges can be prohibitively expensive for long distance and toll-free dialing. In the case of telecommuting, the remote access user must be connected for prolonged periods. With a toll-free service, the cost can often run as high as $6/hour. For international access, it is simply not economically feasible to implement long distance dialing as the first option.

Second, modem speed is slow for data communications. Even with the v.90 standard, the highest download speed is 56 kbps, still far from the standard speed offered for cable modem and DSL technologies. Internationally, the digital modulation scheme differs between countries. For example, the United States and Canada use the μ-law digital modulation standard, whereas Europe uses the *a*-law digital modulation standard. These differences, and the line noise due to international telephone circuits, can reduce modem speed to 19.6 kbps or lower.

Most corporate networks are (or are becoming) IP-based, and IP connectivity is readily available from various local, national, and international ISPs. In the dial-up network access case, an unlimited usage account with a wide-coverage national ISP usually costs about $20/month. It therefore makes sense to consider using local Internet connectivity and the Internet itself as the mechanism for providing corporate access to remote users.

A remote access VPN enables remote connectivity using any Internet access technology. For example, cable modem, DSL, and Integrated Services Digital Network

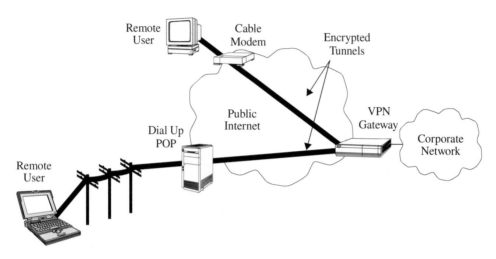

Figure 3-2 Architecture of a remote access VPN

(ISDN) lines can be used to increase the data access speed compared with that of traditional analog modems. Long distance phone calls can be replaced by local phone calls to eliminate toll charges and the a-law-to-μ-law conversion problem. After obtaining Internet connectivity by other means, the remote computer host uses VPN software to create a secure tunnel from the computer through the Internet to access to corporate network resources.

In the most common scenario (see Figure 3-2), the remote user dials in to an ISP's local POP. After obtaining Internet connectivity from the ISP, the remote user launches the VPN client residing on the PC to create a VPN tunnel to the VPN gateway located at the perimeter of the corporate network.

Alternatively, cable modem, DSL, and ISDN customers can use their existing Internet connectivity through the service provider's infrastructure to create the secure tunnel. As broadband infrastructure becomes more prevalent, these cases will be more popular.

3.3 Extranet VPNs

Corporations exchange information and conduct transactions not only within their own organizations but also with other companies. For example, a computer manu-

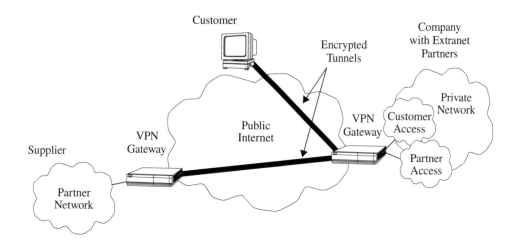

Figure 3-3 Architecture of an extranet VPN

facturer may want to allow its resellers to access its inventory control system so that it can manage its inventory tightly. It also may want to tie that system with its component suppliers so that components can be ordered quickly and even automatically when they are needed. Corporations are also rapidly moving their business transactions to the Internet. These trends make it imperative for a corporation to allow access beyond the perimeter to its network by outside entities.

Clearly, such network access must be tightly controlled, and the data exchanged must be secured. An extranet VPN spans multiple administrative trust domains, increasing the complexity of authentication and access control issues. Additionally, because business needs can change quickly based on market conditions, secure network access also must be added and disabled dynamically. Such dynamic reconfiguration is difficult with the long provisioning process of private circuits.

A VPN can offer the flexibility required by such external communications. The ubiquitous presence of the Internet makes it possible for businesses on the net to create dynamic secure network connections without changing the physical infrastructure. These dynamic secure network connections are referred to as extranet VPNs, as shown in Figure 3-3.

As in a site-to-site VPN, here a VPN gateway can be used on the perimeter of the corporate network. VPN tunnels are created through the Internet between this gateway and a VPN gateway situated in a business partner's network. In another case, a VPN client on a single computer host can allow a customer to access the extranet from a designated remote access computer.

Special access rules and filters can be applied to the tunnel to permit only certain business application traffic to flow across the secure tunnels. The same VPN gateway can be used to establish secure tunnels from multiple business partners. It is important, however, that one business partner not be able to gain access to another partner's information through the use of a poorly constructed extranet; VPNs can keep the data segregated on the wire, but good database design is required to keep the data separate at the host company.

3.4 A Security Services Taxonomy

For VPNs, the tunnel endpoints are where authentication and access control decisions are made, and where security services are negotiated and rendered. The choices of these tunnel endpoints and the rationale behind them are thus critical in the design of a VPN solution. In practice there are three possible kinds of security service endpoint locations. First, the endpoint can be at the end host itself, where the data originates or terminates. Second, the endpoint can be at the corporate local area network (LAN) gateway device, where traffic has been aggregated. Third, the endpoint can be located outside the corporate network, within the ISP's infrastructure (POP), sometimes referred to as "in the cloud."

Because a VPN tunnel has two endpoints, six types of security models can be derived from the possible combinations of the different locations (see Figure 3-4): *End-to-End, End-to-LAN, End-to-POP, LAN-to-LAN, LAN-to-POP,* and *POP-to-POP.*

In the *End-to-End* model, the tunnel goes from one end system to the other. Therefore, security service is negotiated and rendered at the source and destination of the communication. This scenario presents the highest level of security because data always travels securely in any segment of the network, either public or private. However, as the total number of end systems rises, it becomes more difficult to manage the even larger number of security services required by these end systems, unless the security service has only local significance and each end host

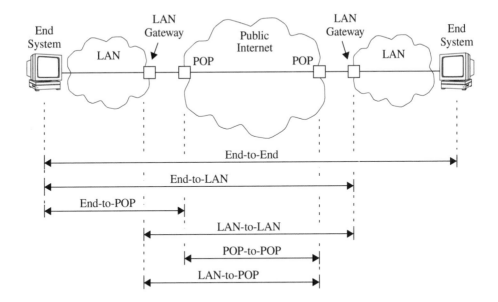

Figure 3-4 Six tunneling models for VPNs

is independent of the others. This security model is most often seen in the higher-layer implementations, as is the case with, for example, the Secure Sockets Layer (SSL). Such higher-layer implementations are generally not considered tunneling.

In the *End-to-LAN* model, the tunnel starts from an end system and terminates at the perimeter of the LAN on which the destination host resides. A VPN device located at the network perimeter is responsible for negotiating and rendering the security service on behalf of the other end systems. In this way, the security of a large number of devices on the corporate network can be managed at a single point, making it much easier to scale. Because the corporate network itself is considered more secure, there is usually no problem for the data to travel in the clear while within the corporate LAN. Most remote access VPNs are implemented in this model.

The tunnel in the *End-to-POP* model starts from a host and terminates at the service provider's network POP. A VPN device, or VPN functions available in an ISP's POP device, is responsible for negotiating and rendering the security service on behalf of one of the destination end systems because the POP is the means by which the destination end system accesses the Internet. Data delivery from the POP to the other end system must be secured either through its physical infrastructure or through a separate secure tunnel. The POP is an even larger traffic aggregation point than the corporate LAN. In addition, this approach may avoid the need to deploy VPN devices or functionality on the customer premises, that is, the corporate network. Remote access VPNs can also use this model.

With the *LAN-to-LAN* model, both hosts use VPN devices situated at the corporate network perimeter to negotiate and render security services. In this way, no security functions need to be implemented on the end systems where data is generated and received. The implementation of security service is completely transparent to them. This approach can drastically reduce the complexity managing security policies. Site-to-site intranet VPNs fit this model.

In the *LAN-to-POP* case, the tunnel starts at a VPN device located at the customer network perimeter and terminates at a VPN device or a VPN function associated with a device at the ISP's POP. This model can be used either alone or in conjunction with another LAN-to-POP or End-to-POP model. As a result combining the models, the data travels through more than one secure tunnel from its source to the destination. Currently, there is not a good example of a VPN scenario that applies to this model.

Finally, with the *POP-to-POP* model, both VPN devices are located within the ISP's network. Therefore, the security service is completely transparent. This model, also known as a network-based model, allows the service provider to provide value-added service easily without altering the customers' network infrastructures. This scheme can also be used in conjunction with the other POP-based security models.

Of the six tunneling models, the End-to-LAN and LAN-to-LAN models are being used extensively today to provide customer premises equipment (CPE)–based VPN solutions. However, the POP-to-POP or network-based security model is attracting increasing attention because of its ability to allow the ISP to provide various value-added services. The RFC "A Framework for IP-Based Virtual Private Networks" [RFC2764] provides a good overview of the various tunneling technologies that can be used in a network-based VPN model. It also presents some essential requirements of the tunneling protocols.

 **Part II**

VPN Technologies

4

Tunnels

View a mountain from different angles,
you will see something different.
—SU SHI, SONG DYNASTY POET

There are two ways to view an internetwork: topologically and architecturally. Topologically, it is a collection of networks linked by computers called gateways or routers. Architecturally, it is a collection of protocol layers that convert user data into manageable units, control their transmission, deliver them to their destinations, and reassemble them into the original data. A *tunnel* is an architectural concept in which one or more protocol layers are repeated so that a virtual topology is created on top of the physical topology.

4.1 Tunneling

Consider the network shown in Figure 4-1. A packet traveling from host A to host I passes through each node along the path—in this case, nodes B through H. There is no way to skip any of these nodes. However, if node C takes the original packet and places it completely within a new packet addressed for node G, then as the new packet passes through nodes D, E, and F, these nodes would only know the packet as if it were addressed to G; they would not know the original destination I. In this case, we say that the original packet is tunneled from C to G, represented by the heavy line in the figure.

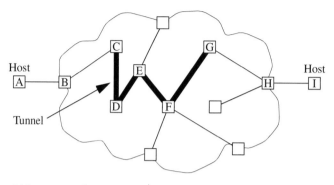

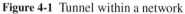

Figure 4-1 Tunnel within a network

Although tunneling can be used in any layer, the two most common layers are layer 2 (the link layer) and layer 3 (the network layer). In layer 2 tunneling, a link layer frame is placed into the payload of a protocol data unit (PDU) from some other layer, including another layer 2 frame. The Point-to-Point Tunneling Protocol (PPTP, see Section 4.3.1), the Layer Two Forwarding protocol (L2F, see Section 4.3.2), and the Layer Two Tunneling Protocol (L2TP, see Section 4.3.3) are examples of layer 2 tunneling protocols relevant to VPNs. Similarly, in layer 3 tunneling, a layer 3 packet is placed into the payload of some other layer or another layer 3 packet, as shown for IP in Figure 4-2. The IPsec protocols AH (see Section 5.2) and ESP (see Section 5.3) tunnel modes are good examples. When the PDU of one layer is placed into the payload of another, it is called *encapsulation* because the new PDU encapsulates, or surrounds, the original.

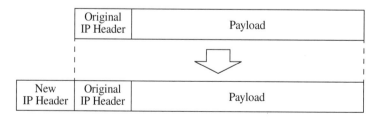

Figure 4-2 Layer 3 encapsulation

Tunneling is useful in several situations. When a common set of services is to be applied to one or more traffic flows, a tunnel is built from the gateway that applies the services to the gateway that extracts the original traffic. Security services such as encryption are often applied this way. The second important situation is when the addresses in one domain are meaningless in another. For example, intranets often use private addressing within the firewall, but packets sent between a pair of intranets may traverse the Internet, where the private addresses are useless for routing. A tunnel is built between the intranets, hiding the private addresses. In the third common situation, two domains run the same protocol, but the interconnect between them runs a different protocol. For example, the Internet uses IP, whereas some intranets use IPX. A tunnel can encapsulate the IPX packets for transport via the Internet so that they can be delivered from one site to the other.

These situations are precisely what makes tunneling an essential element for constructing VPNs.

4.2 Data Integrity and Confidentiality

The Internet is a layer 3 packet-switched network in which each IP packet is an atomic unit that can be independently routed from the source to the destination. Therefore, to ensure the successful delivery of the data through a secure tunnel across the Internet, each IP packet must be secured individually.

There are two important aspects of data security for an IP packet: data integrity and confidentiality. *Data integrity* ensures that a packet cannot be altered without detection. *Confidentiality* means that the packet's contents cannot be read by others without knowledge of the encryption keys. Methods invoked to provide data integrity can also be used to provide authentication of the packet.

Data Integrity

It is crucial that the message received be identical to the message sent. A great deal of effort in communication protocols is devoted to guaranteeing the reliable delivery of the data. In the TCP/IP protocol suite, a TCP checksum is used to protect the entire packet from random errors in the network infrastructure, and the IP header checksum is used protect the IP header.

However, the simple checksum used in TCP/IP is not strong enough to protect the data from active attacks. First, the checksum algorithm is not sufficiently collision resistant. Second, because the algorithm is well known and no secret keys are used to process the checksum, someone intercepting the packet can alter the data arbitrarily and recalculate a new checksum for the modified data. Actually, the IP checksum was designed specifically to make this easy because the TTL field changes from hop to hop.

Maintaining the integrity of an IP data packet in a VPN environment requires stronger methods. Message authentication code (MAC) functions (as discussed in Section 2.5.4) are usually used for per-packet authentication purposes. These functions are one-way hash functions that take as input a secret key as well as the message. The resulting MAC is a digest of the message. The secret key makes it impossible to alter a packet and replace the MAC value with a valid new one without knowing the secret key.

To ensure integrity in a VPN, each IP packet has an extra authentication field associated with it. The value of the field is calculated by the integrity checking function over the appropriate fields of the IP packet. Some fields in the IP header, such as the TTL and fragmentation fields, are subject to change when the packet travels across the Internet. Therefore, the authentication calculation does not cover these fields.

Confidentiality

Simply guaranteeing the integrity of data is not enough when transporting sensitive data through the VPN. Confidentiality is provided by encrypting the data in the packet.

Both symmetric and asymmetric encryption algorithms can be used to keep the data confidential. However, the commonly used algorithms for data confidentiality are all symmetric algorithms. This is because asymmetric algorithms (e.g., RSA) are much more computationally intensive. Because every IP packet must be encrypted and decrypted when it passes through the VPN tunnel, efficient—and preferably hardware-implemented—algorithms are used.

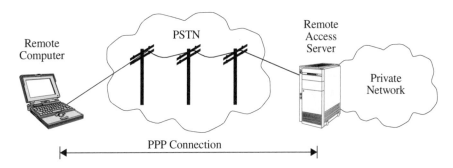

Figure 4-3 Remote user dial-in using the PPP

4.3 VPN Tunneling Protocols

Tunnels serve three major purposes in VPNs. The first is to encapsulate one protocol within another so that different protocols can be transported over an IP infrastructure. The second is to route privately addressed packets through a publicly addressed infrastructure. The third is to provide data integrity and confidentiality.

The layer 2 tunneling protocols (PPTP, L2F, and L2TP) are specifically designed to tunnel Point-to-Point Protocol (PPP) [RFC1661] frames through an IP network. PPP is the most popular way to connect two computers over serial or phone lines, such as dialing in to an ISP. This arrangement is particularly useful for people on the road or telecommuting—they connect on demand into the private network through PSTN (public switched telephone network) or ISDN lines. The remote user sets up a PPP connection from the remote computer to the remote access server (RAS) at the home network, as shown in Figure 4-3. After the PPP connection is established, the remote computer can start sending IP or any other protocol's datagrams inside PPP frames (PPP is called "multiprotocol" because it can carry datagrams from multiple protocols). The RAS removes the datagrams from the PPP frames and inserts them into the private network.

There are several problems with this PPP model. First, the company must provide a suitably large modem bank to serve its remote user population. This can be expensive and equipment-intensive. Second, the remote user must call directly into

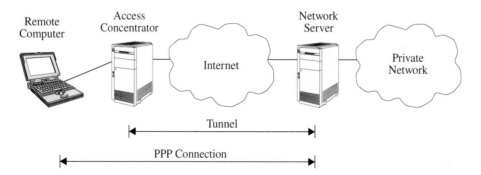

Figure 4-4 Remote user dial-in using a layer 2 tunneling protocol

the home network's RAS even if that requires a long distance call. Third, data applications are bursty—sometimes they have a large amount of data to send, and sometimes they have none—but the telephone circuit bandwidth nevertheless is constant.

The idea behind the layer 2 tunneling protocols is to tunnel PPP frames though the Internet to the home network. To do this, the functionality of the tunneling protocols is divided into two parts: a client part and a server part. The client part, called the *access concentrator*, resides close to or inside the remote computer and encapsulates the PPP frames into something that can be routed over the Internet. The server part, called the *network server*, resides close to the private network and is responsible for stripping the encapsulation and delivering the PPP frames to a PPP terminator. Consequently, the remote user and the home network treat the connection like any other dial-in PPP connection, even though some part of the journey was not made over telephone lines, as shown in Figure 4-4. An added benefit is that the addresses of the packets carried within this end-to-end PPP connection need be meaningful only in the home network and not in the Internet. Furthermore, because PPP is multiprotocol, the packets carried within the PPP frames need not be IP at all; again, they need be meaningful only in the home network.

Notice that the network server is attached to the Internet and not to telephone lines. One of the attractive features of layer 2 tunneling is the possibility of outsourcing all dial-up access to an ISP or telecommunications company (telco). The advantage to the company is that it no longer has to run a modem bank. The advantage to the ISP or telco is that it can charge for providing this service.

Layer 3 tunneling is most useful for VPNs within an IP network, as may happen when one corporate intranet site is connected to another. The two major issues are addressing and security. Intranets may use a protocol other than IP for intrasite communication, or, even if they use IP, the addressing of the IP packets may be privately allocated [RFC1918]. Placing layer 3 packets into an encapsulating mechanism can hide the addressing and protocol issues while at the same time joining two or more intranet sites. The trouble with this arrangement is that when these private packets are sent over the public Internet, the private data within may be viewable by anyone. Security tunneling protocols such as IPsec's Authentication Header (AH) and Encapsulating Security Payload (ESP) can provide confidentiality or authentication or both over the public Internet while at the same time solving the problem of private addressing. IPsec, however, is designed only to encapsulate IP packets, so a separate layer 3 encapsulation is required if the intranet protocol is not IP.

There is one other type of tunneling that somewhat spans both layer 2 and layer 3 because a label is placed between the layer 2 and the layer 3 headers. It is called *label switching*, and the Multiprotocol Label Switching (MPLS) protocol is the prime example. The label is used by each switch along the path to index into a table to quickly find the next hop. This implies that some mechanism has set up the labels along a path, creating what looks like an ATM virtual circuit. Because these paths are preestablished, resources can be allocated to that path, ensuring the packets the same level of quality of service. QoS is, in fact, one of the major reasons for using a label switching protocol.

4.3.1 PPTP

The Point-to-Point Tunneling Protocol (PPTP) [RFC2637] was developed by the PPTP Forum to facilitate PPP access by remote computers to a private network through the Internet or some other IP-based network. To do this, the functionality of PPTP is divided into two parts: the PPTP Access Concentrator (PAC) and the PPTP Network Server (PNS).

PPTP is implemented between the PAC and the PNS—no other systems are involved. A typical scenario is shown in Figure 4-5, where the PAC resides in the remote computer. The remote user dials in to the local ISP network access server

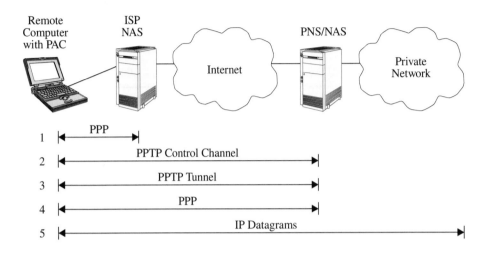

Figure 4-5 Remote user dial-in using the PPTP

(NAS) using PPP (step 1). This action connects the remote user with the Internet. Next, the PAC establishes a control channel across the PPP connection and through the Internet to the PNS attached to the home network (step 2). TCP is used for this. Parameters for the PPTP tunnel are negotiated over the control channel, and the PPTP tunnel is established (step 3). Next, a second PPP connection is made from the remote user, through the PPTP tunnel between the PAC and the PNS, and into the private network's NAS (step 4). Now that a PPP connection exists from the remote computer all the way into the private network, the remote computer can start sending IP or any other protocol's datagrams inside the PPP frames (step 5), just as described earlier.

Another way to look at this scenario is in terms of the packets that are used (see Figure 4-6). Assume that all the connections and tunnels are established and that the remote user has an IP datagram to send to a host on the home network. This datagram (step 1) is placed inside a PPP frame (step 2). This PPP frame is encapsulated inside the PPTP packet structure consisting of a Generic Routing Encapsulation (GRE) [RFC1701] header and an IP header (step 3). This whole package is placed inside another PPP frame (step 4). This PPP frame is sent to the ISP NAS over the first PPP connection. Here, the PPP header is stripped off (step 5), and the IP/GRE packet is sent across the Internet to the PNS. This is the tunnel stage. At the PNS, the IP and GRE headers are removed and the NAS accepts

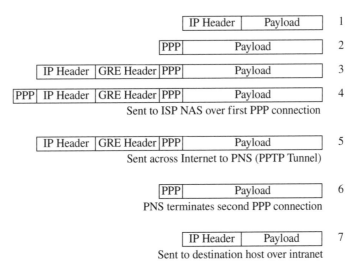

Figure 4-6 PPTP encapsulation of an end-to-end IP datagram

the resulting PPP frame (step 6). The NAS removes the PPP header and inserts the IP datagram into the private network (step 7), where it will find its way to the destination host.

A second scenario has the PAC residing within the ISP NAS. The advantage here is that special PPTP client software is not required on the remote or mobile user's computer, but it does assume that the ISP has the capability to do PPTP tunneling. In the first scenario, no assumptions are made about the ISP's capabilities. This second approach can reduce any extra PPP encapsulation overhead on the dial-up telephone link. However, the PAC functionality does put an extra burden on the ISP's NAS. Because most NAS products are optimized to handle as many dial-up sessions as possible, the PAC function is not widely implemented on the NAS, and thus this second approach is rarely used.

In general, there is a many-to-many relationship between the PACs and the PNSs. There can be many PACs scattered throughout the network concentrating the traffic from geographically dispersed sites connecting back to one central location. Similarly, there can be a single PAC that directs traffic to one of several PNSs, perhaps belonging to different companies.

The first PPTP draft specification was submitted to the IETF in June 1996 by the PPTP Forum. The PPTP Forum includes Microsoft and NAS manufacturers Ascend Communications (now part of Lucent), 3COM, US Robotics (now part of 3COM), and ECI Telematics.

PPTP was intended by Microsoft as an essential VPN technology [MICR96, MICR97]. However, PPTP itself does not provide data security functions but relies on PPP for its authentication and encryption services. PPP uses several methods for authentication: the Password Authentication Protocol (PAP) [RFC1334], the Challenge Handshake Authentication Protocol (CHAP) [RFC1994], and the Extensible Authentication Protocol (EAP) [RFC2284]. As we shall see in Chapter 6, these authentication protocols can have vulnerabilities when used in a networked environment. Microsoft extensions to PAP and CHAP are supported under Microsoft's remote access service. Encryption is also provided by PPP based on a shared secret (the user's password). As with all security schemes, protection is no better than the implementation. Early Microsoft implementations of MS-CHAP [RFC2433] had major security weaknesses [SCHN98], and an upgrade—MS-CHAP version 2 [RFC2759]—was subsequently released and also critiqued [SCHN99]).

4.3.2 L2F

About the same time that PPTP was being developed by an operating system manufacturer and several remote access equipment vendors, Cisco, Northern Telecom (Nortel), and Shiva Corporation (now part of Intel) were developing a virtual dial-up protocol suited for managed networks. This draft standard, called the Layer Two Forwarding protocol (L2F) [RFC2341], is designed to allow telecommunications carriers and other service providers to offer dial-up remote access to private networks as an outsourced solution—that is, a company would not need to buy its own bank of modems and remote access equipment but rather would purchase that service from a telco or an ISP.

Figure 4-7 shows the L2F architecture. L2F is similar to PPTP in that a remote user dials in to the NAS of a local service provider, connecting either to the Internet or some other IP-based network (step 1). This dial-up connection is either PPP or SLIP (serial line IP [RFC1055]) over a PSTN or an ISDN line. Either way, the NAS accepts the call if the remote user can be authenticated using CHAP or PAP. The user's name and home network are gleaned from this authentication, and L2F

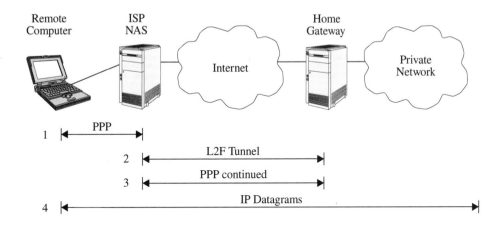

Figure 4-7 Remote user dial-in using L2F

builds a tunnel from the NAS to the private network (step 2). Whereas PPTP uses GRE as the encapsulating protocol, L2F uses any packet-oriented protocol that can provide end-to-end connectivity, such as UDP, X.25, or frame relay.

The terminating endpoint of the L2F tunnel is another important difference between L2F and PPTP. L2F's assumption is that a home network generally sits behind a router that provides firewall protection from and connectivity to the outside Internet, hence Cisco's lead in developing L2F. This router is called the *home gateway* in L2F terminology. When the tunnel is built between the NAS and the home gateway, L2F sends the connection indication, along with some authentication information, to the home gateway. The home gateways accepts the extended SLIP or PPP connection (step 3) and creates a *virtual interface* for the SLIP or PPP connection; this is directly analogous to a dial-up connection except that it is done within the router. At this point, the connection from the remote user through the tunnel and into the home gateway can be treated normally, so authentication, authorization, and accounting can be done as the point-to-point protocol (SLIP or PPP) dictates. Because SLIP has no built-in facilities for these functions, L2F supports ancillary methods such as RADIUS [RFC2138], TACACS [RFC927], and TACACS+ [RFC1492]. IP packets are now sent over PPP (step 4).

Notice that L2F at the home gateway provides the same service as a remote access server but without phone lines or modem banks. This is the point of L2F: Provisioning for dial-up access is expensive and scales poorly, whereas ISPs and telcos have the infrastructure to handle dial-up access. With tight competition within the telco and ISP markets, providing this value-added service is—it is hoped—a positive distinguishing factor. Also notice, however, that there is no provision for putting an L2F client on a remote computer. L2F must have the cooperation of a third party—the ISP or telco—to set up the tunnel on behalf of the remote user. As with PPTP, L2F does not define encryption for the encapsulated data packet.

4.3.3 L2TP

PPTP and L2F are each appropriate in some circumstances. Because PPTP has the backing of Microsoft and vendors of remote access equipment, it is most useful in so-called *voluntary* mode, in which the tunnels are created from the remote computer and not from the ISP. Because L2F was developed by a router company, it is most useful in the so-called *compulsory* mode, in which the tunnels are constructed from the service provider and not the remote computer. Except for some technical details, however, the two protocols are, as we have seen, remarkably similar. Instead of endorsing one draft standard over another, the IETF commissioned yet another draft standard, the Layer Two Tunneling Protocol (L2TP) [RFC2661], to extend the span of a PPP connection. Consequently, L2TP is most commonly described as combining the best ideas from PPTP and L2F.

Not surprisingly, L2TP (shown in Figure 4-8) looks very much like PPTP. Instead of a PPTP Access Concentrator (PAC) and a PPTP Network Server (PNS), the L2TP client side is called the L2TP Access Concentrator (LAC) and the server side is called the L2TP Network Server (LNS). An L2TP tunnel is established in the same way as a PPTP tunnel, using a control channel to negotiate the terms of the tunnel. Unlike PPTP, however, L2TP does not use a separate TCP connection as the control channel, instead building the control channel protocol out of L2TP packets. Whereas PPTP tunnels are built using GRE as the encapsulating header, L2TP (like L2F) uses UDP (port 1701). Furthermore, efforts are also under way to encapsulate L2TP frames within the ATM [TJOE00] and frame relay [RAWA00] networks.

L2TP is designed to easily support both voluntary and compulsory mode tunnels. Because voluntary tunnels are initiated by the remote user and originate from the remote computer, there is more flexibility in how and to where they are created. This flexibility is particularly important for remote mobile users who may be dialing in from a new place each day. Because the ISP is not involved in the creation

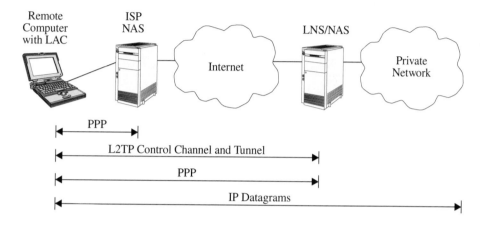

Figure 4-8 Remote user dial-in using L2TP

of the tunnel, the tunnel can span the networks of multiple ISPs without explicit configuration or agreement.

Compulsory tunnels are initiated by the NAS upon dial-in on behalf of the remote user. This implies that the NAS must be preconfigured to know the tunnel's terminating endpoint given a particular user's authentication information. This is done without the explicit intervention of the remote user, and the remote computer needs no special software—the tunneling process is completely transparent to the user.

L2TP, as well as PPTP and L2F, suffers from the lack of solid tunnel protection mechanisms. Because L2TP encapsulates PPP, it inherits PPP's security mechanisms, including authentication and encryption services. PPP authenticates the client to the LNS but does not provide per-packet authentication. L2TP itself includes support for mutually authenticating the LAC and LNS tunnel endpoints at tunnel origination, but it, too, lacks stronger tunnel security mechanisms such as control and data packet protection. Furthermore, L2TP does not provide a key management facility, even though tunnel endpoint authentication relies on the distribution of tunnel passwords. The L2TP Extensions Working Group of the IETF is defining how to use the IP security architecture called IPsec (discussed next) to protect L2TP traffic over IP and other non-IP networks ([PATE99]).

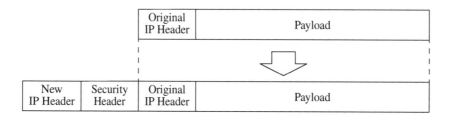

Figure 4-9 IPsec tunnel mode

Because many headers have been added for the various encapsulation methods, the overhead can be large for short packet. Consequently, header compression is advantageous. Compression methods for L2TP are under development in the IETF [VALE00].

4.3.4 IPsec

IPsec is a protocol suite defined by the IETF to secure communication at layer 3—the network layer—between communicating peers. The IPsec Security Architecture [RFC2401] describes the security services offered by IPsec and the protocols used to implement them. In particular, the AH protocol [RFC2402] provides authentication and integrity services, and the ESP protocol [RFC2406] can provide confidentiality with authenticity and integrity, or confidentiality-only services.[1] These protocols are discussed in much more detail in Chapter 5. Cogent to this chapter, however, is the fact that both AH and ESP have a mode of operation called *tunnel mode*, in which IP packets are encapsulated inside IPsec packets to form secure tunnels. IPsec also defines how security associations between the tunnel endpoints can be negotiated and how the encryption keys can be generated.

In tunnel mode, a new IP header is created such that the endpoint of the tunnel is the destination address, and the new IP header, along with a security header, is placed in front of the original IP packet, as shown in Figure 4-9. The original packet remains completely unaltered, holding the original source and the ultimate destination. The new IP header contains the endpoints of the tunnel—that is, the two IPsec devices providing the security services—as its source and destination.

---

1. If NULL encryption is used, ESP can provide authenticity- and integrity-only services.

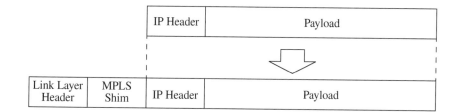

Figure 4-10 MPLS encapsulation

4.3.5 MPLS

The major goal of Multiprotocol Label Switching (MPLS) [ROSE99] is to reduce the amount of processing required at each router to forward a packet, while at the same time allowing the path through the network to be based on information not necessarily contained within the packet's header. In conventional IP routing, each router along the path makes an independent routing decision for each packet. The routing decision is made only on the information available within the IP header. However, the IP header may contain more information than is necessary for routing the packet. Furthermore, the routing decision making is performed at every router along the path, something that is redundant.

In MPLS, packets are forwarded based on a short, fixed-length value—called a *label*—that is inserted between the link layer header and the network layer (e.g., IP) header to the packet, as shown in Figure 4-10. Sometimes, multiple *shim* headers are inserted, commonly referred to as *label stacking*. A router capable of supporting the label switching function is called a label switch router, or LSR. The path the packet takes is called a label switched path, or LSP.

Rather than forward based on the full IP header, the router uses the label as an index into a forwarding table that specifies the next hop and a new label. The old label is replaced with the new one, and the packet is forwarded to the next hop. This process is repeated at each hop along the path until the packet reaches its *egress* router—the router where the packet leaves the MPLS switched network, as shown in Figure 4-11.

The first label is assigned to the packet as it enters the network. This is called the *ingress point*, and analysis of the packet's header is done here. After the packet

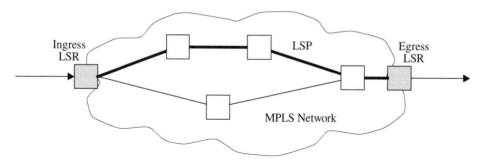

Figure 4-11 Label switching example

has entered the network, no further IP packet header analysis is done; forwarding is completely driven by the labels. Assigning the first label at the ingress point determines the path and class of service for the packet, so this decision is important. Because the assignment is done at or close to the application that generates the packet, additional information from the application (and, in fact, from any aspect of the computing environment) can be used to help determine the appropriate label (and hence the path) assignment.

Notice that, unlike IP addresses used for IP routing, the labels used by each LSR have only local significance. Because of this, the label information must be distributed between the LSRs. The protocol to be used to distribute the switching labels is called a Label Distribution Protocol, or LDP. Because the labels have only local significance, the length of the label to be used for forwarding table lookup can be shorter than the IP address length, enabling a faster lookup than routing table lookups.

Unfortunately, the speed argument no longer holds very well. MPLS labels used to be shorter than IP addresses—20 bits compared with 32 bits—but MPLS labels are now also 32 bits: 20 bits for the actual label and the rest for encoding a TTL and several other fields. Furthermore, today's hardware technology can search a 32-bit table at line speed. Instead of speed, the reasons for using MPLS now are more often to facilitate traffic engineering and quality of service.

The label switching technique is not applicable only to IP packets. As the "multi-protocol" part of the name implies, a label can be applied to any datagram. In fact, the MPLS-capable routers—LSRs—can switch any type of datagram as long as it has an appropriate label. This arrangement matches our definition of tunneling in that an encapsulating header (the label) makes opaque the original packet and treats it as a single payload. However, MPLS tunnels cannot be extended outside the scope of the MPLS network because these labels are not meaningful outside the network, and, in fact, they confuse regular routers looking for an IP or some other protocol's header.

MPLS is attractive as a VPN tunneling mechanism for two reasons. First, it provides a way to construct logically independent routing domains and, within a domain, can map packets onto different levels of service ([RFC2547, ROSE00] and [MUTH00] are examples of MPLS-based VPN architectures). This speaks to the QoS aspect of VPNs, in which exclusive resource consumption is required. Second, an MPLS flow provides a nice way to aggregate the traffic when the same security service can be applied to the already aggregated flow.

However, the MPLS approach provides no direct support for security features such as authentication and confidentiality; it is implicit in the choice of label that the path be secure. Also, this model implies that the intermediate LSRs are trusted and participate in the path security. Conventional tunnels do not need to make this assumption because security is end-to-end, leaving intermediate nodes simply to route packets with opaque payloads and not otherwise to participate in the security.

5

IPsec

Think three times before proceeding.
—CHINESE PROVERB

Layer 3, the network layer, is the lowest layer that can provide end-to-end network connectivity, so it makes sense that security measures be offered within IP. Unfortunately, IP version 4 (IPv4, the current IP version [RFC791]) does not have built-in security mechanisms, so additional protocols and procedures are necessary. IPsec is a suite of protocols that defines the architecture and specifications for providing security services within the IP protocol. Table 5-1 shows the IETF standards that define IPsec.

IPsec [RFC2401] is designed to provide interoperable, strong cryptography-based security for IPv4 and for the next generation of IP, IP version 6 (IPv6, [RFC1883]).[1] In fact, IPsec was first designed for IPv6. *Security* is an umbrella term for many types of protections. IPsec defines a set of security services, including access control, data integrity, data origin authentication, anti-replay protection, data confidentiality, and a limited form of traffic flow confidentiality. IPsec provides these services independent of the cryptographic algorithms used.

5.1 Basic IPsec Concepts

A security architect must first perform risk analysis of the assets in the system. This analysis provides a set of security requirements that dictates which security

---

1. Unless otherwise specified, we use IP to refer to either IPv4 or IPv6.

Table 5-1 IPsec standards documents

Document	Title
RFC 2401	Security Architecture for the Internet Protocol
RFC 2402	IP Authentication Header
RFC 2403	The Use of HMAC-MD5-96 within ESP and AH
RFC 2404	The Use of HMAC-SHA-1-96 within ESP and AH
RFC 2405	The ESP DES-CBC Cipher Algorithm with Explicit IV
RFC 2406	IP Encapsulating Security Payload (ESP)
RFC 2407	The Internet IP Security Domain of Interpretation for ISAKMP
RFC 2408	Internet Security Association and Key Management Protocol (ISAKMP)
RFC 2409	The Internet Key Exchange (IKE)
RFC 2410	The NULL Encryption Algorithm and Its Use with IPsec
RFC 2411	IP Security Document Roadmap
RFC 2412	The OAKLEY Key Determination Protocol

services to use. IPsec is designed to be one piece of the total security package used to protect a communication system.

5.1.1 Security Protocols

IPsec is a specification of mechanisms that provides a set of security services. These services are enabled through the use of two security protocols—the Authentication Header (AH) [RFC2402] and the Encapsulating Security Payload (ESP) [RFC2406]—and through the use of cryptographic key management procedures and protocols, including the Internet Security Association and Key Management Protocol (ISAKMP) [RFC2408] and the Internet Key Exchange protocol (IKE) [RFC2409]. In this regard, IPsec is flexible along two axes: the orthogonality of the protection mechanisms, and the independence of the protocols from the cryptographic algorithms they support.[2] The choice of IPsec protocols and the ways in which they are employed allow security services to meet a variety of security requirements.

---

2. RFC 2411 provides guidelines for the specification of new encryption and authentication algorithms for ESP and AH [RFC2411].

AH is the specification of a protocol that places a new header just after the IP header. AH provides data origin authentication and data integrity (this combination is generally referred to as authentication) and provides partial sequence integrity to prevent replay attacks. This protocol is appropriate when authentication is required but confidentiality is not.

ESP provides confidentiality for IP traffic as well as authentication in the sense provided by AH. Either of these services is optional, but one must be chosen if ESP is employed.

IKE provides the mechanism for two IPsec entities to negotiate the security services and their associated session authentication and encryption keys.

AH, ESP, and IKE are discussed in more detail in Section 5.2, Section 5.3, and Section 5.4, respectively.

5.1.2 Security Associations

The concept of a *security association* (SA) is central to IPsec. An SA defines the kinds of security measures that should be applied to packets based on who is sending the packets, where they are going, and what type of payload they are carrying. The set of security services offered by an SA depends on the security protocol and its options and the mode in which the SA operates. SAs can be negotiated dynamically between the two communication peers when they wish to use one or more of IPsec's security services, based on the security policies given by the security administrator. Alternatively, albeit more rarely, SAs can be statically specified by the administrators directly.

An SA is uniquely identified by three parameters: a destination IP address, a security protocol identifier, and a Security Parameter Index (SPI). The destination IP address is the IP address of the destination endpoint for the SA. The SPI is a 32-bit number usually chosen by the destination endpoint of the SA, and it has local significance only within that destination endpoint. The security protocol identifier is the protocol number for either AH (51) or ESP (50).

Notice that the source IP address is not used to define an SA. This is because an SA is a security services agreement between two hosts or gateways for data sent in one direction. As a result, if two peers need to exchange information in both directions using IPsec, two SAs are required: one for each direction.

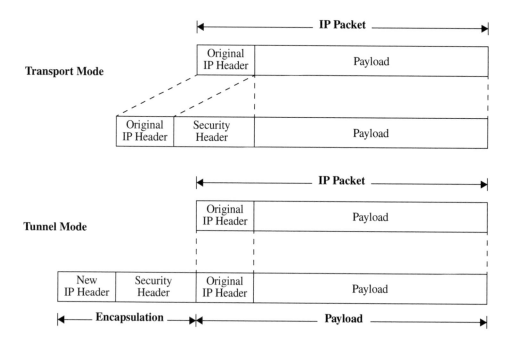

Figure 5-1 Transport and tunnel modes

SAs operate in two modes: *transport mode* and *tunnel mode*. Transport mode is designed primarily to protect the higher-layer protocols (e.g., TCP and UDP). In tunnel mode, an IP packet becomes the payload for another IP packet. This allows the inner IP packet, including its IP header, to be subjected to encryption or other security measures, whereas the outside IP packet serves to steer the data through the network. Hosts can provide both transport and tunnel modes, whereas security gateways can provide only tunnel mode (unless the gateway is acting as a host, in which case it can provide either mode).

Figure 5-1 shows the IP packet structures for transport and tunnel modes. In transport mode, the original IP header remains mostly intact, and a security header is placed between the IP header and its payload. The original IP header is modified only to the extent that it now reflects that a security header follows rather than the payload. In tunnel mode, the original IP packet becomes the payload of an encapsulating IP packet. The encapsulating IP header indicates that a security header follows.

An SA applies a set of security services to IP traffic, but some circumstances require a combination of services that must be applied serially. In these situations, two or more SAs are *bundled* so that one is applied first and then each of the others is applied in turn. SA bundles come in two forms: *transport adjacency* and *iterated tunneling*.

In transport adjacency, both AH and ESP in transport mode are used, and they are applied at the same host. It is easy to see that applying AH over AH or ESP over ESP does not yield any additional benefit. Furthermore, it is desirable to apply AH after ESP because the integrity check of AH covers a wider range than that of ESP, as we shall see in Sections 5.2 and 5.3.

In iterated tunneling, multiple tunnels are used to provide nested layers of security. The tunnel endpoints can be at the same location or at different locations. Unlike in transport adjacency, where only one level of combination is used, iterative tunneling combines any number of tunnels. For example, a host-to-host tunnel can itself be tunneled through a gateway-to-gateway tunnel, and that gateway-to-gateway tunnel can again be tunneled through another gateway-to-gateway tunnel.

5.1.3 Security Databases

Two databases are associated within an IPsec node: the Security Policy Database (SPD) and the Security Association Database (SAD). A policy administrator composes a set of security policies to meet the security needs of all types of IP traffic both into and out of this node. These policies are kept in the SPDs to be used in directing the processing of IP packets and the construction of SAs as needed. All SAs are registered in the SAD, along with the SAs' parameters.

Security Association Database

The Security Association Database is the collection of parameters associated with SAs. Each SA has an entry in the SAD, specifying all the things necessary to perform IPsec processing for the IP packet belonging to the SA:

- The Security Parameter Index (SPI)
- The protocol to be used for the security association (ESP or AH)

- The mode in which the protocol is operated (tunnel or transport)
- The sequence number counter
- The anti-replay window
- The path maximum transmission unit (MTU)
- The source and destination IP addresses of the security association
- The authentication algorithm to be used and its authentication key
- The encryption algorithm and its encryption key
- The lifetimes of the authentication and encryption keys
- The lifetime of the security association

For inbound IP packet processing, the appropriate SA is found in the SAD by matching three values: the destination IP address, the IPsec protocol type, and the SPI. The destination IP address and the IPsec protocol type are obtained from the IP header, and the SPI comes from either the AH or the ESP header. If an SA is found for the inbound packet, the packet is processed according to the security service specified. The processed packet is then subjected to SPD rule processing.

For outbound IP packet processing, SPD processing is done first. If an outbound packet matches a policy that specifies that IPsec processing is needed, the SAD is searched to determine whether a security association is already established. The packet is processed according to the SA if an entry is found. If it is not found, a new SA is negotiated for the packet, and the negotiated SA is then stored in the SAD. The SPD can specify one of three processing options for the packet, as we shall see next.

Security Policy Database

The Security Policy Database is an ordered list of the security policies to be applied to IP packets. Security policies are the general rules that specify how the IP packets should be processed at a higher level of abstraction than the SA. For example, the use of a particular encryption algorithm is specified in the SPD, but the encryption keys are not. The SPD is established and maintained by the policy administrator of the IPsec device. The policy administrator can be a user, a system administrator, or an external application process.

An SPD entry has two components: a set of *selectors* and an *action*. The selectors map an IP packet onto an action. A selector is constructed of a parameter and the value or range of values for that parameter. Parameters generally fall into one of two categories:

- Those carried within the IP packet, such as the IP addresses, protocol number (or next header in IPv6), and upper-layer port numbers
- Those derived from the authentication credential of the communicating entity, such as email addresses or distinguished names (DNs) in digital certificates

To make the policy more flexible and give it finer granularity, the logical operators AND, OR, and NOT can be applied to combine more than one selector. Wildcards, or "don't care" values, can also be used in the selectors to match any value of a particular parameter, helping to reduce the number of entries in the SPD.

When an IP packet contains values that match an entry's selectors, the action in that entry is applied to the packet. There are three choices: to apply IPsec security service, to discard the IP packet, or to allow the IP packet to bypass IPsec. In the first case, the details of the service (i.e., ESP or AH, encryption algorithm, etc.) are also stated in the policy entry. Sometimes, the policy statement is flexible enough to allow the two IPsec peers to negotiate certain parameters (e.g., encryption algorithm, DES vs. 3DES). Table 5-2 shows an example of an SPD.

It is possible for an IP packet to match more than one entry in the SPD. Because the SPD is an ordered list of entries, the first match in the SPD will be the policy selected. In addition, a default policy must be specified for the node. When no match is found in the SPD, the default policy is selected. Usually, the default policy is to discard the IP packet.

The SPD treats inbound and outbound traffic separately. Each network interface has distinct inbound and outbound policies because inbound and outbound IP packets can be subject to different processing. When an inbound IP packet arrives at a network interface, IPsec first searches the SAD for the appropriate SA. When one is found, the system initiates the SAD and SPD processing. After the SPD processing, the system either forwards the packet to the appropriate next hop or subjects it to other processing such as additional firewall rules.

SPD processing is done first to an outbound IP packet as it arrives at the system. If the matching SPD entry specifies that IPsec processing is needed, the SAD is searched to see whether an SA has already been established. The device either maps the packet to an existing SA or negotiates a new SA for the packet.

Because the SPD is checked for every inbound and outbound IP packet, the speed of SPD processing can significantly impact the performance of the IPsec device.

Table 5-2 Example Security Policy Database entries

Inbound	Selectors	Action
	source ip_address = 10.0.0.92 AND source email_address = accounting@newco.com	IPsec (ESP, 3DES, HMAC-SHA-1)
	source distinguished_name = Bob Smith	IPsec (ESP 3DES, HMAC-MD5)
	destination ip_address = 192.89.0.169	Bypass

Outbound	Selectors	Action
	destination ip_address = 10.0.0.92	IPsec (ESP 3DES, HMAC-SHA-1)
	destination distinguished_name = Bob Smith	IPsec (ESP 3DES, HMAC-MD5)
	source ip_address = 192.89.0.169	Bypass

In fact, for a node offering IPsec, the bottleneck is usually the SPD processing. The complexity of the SPD entry makes it difficult to index SPD entries for fast searching. Caching techniques can be applied to SPD processing where all SPD entries are independent of each other and the order of the entries is irrelevant.

Notice that the SPD entries listed in Table 5-2 contain selector information, such as the distinguished name or email address, that is not available from an IP packet alone. It is not possible to match an IP packet against such selectors, so the SPD entries containing higher-level names must be resolved into values that can be used in the matching process. This resolution is done during the negotiation phase of the security association (the Internet Key Exchange, a process described in detail later in this chapter). During the IKE negotiation, SPD entries containing higher-level names are translated into SPD entries containing IP addresses. It is these translated SPD entries that are matched against each IP packet.

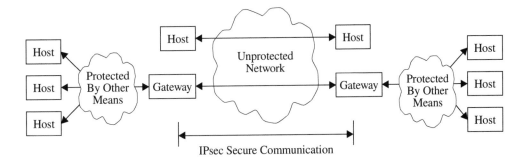

Figure 5-2 Host-to-host and gateway-to-gateway secure communication

5.1.4 IPsec and VPNs

IPsec is designed to work at several traffic granularities, from the set of IP packets related to a particular communication stream to the aggregation of all IP traffic from one site to another. Figure 5-2 shows a large, unprotected network, such as the Internet, with two traffic streams traversing it. In the first, two hosts use IPsec to secure the direct communication between them. In the second, a gateway aggregates all the traffic from one otherwise protected site and employs IPsec to securely traverse the unprotected network to the gateway at the edge of the other protected site. Individual hosts within the protected network do not need to use IPsec directly, nor do they need to know that IPsec is in the path at all.

Obviously, IPsec is an important tool in building VPNs because of its ability to provide both tunneling (the "virtual" aspect) and security (the "private" aspect). However, IPsec is also a complex set of protocols, and given the many optional requirements in the IPsec RFCs, the interoperability of IPsec implementations among different vendors is expected to be achieved slowly.

5.2 Authentication Header

The IPsec Authentication Header protocol is used to provide per-packet authentication—that is, data integrity and data origin authentication—for the IP payload (upper-layer protocol header and data) and as much of the IP header as possible.

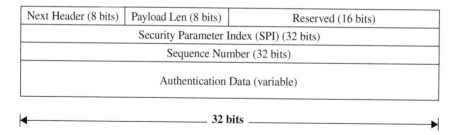

Next Header (8 bits)	Payload Len (8 bits)	Reserved (16 bits)
Security Parameter Index (SPI) (32 bits)		
Sequence Number (32 bits)		
Authentication Data (variable)		

← 32 bits →

Figure 5-3 Authentication header format

As the term *authentication* indicates, the AH protocol makes sure that the data delivered within the IP packet is authentic and that it arrives at the destination without modification. AH also provides an optional anti-replay protection for IP packets. It does not, however, keep the data confidential by encrypting the data.

AH defines how an unprotected IP packet is turned into a new IP packet containing additional information to provide authentication. The fundamental mechanism used by AH to provide authentication is the *authentication header*,[3] shown in Figure 5-3. The new IP packet is formed by placing the authentication header after either a new IP header or a slightly modified original IP header. When the authentication header is inserted, the IP header preceding it must indicate that the next header it will find is the authentication header and not the original payload. The IP header does this by setting the Protocol field to 51, the assigned protocol value for AH. The authentication header, then, takes on the responsibility of indicating what the payload type is.

The authentication header contains six fields:

- **Next Header** The *Next Header* field is an 8-bit field that identifies the type of protocol header immediately after the AH. This is the same set of values used in the Protocol field in the original IP header.
- **Payload Len** The *Payload Len* field is an 8-bit field specifying the length of the authentication header (and not the actual payload, contrary to what the name implies). The Payload Len is the authentication header length in 4-byte words, minus 2. The reason for subtracting 2 is that the authentication header was originally designed as an IPv6 extension header, in which header length

---

3. We use "AH" to describe the protocol, and "authentication header" to describe the header format.

is counted as 8-byte words minus 1. Because Payload Len is counted in 4-byte words, to remain consistent with IPv6, the value is reduced by 2.

- **Reserved** The *Reserved* field is reserved for future use; currently it must be set to zero. This field is now used only for alignment purposes, that is, to cause the SPI field to align on a 32-bit boundary.
- **Security Parameter Index** The *Security Parameter Index* field is an arbitrary 32-bit number for SA indexing. This value is used with the destination IP address and the IPsec protocol type (in this case, AH) to uniquely identify the SA for this IP packet. The SPI value is usually chosen by the destination system when the SA is established.
- **Sequence Number** The *Sequence Number* field is a 32-bit field holding a monotonically increasing number for sequencing the IPsec packets. This value starts at 0 when the SA is established and is incremented for each outgoing IP packet sent using this SA. Anti-replay protection is provided if the destination rejects the packet based on checking the sequence number against a receive window.
- **Authentication Data** The *Authentication Data* field is a variable-length field containing the integrity check value (ICV) for this IP packet. The ICV is calculated with the algorithm selected when the SA is established and is used by the receiver to verify the integrity of the incoming IP packet. The length of the ICV must be an integral multiple of 4 bytes because the Payload Len value is counted in 4-byte blocks. If the computation algorithm obtains a different length, the ICV must be padded or truncated. The default algorithms required by AH are HMAC [RFC2104] with MD5 and SHA-1 ([RFC2403] and [RFC2404], respectively). These algorithms calculate a 96-bit ICV.

In addition to the IP payload, AH provides authentication to as much of the IP header as possible. However, authentication cannot be provided over the whole IP header because some fields in the IP header may change during transit through the Internet. These header fields, called *mutable* fields, include:

- Type of service (TOS)
- Fragment offset
- Fragmentation flags
- Time to live (TTL)
- Header checksum

The TOS field is excluded from the authentication computation because some routers are known to change its value, even though the original IP specification does not consider this to be a mutable header field. Both the fragmentation flags and the fragment offset fields can be changed when the IP packet transits a path having different MTU links. The TTL field decrements every hop, and, of course, the value in header checksum is computed over these changing fields.

To provide authentication, the sender calculates the ICV, places it into the Authentication Data field, and sends it with the IP packet. The ICV is usually a keyed hash value computed over all the fields covered by the authentication. The secret key is negotiated during the SA establishment. The authentication of a received packet is verified when the receiver calculates the hash value and compares it to the ICV from the Authentication Data field.

AH receiver processing is applied only to nonfragmented IP packets. The destination must reassemble the fragments before AH processing is applied. If the packet cannot be authenticated after any necessary reassembly and AH processing, it is discarded. These two measures help prevent the type of denial-of-service attack in which an attacker sends bogus fragments or packets that cannot be authenticated.

Recall that AH specifies placing the authentication header after either a new IP header or a slightly modified original IP header. The transport mode of AH uses the original IP header and changes only the Protocol field. Tunnel mode encapsulates the original IP packet inside a new IP header followed by the authentication header. These two modes are described in more detail next.

Transport Mode

In transport mode, the original IP header is retained as the header of the new IP packet, and the authentication header is inserted between the IP header and the original payload, as shown in Figure 5-4. The picture is a little more complicated for IPv6 than for IPv4 because there are extension headers (some going before the authentication header and others after). But in both versions, the original IP header stays largely intact; only the Protocol field is changed to the value 51 for the AH protocol. The old value of the Protocol field, representing the protocol number of the upper-layer protocol, is put into the Next Header field of the authentication header. The ICV is calculated over the whole of the new IP packet, except for the mutable fields mentioned previously.

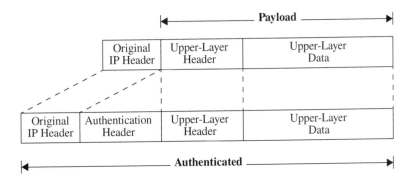

Figure 5-4 AH transport mode

Transport mode has the advantage of adding only a few extra bytes to the original IP packet. However, because the original IP header is used as the header of the new IP packet, only end hosts can use AH transport mode. This limitation is acceptable when both endpoints of the IPsec SA are acting as hosts themselves and are not acting on behalf of other devices. Another disadvantage is that transport mode can be subjected to the traffic pattern analysis, in which an observer gleans information from the number and types of packets traversing the network even if the contents are obscured.

Tunnel Mode

In tunnel mode, a new IP header is created for the new IP packet, and the authentication header is inserted between the original and new IP headers, as shown in Figure 5-5. The original IP packet stays intact and is encapsulated within the new IP packet. In this way, authentication is provided over the entire original IP packet (including the mutable fields of the original IP header), in addition to the authentication header and the immutable fields of the new IP header. Further, more processing power is needed for adding and stripping these extra headers.

The original IP header is completely unaltered and contains the ultimate destination IP address as well as the original source IP address. The new IP header contains the source and destination IP addresses of the IPsec devices between which the new packet will travel. Consequently, tunnel mode can be used whether the endpoints of the SA are hosts or security gateways.

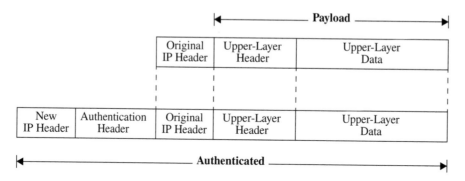

Figure 5-5 AH tunnel mode

If the SA is between hosts, the new source and destination IP addresses are usually the same as the original. The typical reason for using AH in tunnel mode between hosts is to completely authenticate the original packet.

If the SA is between security gateways, the new source and destination IP addresses are those of the gateways. Tunnel mode AH between security gateways allows aggregation of traffic between sites through an authenticated tunnel. In addition, traffic analysis is more difficult because the original IP packet is buried within the payload of the new IP packet and potentially is multiplexed with other traffic traveling between the same sites.

Again, the Protocol field in the new IP header contains the value 51 for the AH protocol, and the Next Header field in the authentication header contains the value for IP (4 for IPv4)

5.3 Encapsulating Security Payload

The IPsec Encapsulating Security Payload protocol provides authentication, data confidentiality through encryption, and optional anti-replay protection for IP packets. Authentication and encryption are also optional, but one of them must be employed; otherwise, this protocol provides no added value. Typically, if confidentiality is required, authentication is also applied because confidentiality without authentication may subject the traffic to certain forms of active attacks.

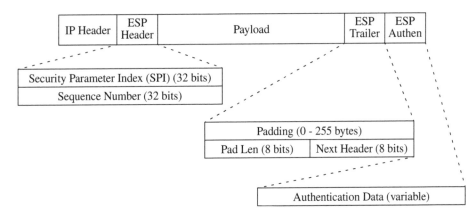

Figure 5-6 ESP header, trailer, and authentication segment formats

Confidentiality is achieved via encryption. The encryption algorithm employed for a particular IP packet is dictated by the SA over which the packet is sent. Because IP is a datagram protocol, each packet must carry enough information to establish cryptographic synchronization to allow the decrypting to work properly. The NULL encryption algorithm [RFC2410], in which no encryption is applied, is also a valid encryption algorithm. In this case, ESP provides a traffic authentication service only.

As with AH, additional fields are inserted into an IP packet to provide these services, and many of the fields have the same meaning as in AH. Unlike with AH, however, these fields are spread throughout the IP packet. Some are in an ESP header, others are in an ESP trailer, and one is in an ESP authentication segment, as shown in Figure 5-6.

The ESP header follows either a new IP header or a slightly modified original IP header, depending on the mode. The ESP trailer follows the end of the original IP packet, and the ESP authentication segment follows the trailer. If authentication is not applied, the ESP authentication segment is not appended. If encryption is applied, everything from the end of the ESP header to the end of the ESP trailer is encrypted.

The fields within the ESP header, trailer, and authentication segments are similar to those within the authentication header. In fact, the SPI, Sequence Number, Next

Header, and Authentication Data fields are defined just as they are in the AH protocol. The variable-length *Padding* field is used to pad the data to be encrypted to a 4-byte boundary or some other boundary appropriate for the encryption algorithm, and to meet IP packet alignment requirements. The *Pad Len* field specifies the length of the padding so that the padding can be stripped after the data is decrypted. Note that an arbitrary additional amount of padding can be used to mask the actual size of the original payload.

It is easy to see that by adding the ESP Header, Padding, and Authentication Data fields, the resulting packet will be larger than the original packet. This growth is problematic if the original packet size is already at or near the maximum transmission unit for the path. Because the MTU dictates the maximum packet size, encapsulating an already large IP packet may cause the new IP packet to be fragmented. ESP processing must be applied only to the whole IP packet and not to fragments. If an IP packet is fragmented, the security gateway must reassemble the entire IP packet before processing.

The Payload field in Figure 5-6 contains what ESP is to protect. When encryption is used, the Payload field may also contain additional structures required for cryptographic synchronization, such as an initialization vector, as used by some encryption algorithms (for example, [RFC2405]). The Payload field is only the upper-layer header and data when ESP used in transport mode. In tunnel mode, the entire original IP packet is placed within the Payload field.

Transport Mode

Figure 5-7 shows how the new IP packet is constructed from the original IP packet by inserting the ESP header between the IP header and payload, and by appending the ESP trailer and authentication segments, if necessary. If the original IP packet already had IPsec security headers, the new ESP header is placed before them (e.g., in SA bundling). Because the original IP header is used, the IP packet's source and destination cannot change. Therefore, ESP in transport mode, like AH in transport mode, can be used only between hosts.

Transport mode is most useful when it is not necessary to hide or authenticate the source and destination IP addresses. Unlike with AH, the authentication is not provided over any fields of the original IP header, immutable or not. Encryption, if performed, provides protection only of the payload and not of the original IP header or the ESP header.

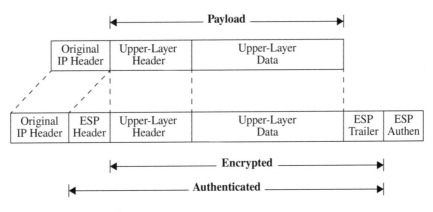

Figure 5-7 ESP transport mode

Tunnel Mode

Tunnel mode encapsulates the entire original IP packet into the new IP packet. Figure 5-8 shows how a new IP header and an ESP header are added to the beginning of the original IP packet, and the ESP trailer and authentication segments are appended to the end. If the tunnel is between hosts, the source and destination IP addresses in the new IP header can be the same as the addresses in the original. If the tunnel is between two security gateways, the addresses in the new IP header will reflect the gateway addresses. Running ESP in tunnel mode between security gateways can provide both confidentiality and authentication for the transit traffic between the two gateways. It protects the ultimate source and destination from observers because the original IP header is within the payload of the new IP packet.

5.4 Internet Key Exchange

Although the IPsec ESP and AH protocols specify how the data security services are to be applied to each IP packet according to the SAs negotiated between the IPsec devices, they do not tell how these SAs are actually negotiated. The SAs can be manually configured by the system administrators or, more importantly, they

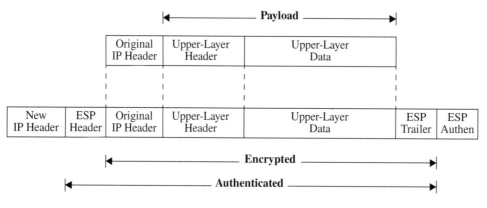

Figure 5-8 ESP tunnel mode

can be dynamically negotiated via a key management protocol such as Internet Key Exchange [RFC2409].

There are two reasons for dynamic negotiation of IPsec security associations. First, it is not possible to anticipate the need to establish a new SA whenever data must be secured outside the currently established SAs. Second, security associations should not have long lifetimes because the longer that keying material is exposed, the greater the chance that it can be cracked. To avoid this risk, keying material must be regenerated and SAs renegotiated periodically.

IKE is based on the framework defined by the Internet Security Association and Key Management Protocol [RFC2408]. It implements part of the Oakley [RFC2412] and SKEME (Secure Key Exchange Mechanism) [KRAW96] key exchange methods, as well as two exchange methods of its own.

ISAKMP defines how the two communicating peers can go through a set of procedures to secure the communication channel between them. It provides the means for two peers to authenticate each other, exchange key management information, and negotiate security services. It does not, however, specify how the authentication is done or what keys are generated. More plainly, it provides a vehicle for transportation, but which goods will be transported is left for others to specify.

An ISAKMP message consists of an ISAKMP header and one or more ISAKMP payloads chained together in a UDP (port 500) packet. This is shown in Figure

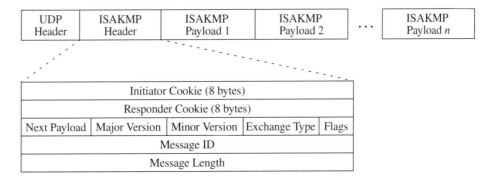

Figure 5-9 ISAKMP message format

5-9. The *initiator cookie* and the *responder cookie* are special values generated by the ISAKMP peers to provide some protection against denial-of-service attacks, in which an attacker might try to generate a lot of bogus ISAKMP messages and overwhelm the ISAKMP processor. A cookie affords some protection by permitting ISAKMP to discard bogus messages quickly before too many of the processing resources have been wasted.[4] The two cookies are also used for identifying the security association between the two ISAKMP peers after the negotiation has been completed successfully.

ISAKMP defines two phases in the security association negotiation. The first phase is the negotiation between the two ISAKMP peers. In this phase, two peers agree on how to protect further communications between them, thus establishing an ISAKMP security association. Although it is called a "security association," an ISAKMP SA is not to be confused with the IPsec SA discussed previously. An ISAKMP SA is bidirectional, and does not actually apply to the IPsec traffic.

In the second phase, security associations for other protocols (IPsec in particular, although in theory an ISAKMP SA can be used by other protocols) are negotiated between the two ISAKMP peers. Because the communication channel between the negotiators is already secure, these subsequent negotiations can proceed more quickly. In many cases, a security gateway will negotiate IPsec SAs on behalf of

---

4. Cookies are useful only when one assumes that an attacker cannot passively eavesdrop or cause redirection of an initial IKE exchange.

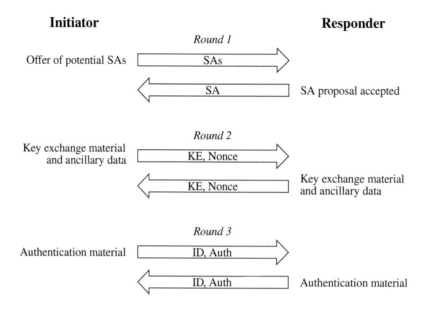

Figure 5-10 IKE phase 1 main mode exchange

the hosts it protects. One ISAKMP SA can be used to negotiate many IPsec SAs, reducing negotiation overhead.

5.4.1 Phase 1 Negotiation

IKE defines two modes when negotiating a phase 1 SA: main mode and aggressive mode. The message exchange of main mode is shown in Figure 5-10.

There are three negotiating rounds in the IKE phase 1 main mode exchange. In the first round, one ISAKMP entity (the *initiator*) sends multiple SA proposals to another entity (the *responder*). The responder chooses one proposal and sends it back to the initiator. In the second round, the two peers exchange their key exchange parameters and random use-once values called *nonces*. The use of nonces is intended to guard against replay attacks. In the third round, all the exchanged information is authenticated through one of three authentication mechanisms: shared secret, digital signature, or public key encryption.

Initiator   **Responder**

Offer of potential SAs,
key exchange material,
nonce, and identifier

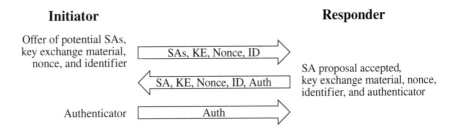

SA proposal accepted,
key exchange material, nonce,
identifier, and authenticator

SAs, KE, Nonce, ID

SA, KE, Nonce, ID, Auth

Authenticator   Auth

Figure 5-11 IKE phase 1 aggressive mode exchange

When a shared secret mechanism is employed, the two peers use a secret key derived from a shared secret to create the keyed hash. The keyed hash is then exchanged between the two peers and serves as the authenticator. With the second alternative—digital signature—the authentication between the initiator and the responder is carried out using the digital signature of the negotiation entities. The two peers exchange digitally signed hashes of their identities, public key values, and SA proposals. The third alternative is public key encryption. Here, the two peers exchange the public-key encrypted value of their IDs and nonces, as well as a keyed hash value.

In aggressive mode, shown in Figure 5-11, the SA proposals, key exchange parameters, nonce, and identity information are all exchanged in a single message. In addition, the authentication information exchanged between the initiator and responder is not encrypted.

After completion of the phase 1 negotiation, an ISAKMP SA is established. The ISAKMP SA is a bidirectional SA used to protect subsequent phase 2 security association negotiations.

5.4.2 Phase 2 Negotiation

During phase 2, security associations are negotiated on behalf of services such as IPsec or any other service that needs keying material or parameter negotiation. Because a secure channel has already been established in phase 1, the negotiation can be performed more quickly; thus, it is referred to as *quick mode*. The message exchanges in quick mode are shown in Figure 5-12.

Initiator   **Responder**

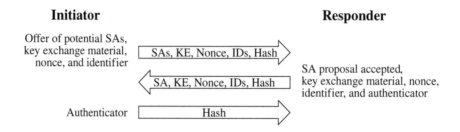

Offer of potential SAs,
key exchange material,
nonce, and identifier

SA proposal accepted,
key exchange material, nonce,
identifier, and authenticator

Authenticator

Figure 5-12 IKE phase 2 quick mode exchange

The identity of the IKE peers has already been verified in phase 1, and exchanges between the IKE peers are already protected by the ISAKMP SA. Therefore, the identities passed in quick mode are not the identities of the IKE peers but rather the identities of the selectors to be used in the IPsec security policy database.

A phase 1 ISAKMP SA is required when negotiating a phase 2 SA. Once established, a phase 2 SA can exist independently of the phase 1 SA even if the phase 1 SA is later destroyed.

5.4.3 Key Generation in IKE

Recall that the key exchange (KE) parameters are passed between the two IKE peers. How do the IKE peers use the exchanged parameters to generate the various keys used for authentication and encryption?

Central to key generation in IKE is the Diffie-Hellman algorithm [DIFF76]. The Diffie-Hellman algorithm allows two parties to derive a secret key from publicly known parameters as long as these parameters satisfy certain mathematical properties. Specifically, the two known parameters are a large prime number p, and g, one of p's *primitive generators*. A primitive generator is defined as a value g such that every number from 1 to $p-1$ can be expressed as $g^a \bmod p$ for some a.

The initiator and responder will use these values p and g to generate a pair of keys in the following way. First, the initiator picks p and g, chooses a large number x, and calculates z_I:

$$z_I = g^x \bmod p$$

The values z_I, g, and p are sent to the responder as the KE parameters in round 2 of phase 1. Similarly, the responder calculates z_R from some large number y:

$$z_R = g^y \bmod p$$

Then z_R is sent to the initiator. Now each side generates a key:

$$k_I = z_R^x \bmod p$$

$$k_R = z_I^y \bmod p$$

Without exchanging anything secret, k_I and k_R turn out to be equal:

$$k_I = z_R^x \bmod p$$

$$= (g^y \bmod p)^x \bmod p$$

$$= g^{xy} \bmod p$$

$$= (g^x \bmod p)^y \bmod p$$

$$= z_R^x \bmod p$$

$$= k_R$$

Because of the difficulty of computing discrete factors when the prime number p is large, it is not feasible to derive x from z_I. Therefore, it is not practical for an eavesdropper to derive the same secret as the two exchange entities can. The Diffie-Hellman algorithm, however, is vulnerable to a man-in-the-middle attack, in which someone intercepts the message exchanges and impersonates one of the peers, effectively hijacking the SA negotiation. Consequently, in the IKE exchanges, the two exchanging parties must be authenticated.

The Diffie-Hellman secret key g^{xy} generated from the phase 1 exchange is called the *ISAKMP master key,* and the Diffie-Hellman secret key generated from the phase 2 exchange is called the *user master key.*

The Oakley [RFC2412] key determination protocol uses the Diffie-Hellman scheme to exchange secret keys securely between two authenticated parties. Oakley defines three modes of key exchange: aggressive mode, conservative mode, and quick mode. Aggressive mode uses a three-way message exchange for negotiation, but the identities of the negotiating parties are not protected. In conservative mode, six messages are used, and the identities of the negotiating parties are protected. Quick mode is used when an old key is already present (e.g., from the previous exchanges), permitting a simpler exchange using only three messages but still protecting the identities. The Oakey protocol also defines five groups for the Diffie-Hellman key exchange. Each group defines the set of parameters—that is, the p and g pair—used for the exchange. For example, Oakley group 1 defines p as follows (in hexidecimal):

```
FFFFFFFF FFFFFFFF C90FDAA2 2168C234 C4C6628B 80DC1CD1
29024E08 8A67CC74 020BBEA6 3B139B22 514A0879 8E3404DD
EF9519B3 CD3A431B 302B0A6D F25F1437 4FE1356D 6D51C245
E485B576 625E7EC6 F44C42E9 A63A3620 FFFFFFFF FFFFFFFF
```

The primitive generator g for group 1 is 2. IKE uses the exchange modes and groups defined in Oakley for its key exchange negotiation.

5.5 IPsec Implementation

IPsec's role in providing security in the Internet is increasing. The richness and flexibility of IPsec make it possible to address a wide range of security needs for IP traffic. Its status as an IETF standard also makes it the protocol of choice for Internet security.

However, the richness and flexibility of IPsec also make it difficult to create simple implementations from different vendors that can interoperate. The IPsec RFCs contain several hundred instances of *should* and *optional*. Each *should* and *optional* means that an implementor can choose whether to implement the feature.

To illustrate how the various components of IPsec work together, consider a host with a single network interface running an IPsec implementation with the following components, as shown in Figure 5-13:

• **IPsec Base Protocols** This component implements the ESP and AH encapsulation procedures and interacts with the SAD to determine the security

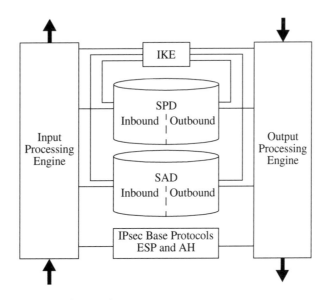

Figure 5-13 IPsec component interactions

measures to apply to an IP packet. This component usually resides within the kernel of the computer operating system.

- **IKE** This component is responsible for negotiating and establishing SAs (both ISAKMP and IPsec) and for keeping a list of SAs whose endpoint is this host. The IKE component populates the SAD through IKE negotiation. This component is usually a user-level process.
- **Security Association Database** This component contains all the active IPsec SAs. Outbound and inbound SAs are listed separately. The database is populated during the IKE negotiation, and each entry is deleted after its expiration.
- **Security Policy Database** This component contains policy entries. Outbound and inbound policies are listed separately.

5.5.1 Inbound Packet Processing

When an inbound IP packet arrives from the network, the IP layer input processing engine (e.g., the *ip_intr* function in BSD UNIX) is invoked by the layer 2 software interrupt. If the IP packet is an IPsec packet, the following steps are taken:

1. The processing engine extracts the SPI, protocol (AH or ESP), and destination IP address contained in the IP and either AH or ESP headers.

2. The processing engine retrieves the SA information from SAD. If an active SA is not present, this function fails and an error is logged.

3. If the SA retrieval is successful, the IPsec function processes the packet and returns the decapsulated IP packet.

4. The decapsulated IP packet is checked against the policies in the inbound side of the SPD to determine whether the packet is allowed. If the packet is not allowed, it is dropped and an error is logged.

5. If the packet conforms to the security policy, the packet is passed to the upper layer.

5.5.2 Outbound Packet Processing

Outbound packet processing is more complex than inbound processing because there may not be an established SA for the packet at the time the packet arrives from the upper layer, so an IKE negotiation session may be invoked. In addition, unlike the easy match of SPI, protocol, and destination IP address to an SA in the SAD, the outbound side of the SPD must be searched to determine the appropriate SPD entry to apply.

When an outbound IP packet arrives from an upper-layer protocol, the IP layer output processing engine (e.g., the *ip_output* function in BSD UNIX) is invoked. The following steps happen in sequence:

1. The processing engine searches the SPD to find the first matching entry for the packet. If there is no match, the packet is dropped and an error indication is returned.

2. If a matching SPD entry is obtained, the processing engine determines whether an active SA has already been established for the packet. This is usually done by a pointer associated with the matching entry that points to the location of the appropriate SA in the SAD.

3. If there is currently no active SA established, the IKE function is invoked to negotiate and establish an SA for the policy entry. While waiting for the SA to be established, the output processing engine determines whether to queue the packet and wait for an SA establishment signal or simply to drop the packet (remember, IP is best effort).

4. If an active SA has been established or if the IKE function returns with a successfully established SA, IPsec protocol processing is invoked to encapsulate the packet according to the parameters specified in the SA entry. When IKE returns a newly established SA, a pointer can be created from the SPD entry to this new SA entry to speed the search for subsequent packets.

5. The IP output function continues to process the resulting IPsec packet, preparing it for transmission.

6

Authentication

> *Know yourself and know your enemy,*
> *and you will not be defeated.*
> —SUNZHI, THE ART OF WAR

Identity is the key to many things—it is the map from our person to our possessions and permissions. But in a world of six billion people, it is not enough to simply declare that we are who we say we are. We must prove it.

Authentication is the act of verifying the identity of someone or something within a defined context.

The concept of an authentication context is important because proof of identity in one circumstance may not be proof of identity in another, and an identity in one context may fail to be meaningful in another. For example, a passport identifies a person with respect to a country, an employee badge identifies the person as an employee of a company, and a private club membership card is valid only within that club. In computer security, the authentication of a user is always explicitly associated with the context of the authentication.

Authentication is usually an interaction between two entities: the object of the authentication (a user or a client) wishing to assert its identity, and an authenticator (a peer or a server) performing the identity verification. The user provides *authentication information*—which includes its claimed identity and supporting information—to the authenticator. To perform the verification, the authenticator applies an *authentication function F* to the provided information and compares the result with the expected result:

$$F(\text{authentication information}) = \text{expected result}$$

If the result of the function F matches the expected result, the user's identity is verified.

The authentication information can be a simple password or a complex set of parameters and messages. Similarly, the function F can be a simple function (as in the case of mere password comparison) or a complex application of cryptographic algorithms (as in the case of digital signatures).

If the authentication information and the authentication function F are totally under the control of the two entities, the authentication scheme is called a *two-party* scheme. However, in many cases, it is more scalable and secure to enlist the help of a third party (or more than one third party) for the authentication. These schemes are called *trusted third-party* schemes.

Another factor to consider is the integrity and confidentiality of the authentication information. It is important that the information used for authentication be secure and not be obtainable by unauthorized parties. Measures must also be taken to secure the authentication information during network transit. The transit risk is particularly important in the case of VPNs, where the authentication information must be transmitted across the Internet.

6.1 Two-Party Authentication

Two-party authentication can have both one-way and two-way schemes. In a one-way scheme, a client must be authenticated to its server, but the server need not be authenticated to its client. In a two-way scheme, the client and server must be mutually authenticated to each other. A two-way protocol can consist simply of two independent one-way protocols. Sometimes, mutual authentication can be performed with the same protocol exchanges.

Many two-party authentication schemes rely on both the user and the peer knowing one or more pieces of information that no one else knows. This information is usually called the *shared secret*. Knowledge of the secret is proof of identity for the user.

Strictly speaking, the user and the peer need not actually know the same piece of information. The peer may know a piece of information that can be derived only from the secret held by the user. In other cases, the information shared is not secret at all, as in the use of public key cryptography for authentication, when the user simply shares its public key with the peer.

The difference between various two-party authentication schemes lies in how the authentication information, the authentication function, and the expected results are created, stored, and transmitted between the two authenticating parties.

The authentication information can be either static (e.g., a fixed password) or dynamic (e.g., a one-time password). If the authentication information is dynamic, its change may depend on the client, the server, or both. Similarly, the expected results can have the same kinds of variations. The authentication function can employ either a symmetric or an asymmetric cryptographic algorithm.

A great many two-party authentication schemes rely on the two parties—the user and the peer—to share the same piece of secret information. In these cases, the creation mechanism must ensure that only the two parties know the secret and that as few other parties as possible are involved. Generally, the secret information must be distributed outside the normal communication channels for which authentication is performed.

Once the secret is created, the user and the peer must store it or some derivative of it. Depending on the authentication scheme, the peer may have to store the secret, some representation of the secret, or some value derived from the secret. The two parties must have mutual confidence in the effectiveness of the storage arrangement: If the user loses control of the secret, the peer may give an impostor access to a valuable resource; if the peer loses control of the user's secret, the user's identity is compromised.

The act of authentication in a communications environment requires the user and the peer to exchange information over a communications channel. In a networked environment, authentication schemes must assume that others can listen to what is transmitted over the channel.

One drawback of two-party authentication schemes is that the authentication information for each user-peer pair must be independently established. Suppose that there are N communication entities and that each one must be able to authenticate all the others. This will result in a total of $N(N-1)/2$ independently managed authentication sessions. When shared secrets are used, there will be $N(N-1)/2$ total shared secrets in the system. When N becomes large, this arrangement can be quite difficult to manage.

There are many variations of two-party authentication schemes: passwords, challenge/response, one-time passwords, token cards, and others. These types are not mutually exclusive and an authentication scheme can usually have characteristics of more than one type.

Passwords

Password authentication schemes are perhaps the simplest and still the most widely used form of two-party authentication. The user and the peer have previously worked out a secret word or phrase that only they know. The provided information from the user is the password itself. At its basic level, the authentication function is a simple comparison operation.

The password scheme has several major drawbacks. First, passwords are often either hard to remember (and consequently are written down) or easy to guess. Because passwords are typically generated by humans, they have certain characteristics that make some combinations of letters (such as those that form words) more likely than others. Exploiting this fact is called a *dictionary* attack, and studies have shown that as many as 40 percent of the passwords on an average computer system can be guessed by using simple words and word combinations [KLEI90]. Adding a random value to the password during storage, called a *salt* or a *seed*, increases the *entropy* of the password (that is, makes it harder to guess). Even so, researchers have developed a list of common salt values applied to dictionary words and derivatives, and they estimate that the list can match as many as 30 percent of passwords on any given host [FELD90].

In 1985, the National Institute of Standards and Technology (NIST) developed a set of guidelines for choosing passwords [NIST85], but these guidelines are generally not enforced by the computer host, and many users do not know of or comply with them. Although the studies cited in the preceding paragraph may suggest that users are careless in password choice, other researchers argue that the designers of security systems are more to blame than the users [ADAM99], suggesting that organizations do not teach users how password systems work for fear they may try to defeat them. As a result, the users do not necessarily realize what makes a password weak.

A second drawback is the need for storage. The peer must store the password, so the user must rely on the peer's physical security. One way to reduce the risks of storing the password at the peer is for the peer to store a different set of values using a one-way hash (see Section 2.5). In this case, the authentication function is the one-way hash function, and the expected result is the hashed value of the password. Because one-way hashes are designed so that inversion is infeasible, someone stealing the stored hash cannot reconstruct the original.

Because hashing algorithms are well known, an attacker can launch a brute force attack by hashing every possible combination of characters of certain lengths and comparing them to the stored hash value. Consequently, simply storing the hashes of passwords is not enough; you must also control access to the files where they are stored.

Third, the password is transmitted from the user to the peer over a network. Depending on the security of the network or the means used to secure the transmission, the password may be subject to eavesdropping. It does not matter how well a password has been chosen if someone can watch it go past on the wire. Because this attack is passive, it may be quite a while before either the user or the peer realizes that the password has been compromised, if they realize it at all.

Finally, the peer may have no way of disqualifying an attacker from simply submitting hundreds of guesses, hoping one will work. When a user tries several passwords in quick succession, either the user has forgotten the password and is desperately trying to remember, or a trial-and-error attack has been mounted. Some systems recognize this possibility and place the user into a so-called penalty box hoping to fend off the attacker.[1]

The Password Authentication Protocol (PAP), from the group of authentication protocols used by the Point-to-Point Protocol (PPP), is an example of a straight password-based scheme. PAP is discussed in Section 6.1.1.

Challenge/Response

A *challenge/response* authentication scheme is a password-based scheme in which the peer asks the user a question—that is, presents a challenge—and the user must answer the challenge appropriately or the authentication will fail. Here the authentication information is dynamic. For example, say both the user and the peer have a list of 100 random words, and the lists are exactly the same. These lists are the shared secret. The peer could ask for the 82nd entry, and the user would have to

---

1. This approach, of course, also locks out legitimate users.

supply it. Another example is the use of a shared secret as the key to an encryption algorithm. The peer sends the user a random phrase, and the user processes it using the shared key and sends it back. The peer also processes the phrase with the shared key and then compares the user's results to its own processed version. In this case, the provided information from the user is the random phrase processed by the secret key.

Because the challenge is initiated by the peer, the peer can readily determine how many tries to allow the subject before giving up. The peer can also determine that a constantly failing user is wasting valuable resources and can lock access to the resource for a predetermined period.

Like PAP, the Challenge Handshake Authentication Protocol (CHAP), also discussed in Section 6.1.1, is an authentication mechanism defined for use in PPP.

One-Time Passwords

One of the major drawbacks of password schemes, as mentioned earlier, is that someone can learn the shared secret by eavesdropping on the transmission of the password from the user to the peer. Even if the shared secret is a key used to encrypt a challenge value, collecting enough samples aids in cracking the key if the choice of challenge/response pairs is not well designed.[2] The attacker can then, at his or her convenience, replay the password or the response to the peer and assume the identity of the original user. One way to avoid this is to use a scheme called *one-time passwords*, in which the password is valid only for a single authentication session—not before and not after. In this case, an attacker cannot replay an eavesdropped password or response.

Typically, a list of one-time passwords is mutually generated by the user and the peer. The user uses the passwords in order, and, upon successful completion of a session using one password, it is crossed off the list and the next password is used for the next authentication session. Of course, keeping a list of passwords is much more complicated than keeping only one, and one-time passwords per se do not mitigate a breach of physical security at the peer. But some clever one-time pass-

---

2. In theory, the challenge/response scheme can also be viewed as a one-time password scheme in which the authentication information is dependent on the challenge from the peer. We separate them here based on the distinction that in most other one-time password schemes, the authentication information is not dependent on the peer or server.

word schemes do provide solutions to both problems, as we shall see with S/KEY (described in Section 6.1.3).

Token Cards

Password-based authentication methods have one serious flaw that no algorithm or protocol can fix: There is a human factor in the loop. Passwords should be hard to guess and should be changed often. Unfortunately, "hard to guess" generally means "hard to remember." Users tend to choose passwords that mean something to them: a birthday, a child's name, or some common word six to eight characters in length. Such passwords have poor entropy and are easily guessed with brute force methods such as the dictionary attack. Good passwords are long and random. However, any password, no matter how long or how random, can be guessed given enough time. Users tend to use the same passwords too long for fear of forgetting new ones. Fear of forgetting passwords also leads many users to write them down. A shared secret works only if the shared information is kept secret, so the scheme is compromised the moment the crib sheet falls into the wrong hands.

One way to get around the shortcomings of human factors is to have a device pick the passwords. A *token card* serves this purpose. A token card generates a different octet stream every time it is used, and so it is a special case of a one-time password scheme. The important aspect about token cards is that they keep the token stream from being predicable. Some token cards keep the token generation algorithm secret; others use secret seeds with known algorithms. The generation mechanism is known only to the authenticator and the token card. After the token card is synchronized with the peer, the user can use the tokens generated by the card as the password.

SecurID, from RSA Security (formerly Security Dynamics), is perhaps the most widely used token card. Each SecurID card has a unique 64-bit seed value that is combined with a random number generator algorithm to generate a new code every 60 seconds. Only the associated server knows which number is valid at that moment for that user and card combination. A user-entered PIN is combined with the token value to form the authentication information, so merely possessing the SecurID card is not enough to prove identity.

Smartcards

The term *smartcard* describes a suite of small, credit-card–size electronic devices used for storage and identification. What we think of today as a smartcard has integrated circuitry providing memory and possibly processing power. Smartcards with processors may have their own operating systems and can run programs. In particular, smartcards are proving to be an ideal place to implement cryptographic algorithms and store keys, especially when a cryptographic coprocessor is included to speed up the algorithms.

The International Organization for Standardization (ISO) has several standards under development governing the types and interfaces to what it calls *identification cards*. ISO 7816 [ISO7816] specifies the identification cards with electronic contacts, their physical characteristics, locations of contacts, and transmission protocols for data onto input and output.

Smartcards have several advantages in a communications environment. Secret key information is written into electrically erasable programmable read-only memory (EEPROM) surrounded by tamper-resistant mechanisms such as irreversible fuses and voltage fluctuation sensors. Because the key never leaves the card, authentication using a smartcard instead of a human at a keyboard is strengthened. The card is portable, so keys can follow the person. Because every use of a key provides a cracker one more piece of information that can be used to help crack the key, a smartcard may keep an accurate count of the number of uses of a particular key. Smartcards still have vulnerabilities. In particular, because a signal must be transmitted from the smartcard to the authentication device, the signal is subject to eavesdropping.

Smartcards have been fairly slow to catch on in the United States, although they enjoy wide acceptance in Europe and Asia. Lack of widely adopted smartcard standards, and the cost of converting from an infrastructure dominated by magnetic stripe technology, may be to blame.

Smartcard technology is a mechanism for secure storage of authentication credentials and facilitates the portability of the credentials. Therefore, smartcards can be used in both two-party schemes and trusted third-party schemes.

6.1.1 PPP Authentication

Recall that the Point-to-Point Protocol provides a standard method for encapsulating network layer protocol information over point-to-point links. To establish a connection over the link, each end of the link must first exchange Link Control Protocol (LCP) packets to negotiate the configuration of the connection. Among the things configured is which protocol, if any, will be used to authenticate the user of the link. If an authentication algorithm is agreed upon, an authentication phase begins. Authentication in PPP is only unidirectional; if the connection is full duplex, both client and server may perform authentication phases (and they can be different protocols), as the LCP negotiations dictate.

Usually a database within each PPP server associates a user with its authentication information. For any authentication mechanism to be viable, this information must be stored so as to limit access to it as much as possible. Similarly, the distribution of the shared secret must also limit the number of entities that must handle it. Even if the authentication material is handled and stored securely, all that is for naught if the implementation of the authentication protocol is not itself free of security holes.

PAP

PAP, the Password Authentication Protocol [RFC1334], provides a simple method for a user to establish its identity using a two-way handshake, as shown in Figure 6-1. A user ID and password pair are repeatedly sent by the user to the peer until the authentication is acknowledged or the connection terminated. This authentication is done only once—at the initialization of the connection—and remains valid for the lifetime of the connection.

Of course, PAP is not a very strong authentication method: Passwords are sent in the clear along with the ID, and there is no protection from replay or repeated trial-and-error attacks. Moreover, the authenticating peer has no control over the frequency or timing of the authentication requests. PAP is most appropriately used where the serial link is considered physically secure. When PPP is tunneled—as it would be with PPTP, L2TP, or L2F (see Chapter 4)—the assumption of physical security must be utterly disregarded.

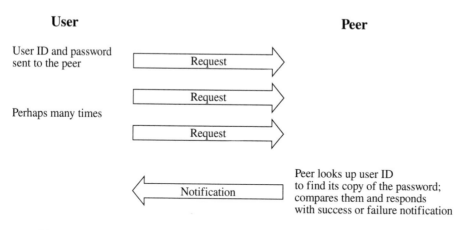

User   **Peer**

User ID and password
sent to the peer   Request

Perhaps many times   Request

                                    Request

                                                        Peer looks up user ID
                                    Notification   to find its copy of the password;
                                                        compares them and responds
                                                        with success or failure notification

Figure 6-1 Two-way PAP handshake

CHAP

CHAP, the Challenge Handshake Authentication Protocol [RFC1994], is a three-way handshake used to verify the identity of the user on a PPP link (see Figure 6-2). After the link is established, the peer issues a challenge to the user. This challenge should be a unique and unpredictable value and should be changed on each subsequent challenge. The user responds with a value calculated by using a keyed

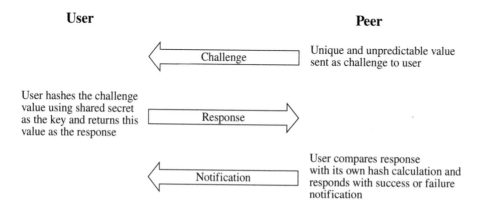

User   **Peer**

                                    Challenge   Unique and unpredictable value
                                                            sent as challenge to user

User hashes the challenge
value using shared secret
as the key and returns this   Response
value as the response

                                                            User compares response
                                    Notification   with its own hash calculation and
                                                            responds with success or failure
                                                            notification

Figure 6-2 Three-way CHAP handshake

one-way hash function run over the challenge value. The key used in the one-way hash is the shared secret between the user and the peer. The peer checks the response against its own calculation of the hash value using the shared secret. These values will be the same only if the hashes used the same key, so the peer replies with a success or failure message depending on whether the two hash values are the same.

CHAP has several advantages over PAP. The shared secret is never transmitted in the clear from the user to the peer. Playback protection is provided if the challenge is indeed unique and unpredictable, because the response message is valid only for one particular challenge, and that challenge is valid only one time. The peer controls the timing and frequency of the authentication, so it can limit the number of challenges and ignore users who habitually misbehave. Finally, the authentication can be repeated at any time during the connection.

The major drawback of CHAP is that the shared secret must be stored at the peer and used in a cleartext form because the secret is the key to the one-way hash. Even if the secret were stored in encrypted form, it would have to be decrypted for use.

EAP

EAP, the Extensible Authentication Protocol [RFC2284], is a general authentication protocol that supports multiple authentication mechanisms. Because PAP and CHAP are single-mechanism protocols, choosing one or the other during the LCP negotiation implies the mechanism used during the authentication phase. If EAP is chosen during the LCP negotiation, the actual choice of mechanism is postponed until the *Authentication Phase*. This may sound like a subtle point, but it more completely separates the link establishment from the authentication mechanism.

Three authentication types are defined by the RFC: MD5 challenge (like CHAP), one-time password (as per the scheme described in [RFC1938], which is similar to S/KEY but more generic), and generic token card. Others can be added (hence the name "extensible") without losing backward compatibility.

The authentication exchange is shown in Figure 6-3. The peer sends an identity request (unless the user is already known by some other means). The user responds with its purported identity. The peer then sends one or more requests for authentication using one of the previously mentioned authentication types. The

User   **Peer**

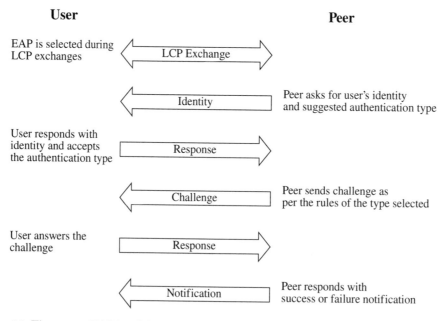

EAP is selected during
LCP exchanges

LCP Exchange

Identity

Peer asks for user's identity
and suggested authentication type

User responds with
identity and accepts
the authentication type

Response

Challenge

Peer sends challenge as
per the rules of the type selected

User answers the
challenge

Response

Notification

Peer responds with
success or failure notification

Figure 6-3 Three-way EAP handshake

user can reject a request if it cannot provide authentication credentials under that mechanism, and it can ask for the use of an alternative authentication type. When the user gets an authentication request it can answer, it sends back a type-specific response. The peer either accepts that response—and the user is authenticated—or rejects it with a failure message.

Although EAP provides the framework for a user to be authenticated via multiple authentication mechanisms, it is anticipated that a named user will be authenticated by only one mechanism. Having multiple mechanisms authenticate one named user allows an attacker to focus on the weakest of the mechanisms when, by gaining entry, the attacker has effectively defeated the strongest of the mechanisms. Although EAP is extensible and flexible, it is not widely used.

6.1.2 RADIUS

Managing authentication for simple resource access is one thing, and managing network access in a heterogeneous environment such as the Internet is quite another. In such an environment, well-defined protocols and standards, and widely available implementations that can interoperate with each other, are critical. The Remote Access Dial In User Service (RADIUS) [RFC2138] was developed in such a context. With RADIUS, remote dial-in users can be authenticated easily with widely available products and services. The majority of Internet users still use telephone dial-in as the network access method, and many of them use RADIUS for authentication. RADIUS is also being widely used in network services other than dial-in services.

RADIUS was first developed by Livingston Enterprise, now a division of Lucent Technologies. RADIUS uses a client-server architecture and includes two components: an authentication server and a client protocol. The server is installed on a central computer. The client protocol is implemented on the network access server (NAS).

RADIUS authenticates users through a series of communications between the client and the server. After a user is authenticated, the client provides that user with access to the appropriate network services.

A typical RADIUS authentication session in a dial-in scenario works as follows:

1. A remote user dials in to a modem connected to an NAS. When the modem connection is completed, the NAS prompts the user for a name and password.

2. Upon receiving the username/password pair, the NAS creates a data packet, called the Authentication Request, from this information. This packet includes information identifying the NAS sending the authentication request, the port that is being used for the modem connection, and the username and password. For protection from eavesdropping hackers, the NAS, acting as a RADIUS client, scrambles the message using a predetermined shared secret between the NAS and the RADIUS server.

3. The Authentication Request is sent over the network from the RADIUS client to the RADIUS server. This communication can be done over a local or wide area network. If the RADIUS server cannot be reached, the RADIUS client can route the request to an alternative server.

4. When an Authentication Request is received, the RADIUS server validates the request and then verifies the username and password information. This information can also be passed to the appropriate security system being supported.

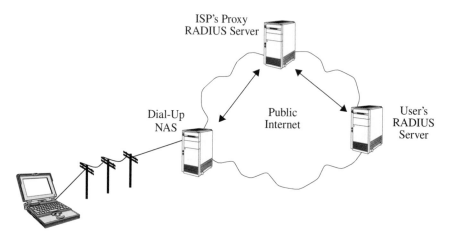

Figure 6-4 RADIUS proxy server

This could be a UNIX password file, Kerberos, a commercially available security system, or even a custom developed security system.

5. If the username and password are correct, the server sends an Authentication Acknowledgment that includes information on the user's network system and service requirements. For example, the RADIUS server can tell the NAS that a user needs IP over PPP or IPX over PPP to connect to the network. The acknowledgment can even contain filtering information to limit a user's access to specific resources on the network (the authorization feature of RADIUS).

6. If at any point in this log-in process conditions are not met, the RADIUS server sends an Authentication Reject message to the NAS, and the user is denied access to the network.

RADIUS also employs a distributed architecture in the event that an NAS must support authentication for multiple authentication domains (where the different domains serve as different contexts for the authentication). The ISP in control of the NAS can have a centralized RADIUS proxy, as shown in Figure 6-4.

The proxy RADIUS server resides at the ISP. When a dial-up user enters its username and password, it uses the format "joe@mycorp.com." Then the NAS sends an Authentication Request to the ISP's proxy RADIUS server. After finding that the request is for "mycorp.com," the ISP's proxy RADIUS server forwards the request to the appropriate RADIUS server for that user.

A shared secret between the NAS and the RADIUS server is used to protect the communication between the NAS and the ISP's proxy RADIUS server. A separate secret password is used to protect the communication between the proxy server and the user's real RADIUS server.

Although the NAS and the RADIUS proxy server are involved in the authentication exchange, their role is relegated to the delivery of the authentication information from the remote access user to the user's authentication server. Thus, the RADIUS authentication scheme is still regarded as a two-party scheme.

6.1.3 S/KEY and OTP

S/KEY [RFC1760] is a one-time password scheme developed by Bellcore (now Telecordia). OTP, which stands for one-time password [RFC1938], evolved from S/KEY and is very similar. The idea is that the user and the peer each construct a long list of one-time passwords, each successive one derived from the preceding one. The initial password, called S, plus a salt, is hashed with MD4 [RFC1320] (S/KEY) or MD5 [RFC1321] (OTP) to create the first entry x_1. The x_1 entry is then hashed to create x_2 and so on until some number of them (say N) are created. So, for x_i, the hash function is applied a total of i times:

$$x_1 = H(S)$$

$$x_2 = H(H(S))$$

$$= H((x_1))$$

$$x_i = H(x_{i-1})$$

The last entry is x_N. The user holds onto this list and keeps it confidential (actually, as long as the user has S and the salt, it can re-create the list at any time). The peer need keep only one entry: x_{N+1}, that is, S plus the salt hashed $N+1$ times.

The passwords are then used one at a time, working backward through the list. Because x_{i+1} can be derived from x_i, an eavesdropper can learn x_i and know all subsequent passwords. However, because MD4 and MD5 are one-way hashes, knowing x_i does not give the eavesdropper any clue about what x_{i-1} is.

When the user is ready to be authenticated, the user sends x_N to the peer. Recall that the peer has x_{N+1} stored, so all it has to do is to hash x_N once and compare the result with x_{N+1}. If they match, the user is authenticated. Now the user must scratch x_N off its list, and the peer must disregard x_{N+1} and save x_N. The next time the user must be authenticated, it uses x_{N-1}, and the peer hashes that to get x_N, which it has stored. Again, both sides back up one on the list. When the list runs out, or when either side chooses, a new S is picked and the list is regenerated.

Notice that, after the initial use of the shared secret S, the peer discards it. Even if someone steals the authentication information kept by the peer—that is, x_i—it is useless because it cannot be used to derive S, and it has already been used as a password.

S/KEY and OTP can be used in a challenge protocol. In this case, the user need know only the value of S. The peer challenges the user with a number C and the salt. The user adds the salt to S and hashes that value C times. This is the response value. The peer hashes this response one more time and compares it with the value it has stored, that is, x_{C+1}.

S/KEY is vulnerable to a server spoofing attack in a one-way scheme. An attacker may pretend to be the authentication server and trick the user into sending it the next value in the list.

6.2 Trusted Third-Party Authentication

As discussed in Section 6.1, using a two-party authentication scheme requires the user and the peer to share a piece of secret information. Every pair of users and peers must share a different piece of secret information. As the amount of secret information proliferates, it makes the creation, storage, and transmission of the secret information more difficult to manage.

Trusted third-party schemes employee a special entity (or sometimes more than one) whose responsibility is to aid authentication. When a user must be authenticated to a peer, a trusted third party can vouch for the user's identity or can provide information that can be used in authentication. Both the user and the peer trust the third party to provide the service.

Trusted third-party schemes can employ both symmetric and public key cryptography. In Kerberos, an example of the former, users authenticate themselves to an authentication service to receive a credential for use with other servers in the network.

Public key cryptography has a built-in mechanism for authentication. As long as there is a unique mapping from the public key to the user that created it, and as long as the user has kept the private key secure, the act of encrypting or signing is the proof of identity. The problem in this scheme is to establish a believable mapping from the user to the user's public key. A practical solution is to employ a trusted third party to vouch for the mapping. There are two approaches: a hierarchical authority, as used by the X.509 Public Key Infrastructure, and a web of trust, as used by Pretty Good Privacy.

6.2.1 Kerberos

The Kerberos network authentication system [RFC1510] provides a means of verifying the identities of entities (called *principals* in the RFC) on an open, unprotected network using a trusted third party. Kerberos was developed as part of a distributed computing project at MIT called Project Athena (the project also responsible for developing the *X* window system).

A distributed system has clients and servers, and the clients occasionally must communicate with the servers to access a resource of some sort. Kerberos does not require that servers authenticate clients directly; rather, the servers rely on the good judgment of a centralized *authentication server* (AS) as the trusted third party. Doing so relieves each server of the need to perform the authentication process with each client. Suppose that there are N clients and M servers. With a two-party scheme, each of the M servers would need to keep an up-to-date database of each of the N client's shared secret key. This means that there are $M{\times}N$ keys in the network, and M copies of any client's key. With this many keys, an attacker has a lot of opportunities to find at least one weakness.

The security of the whole system rests on the Kerberos AS. The AS is responsible for maintaining a database of principals and their secret keys, so the AS must be running on a secure host to protect the database.

When a client needs to gain access to the server, the client sends a request to the AS for a set of *credentials* it can present to the server to prove its identity. These credentials consist of a *ticket* and a *session key*. The ticket is the AS's assertion of the client's identity, and the session key is used to authenticate that assertion. The

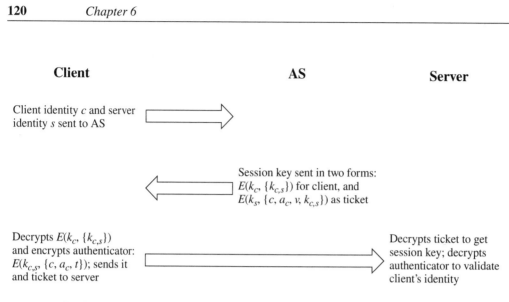

Figure 6-5 Kerberos authentication

client sends the server the ticket and a special message called an *authenticator*. The ticket asserts the client's identity but does not prove it; the authenticator, taken with the ticket, proves the client's identity.

Now let us look at that protocol again, this time more formally (see Figure 6-5). Consider a client c and a server s with secret keys k_c and k_s (shared with the AS), respectively. The client sends a cleartext message consisting of who it is (c) and whom it wants to talk to (s). The AS generates a session key $k_{c,s}$ that will be used only for the session between the client and the server.

The AS makes two copies of the session key. The first copy is encrypted[3] with the client's key: $E(k_c, \{k_{c,s}\})$. The second is encrypted with the server's key and includes the client's identity c, its address a_c, and a period of validity v: $E(k_s, \{c, a_c, v, k_{c,s}\})$. This copy is the ticket. Note that the ticket is in a form that the client can neither construct nor alter. Both copies are sent back to the client.

The client decrypts its copy of the session key and uses it to create an authenticator message. The authenticator message consists of the client's identity and address, as well as a timestamp, all encrypted with the session key: $E(k_{c,s}, \{c, a_c, t\})$. The client sends the ticket and this authenticator to the server.

---

3. Recall our notation from Chapter 2, where $E(k, m)$ means that the function E is used to encrypt the message m with key k.

The server first decrypts the ticket to get the session key and the information about the client. The server cannot necessarily believe the client yet because an eavesdropper could have captured a copy of the ticket and is now replaying it. The thing that validates the client is the authenticator; the session key is used to decrypt the authenticator to reveal the client's particulars and the timestamp, and the result is compared with the information contained in the ticket. Because the client could get the session key only by proving its identity to the AS (only the holder of k_c—that is, the client—could have decrypted the session key), and because only the server and the client know the session key, the server believes the client is who it says it is. The timestamp makes the authentication valid only right now; any captured authenticator is useless without matching it with the proper time inside.

Note that the ticket can be used by the client multiple times—as long as the period of validity has not expired—but a new authenticator is required for each use. Also note that, although its main purpose is to authenticate the client, the session key can be used to encrypt subsequent client-server communications.

Figure 6-6 shows a more general Kerberos model. In it, the AS is used only to authenticate the principals, and another special server—the Ticket-Granting Server (TGS)—governs which servers a client can access. Consequently, the client must go through two phases of authentication: one to prove its identity to the TGS, and another to prove its identity to the server (and, by implication, its right to access it). In the first phase, the client performs the protocol just described to get a special ticket called a TGT, or Ticket-Granting Ticket, from the AS. In the second phase, the TGT is presented to the TGS, where a server-specific ticket is granted for the client to access the server. The TGS can be viewed as an access control server.

Kerberos is a popular and widely used authentication protocol. Even so, there are some potential concerns about its security. The whole scheme relies heavily on synchronized clocks, a hard problem in itself.[4] If the time at the server is ahead or behind the time of the client and AS, the server will reject a bona fide ticket thinking it may be a replay attack. If the time at the server is really ahead of everyone else, an eavesdropper can capture the ticket and authenticator messages and replay them when they are valid, sometime in the future. To cope with minor clock skew,

---

4. The Network Time Protocol (NTP) [RFC1305] can be used to synchronize the clocks of the involved parties. Of course, the NTP exchanges must also be secured.

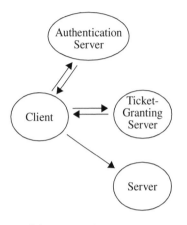

Figure 6-6 Generalized Kerberos model

the server usually has a window of acceptance in which a time plus or minus some delta is considered valid. Even this leaves open the possibility of a replay attack. Some implementations keep a copy of all received authenticators and reject any new ones that have exactly the same timestamp as an old one.

There is no built-in method for refreshing the principal's secret keys. The more a key is used, the more examples a cracker has to work with to break the cipher. Also, a lot of trust must be placed on the Kerberos implementation at hand: Why waste time trying to break the cipher if you can insert malicious code into the implementation that records the keys as they are used (e.g., a Trojan Horse attack)?

6.2.2 X.509 Public Key Infrastructure

The public key infrastructure (PKI), specified by the International Telecommunication Union (ITU) X.509 standard [ITU97] (formally CCITT X.509), defines a framework for providing authentication across networks using public key cryptography. In particular, X.509 defines a data structure called a *certificate*. A certificate communicates the identity of a party—called the *subject*—and its public key in a secure way. A certificate is generated by a trusted third party—called the *certification authority* (CA)—which validates the subject's identity with respect to its public key. A CA is the digital equivalent of a notary public.

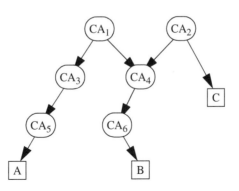

Figure 6-7 X.509 certification hierarchy

X.509 is part of the X.500 series of recommendations that defines a directory service. The X.509 certificate format was initially issued in 1988 (version 1), revised in 1993 (version 2), and finalized in 1997 (version 3). In the fall of 1995, the IETF established the PKIX Working Group with the intent of developing Internet standards needed to support an X.509-based PKI. RFC2459 [RFC2459] profiles the X.509 version 3 certificates for use on the Internet.

To establish authenticity, a user approaches a CA with proof of identity and a public key. The CA constructs a certificate with a name for the user that is unique in the whole system (called the *distinguished name*), the user's public key, and several other pieces of information used to clarify and validate the certificate. The certificate is then digitally signed (see Section 2.5.3) by the CA. Anyone who believes the legitimacy of the CA will believe the contents of the certificate and hence the identity of the user. Issued certificates are usually stored in databases of the system, and the CA keeps a copy in case of dispute.

A CA is born trusted within the context of the system that the CA serves. It can therefore issue its own certificates. An important one is the certificate that maps the CA to its own public key; the self-signed certificate is usually referred to as the *root certificate*.

Sometimes there is only one CA for the whole system, but often this arrangement puts too much burden on one authentication entity. CAs can be arranged in a hierarchy, as shown in Figure 6-7. A CA's certificate is signed by the CAs directly above it: CA_1 signs certificates for CA_3 and CA_4, and CA_4 signs certificates for CA_6.

When user A, with a certificate signed by CA_5, wishes to be authenticated to user B, there must be a *certificate path* from A to B: A is signed by CA_5, who is signed by CA_3, who is signed by CA_1, who signed CA_4, who signed CA_6, who signed user B. The two users must have a single common point of trust in the certificate hierarchy—in this case, CA_1. User A cannot be authenticated to user C because there is no single common point of trust.

Certificates carry a period of validity, so eventually they expire. When a certificate is no longer valid for some other reason, as when the named user's attributes have changed, it is important to *revoke* the certificate. The CA publishes a *certificate revocation list* (CRL). Any certificate listed in the CRL is deemed invalid. The problem with CRLs is that they are not particularly timely, inasmuch as the revocation is usually not predictable, and the CRL publication is usually periodic and cannot be too frequent.

PKI is a particularly rich and complex authentication system. This discussion serves only to set PKI in context with other trusted third-party schemes; PKI is emerging as a particularly important system for Internet authentication. There are now many companies that serve as certification authorities, driven by the need for authentication in e-commerce. In addition to this brief introduction, Chapter 7 is devoted solely to the issues and protocols involved in constructing a public key infrastructure.

6.2.3 Pretty Good Privacy Trust Model

Pretty Good Privacy (PGP) [ZIMM95] is a family of software systems developed by Philip R. Zimmermann for securing email, both encrypting its contents and authenticating its sender. The authentication mechanism is an ad hoc approach to trust; there is no centralized certificate authority to map public keys to their creators. Instead, PGP uses a *web of trust* that is somewhat analogous to social trust. In your circle of friends, you trust some more than others. Of those you trust, you will be more likely to trust their friends. A PGP web of trust is similarly transitive. There is no specified policy about whom to trust, so each user must decide that for itself.

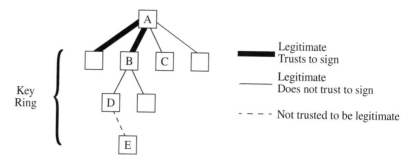

Figure 6-8 PGP web of trust

Like X.509, PGP uses public key cryptography, but instead of a CA signing a user's public key (and thus establishing the mapping of the key to the user), other users sign the public key. If user A generates a public key k_A and B knows and trusts A, A may get B to sign it: $k_A{}^B$. Now B vouches for A, and anyone who trusts B can trust A.

There are two statements of trust: One speaks to the degree a user believes the key to be legitimate, and the other speaks to the degree the user trusts the owner of the key to sign others' keys. It is the user's responsibility to determine how much a signed key is to be trusted on both accounts.

Consider the example shown in Figure 6-8. Three users—A, B, and C—agree to meet one evening over beer and sign each other's keys. This is called a *key signing party*. After the party, A has signed keys from B ($k_B{}^A$) and C ($k_C{}^A$). These keys are added to A's *public key ring*, a set of keys A collects.

User A really knows and trusts B, so A marks $k_B{}^A$ with a high level of legitimacy and a high level of trust for signing others' keys. User A does not know C so well; A trusts k_C to be legitimate but does not trust C to sign others' keys.

If user A receives a key from a stranger, D, but D's key is signed by B ($k_D{}^B$), A will believe it because A trusts B's choice of whose keys it signs. User D's key is added to the key ring without A having had to sign it. User A decides, however, not to trust D's ability to sign others' keys. If A then receives a key from E signed by D ($k_E{}^D$), A will not trust it as legitimate.

Key revocation is the weakest part of PGP. It is impossible to guarantee that no one will use a compromised key. When a key becomes compromised, a key revocation certificate is issued, but because the web of trust is ad hoc and distributed, there is no formal mechanism for ensuring that everyone who has the compromised key will also get the key revocation certificate.

6.3 Authentication in VPNs

The role of authentication in VPNs is to verify the identity of the parties involved in the establishment of VPN tunnels. When the tunnel connects two VPN gateways, the identities to be verified are those of the VPN gateways and not of the hosts and servers located in the intranets behind the gateways. When the tunnel connects a VPN client with a VPN gateway, the identities of the remote access client and the VPN gateway must be verified.

Consider the example shown in Figure 6-9. Two VPN gateways—X and Y—are located in two geographically separate sites. A VPN tunnel needs to be established between gateway X and gateway Y on behalf of the subnets behind them. In addition to the site-to-site VPN tunnel, gateway Y serves as the remote access VPN gateway for the several VPN clients.

6.3.1 Gateway-Gateway Authentication

In our example, gateways X and Y must mutually authenticate each other before establishing the VPN tunnel between them; several appropriate authentication schemes have been presented in this chapter. But identifying an appropriate authentication scheme alone is not sufficient; a mechanism is needed to carry the authentication information between the two gateways and to create a VPN tunnel between gateway X and gateway Y after the authentication is successful.

In IPsec, the protocol for carrying out the authentication between the two VPN gateways is IKE (see Section 5.4). The simplest way is for the two gateways to share a secret. The shared secret is entered by the gateway administrator. For security reasons, the secret is usually stored in encrypted form on the gateway. This shared secret can change as long as the same secret is entered in both gateways.

A VPN gateway establishes VPN tunnels with multiple corresponding VPN gateways in a pair-wise fashion using a different shared secret for each corresponding

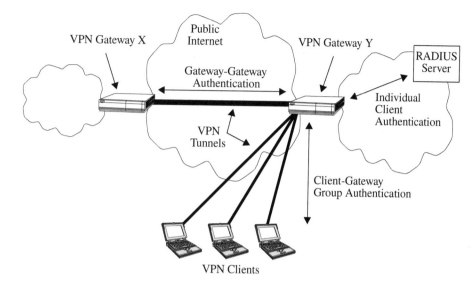

Figure 6-9 Authentication in VPN

VPN gateway. Although this pair-wise authentication does not scale well, the number of corresponding VPN gateways is usually small enough that scaling does not matter.

6.3.2 Client-Gateway Authentication

Scaling is a factor, however, for client-gateway authentication. Often there are considerably more VPN clients than VPN gateways, so the client-gateway authentication is not typically done in the same pair-wise fashion as gateway-gateway authentication. The issue is the difficulty of maintaining the database of shared secrets for each individual client.

Ideally, the VPN gateway would like to treat the whole collection of VPN clients as a group so that it can authenticate every member of the group using the same shared secret. This group authentication approach causes each client to share its fate with all other clients, so if the secret is compromised in any one of them, it is compromised for all. A two-tiered approach can reduce the fate sharing: A client and the gateway use a group password to mutually authenticate each other. The client is identified as a member of the group allowed to access the VPN gateway.

The gateway then relies on an authentication server to authenticate the individual client. RADIUS works this way. When the client and gateway are mutually authenticated using the group passwords, the client's username and password are sent to the RADIUS server for authentication of the individual client. This two-tier arrangement is shown in Figure 6-9 for VPN client remote access to gateway Y.

Public Key Infrastructure

It takes two hands to make a clapping sound.
—CHINESE PROVERB

As electronic commerce and business communications increasingly rely on the Internet, authentication becomes crucial. Public key cryptography can be used to address this issue: In particular, Diffie and Hellman [DIFF76] suggested that the proper management and use of public-private key pairs could provide a powerful authentication service.

Public key cryptography offers a useful mathematical tool to facilitate authenticity, but the real problem is how to publish and manage public keys for everyone in such a way that a powerful statement of authentication could be made. A PKI—*public key infrastructure*—is the set of services and policies that lays the framework for binding a public key to an identity and distributing that binding.

A PKI has three basic processes: certification, validation, and certificate revocation. *Certification* is the binding of an identity or attributes to a public key. The public key and the identity or attributes—that is, some unique naming information—are placed inside a digital document called a *certificate*. A trusted third party digitally signs the certificate, vouching for the correctness of its contents. The trusted third party in a PKI is called a *certification authority*, or CA.

Validation is the process of verifying the authenticity of the certificate so that the certificate's contents can be believed. This involves verifying the signature of the CA by using the CA's own public key and by checking the certificate against a *certificate revocation list* (CRL). A CRL contains a list of certificates that have been revoked by the CA, indicating that the binding is no longer valid. Validation also involves checking the validity period contained in the certificate itself.

Certificate revocation is the process of disavowing a previously issued certificate before its expiration date. This happens when some aspect of the information contained in the certificate changes; perhaps the user's identity has changed (e.g., the user has moved or changed email addresses), or the user's private key has somehow been compromised. The CA must keep track of all the certificates it has issued and must be prepared to revoke any one of them at any time, typically by entering the certificate's serial number in a CRL. The CA is responsible for issuing an updated CRL.

A fundamental aspect of the application of a PKI is the trust that is placed in the CA. Without such trust, the digital certificates issued by the CA are worthless. Delegation of trust is a social, political, and commercial issue and, consequently, outside the scope of a PKI. The PKI is a mechanism to use after trust delegation has been established.

Recall that authentication is contextual: The act of verifying the identity of an entity is meaningful only within a defined context. The same is true for the authenticity of the identity information in the digital certificate. The context affects not only whether the trust can be delegated but also the length of the certificate validity period because the social, political, and commercial environments are bound to change. The more specific the information, the more likely it is that it will change over time.

7.1 PKI Architecture

A PKI includes the certification authority and all other components that enable certification, validation, and revocation. Figure 7-1 shows the major components of a PKI: the *user* (also called the *subject*, *principal*, or *certificate holder*), the *validator*, the *registration authority* (RA), the *certification authority*, and the *certificate and CRL repository*. The components interact to facilitate the acquisition and use of digital certificates.

The CAs, the RAs, and the repository are *management entities* because they are responsible for generation, distribution, storage, and revocation of the digital certificates. The users and validators are *user entities* because they use the digital certificates and PKI functions to achieve their goals. The user entities make

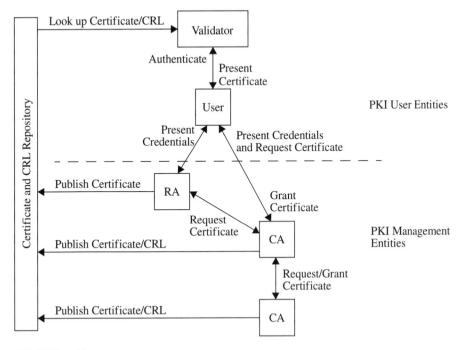

Figure 7-1 PKI architecture

requests to the management entities, either for the purpose of acquiring a certificate or validating one presented by another user entity. The certification request can be addressed directly to the CA, or to an RA working on behalf of the CA. After credentials are presented and verified, a certificate is issued to the user and published in the repository. When a validator needs to authenticate a user, it uses the valid public key contained in the certificate to verify a message signed by the user's private key. CAs also publish CRLs to the repository, so the validator can check whether the user's certificate is still valid. Alternatively, CRLs may be received periodically, without an active retrieval. A set of protocols has been developed and standardized to govern the transactions between the entities.

How all these components are assembled to provide these processes depends on the trust model employed by the PKI. Each process and the trust models are discussed next.

7.1.1 Certification

Certification binds a user entity with its relevant information (sometimes, the information is not related to the identity but to other attributes of the user entity). To ensure the authenticity and integrity of such binding, the CA signs the document using its private key.

Several steps must happen during certification. First, the CA must verify that the information to be contained in the digital certificate is authentic and accurate. This implies a certain level of security in the request channel and careful handling by authorized personnel of the information as it is inserted into a certificate. Often, the party that enters the information is not the user to be certified.

The next step is the generation of the key pairs. The user's public key must be included in the certificate. Often the user generates the key pair and passes only the public key to the CA. This facilitates nonrepudiation because only the user ever knows the private key. Sometimes the CA generates the key pair on behalf of the user. The CA can keep a copy of the private key to effect *key escrow* in case something happens to the user's copy of the private key. Companies typically do this so that encrypted documents can be recovered after an employee leaves the firm. Certainly, key escrow weakens the nonrepudiation property of the private key. Therefore, in some applications, two key pairs are generated: one with private key escrow and one without. The one with escrow is used for encryption, and the other one is used for signing.

Next, the CA signs the certificate with its private key. This accomplishes two things: The certificate is vouched for by the CA, and the integrity of the certificate is protected. As long as the community of users trusts the CA and its ability to keep its own private key a secret, the certificate can be validated, and no one can modify its contents.

After the digital certificate is created and signed by the CA, the user can retrieve the certificate from the CA. The user can initiate the retrieval session by presenting a one-time credential to the CA, usually in the form of a reference number and authorization code given to the user through a separate (preferably secure) channel. Or the CA can simply email the certificate to the user.

In many cases, the CA may rely on a separate component, the registration authority, to perform the task of information verification for the certificate request. In doing so, the CA can remain focused on the signing of the certificate and key management.

7.1.2 Validation

A certificate must be validated before it can be trusted. Certificate validation involves the following steps:

1. The integrity of the certificate is checked by verifying the digital signature using the CA's public key.

2. The validity interval of the digital certificate is checked.

3. The CA's CRL is checked to make sure that the certificate has not been revoked.

Obviously, the validation entity must acquire a copy of the CA's public key prior to the first step. Usually, a self-signed certificate is issued by the CA certifying its own key. The CA places its public key into a certificate and signs it with its private key. The signature ensures that the public key has not been modified.

The second step is the examination of the validity interval and other attribute information contained in the certificate. A validity period is not strictly required, but most certificate formats use them (see Section 7.2).

The third step is to check the certificate against a CRL, or through a status-checking protocol. CRLs are issued by the CA to invalidate a certificate before its validity interval expires.

7.1.3 Certificate Revocation

A certificate may need to be revoked before its expiration date if it becomes invalid in some way, as when the private key becomes compromised or the information within it is no longer valid. As with the certification process, the request to revoke a certificate should be received via a secure channel and carefully examined.

The CA revokes a certificate by including it in a list of revoked certificates called the certificate revocation list. A CRL usually contains only the serial numbers of the revoked certificates. Putting all the certificate information into the CRL will result in an unnecessarily large CRL file.

Just as the integrity of the digital certificate itself is protected by the digital signature of the issuer, the integrity of the CRL must also be protected so that there is no question of its authenticity. The CA signs the CRL using its private key.

The CA makes the CRL known by publishing it to a well-known repository. The CRL is updated frequently (e.g., every eight hours). The validation entity can pull the updated CRL from the repository when the CRL in its possession has expired.

Often, the CA must proactively deliver the CRL to the potential validation entities when a new revocation takes place so that the revocation can take immediate effect.

7.1.4 Trust Models

The excellent mathematical properties of public key cryptography cannot solve the problem of how trust is instilled and delegated in a public key infrastructure. The trust that exists among the certificate users, the CAs, and the RAs is a complex issue. Carl Ellison and Bruce Schneier offer an overview of the risks of using PKIs when trust management is not properly handled [ELLI00].

There are many trust models, and taxonomies of trust models, for PKIs (Steve Kent [KENT97] and Radia Perlman [PERL99] offer two). Some people have grand visions of a single, unified PKI across the globe. Others see a confederation of PKIs based on political structures such as nations and municipalities. Still others prefer a model in which the trust placed in the certification authority be limited to the specific purpose for which the CA has been established.

The *single CA* model posits a single PKI for the whole world, with everyone using one CA to get and verify certificates. This is the simplest solution: Everyone knows exactly where to get a certificate, and verification of a certificate requires knowing only the single CA's public key. Unfortunately, this model has several major drawbacks. Politically and socially, there is no single organization with enough clout and trustworthiness to act as the single CA, so one would have to be invented. The demand for certification would tax a single CA because the identity of every requesting entity would need to be verified. If the CA's private key were ever compromised, everyone in the world would have to be told to switch to the CA's new public key, and all certificates signed by the old private key could not be trusted.

A *hierarchical* model has one root CA that in turn delegates trust to other CAs in a hierarchical fashion. PEM (Privacy Enhanced Mail) [RFC1422] and DNSSEC (Secure Domain Name System) [RFC2065] use this approach. In addition to a hierarchy of CAs, the namespace convention can also be hierarchical. CAs are trusted to certify only name-to-key mappings in a subtree of the namespace. This practice is called *name subordination*. By following the pieces of the name, the CA path is also followed, and the certificate is verified. This requires that the root CA be trusted by all. For example, in the DNSSEC case, the root DNS server is trusted by all other DNS servers. Unfortunately, the root CA presents a central point of failure for the entire system.

A *distributed* model assumes that all CAs are created equal. Each CA has its own trust domain and is responsible for configuring its own keys into applications. It is left entirely to the various CAs to decide whether to delegate trust among them. Recall that the PGP model [ZIMM95] is one such example; in PGP, each user acts as its own certification authority.

One issue that arises when different CAs have their own independent trust domains and issue their own certificates is how users between different trust domains can establish trust and exchange secure data. This is the issue of *cross-certification*.

Cross-certification is a process by which two CAs securely exchange keying information so that one CA can certify the trustworthiness of another CA's public key certificates unilaterally, or both CAs can certify the trustworthiness of each other. As with to the certification process for a user, a CA can vouch for the authenticity of another CA's public key by creating a digital certificate for it. This special kind of certificate is called a *cross certificate*.

Of course, there is much more to cross-certification than the technical details of exchanging keying information between the two CAs. Because cross-certification extends the third-party trust in the PKI, it is important for the members of each CA's domain to be completely comfortable with the security policy of the other CAs.

Distribution of the root certificate to the validation entities is another important trust issue. Sometimes the root certificate is distributed manually, but in many cases, the root certificate is already installed in applications. Web browsers offer an interesting example. Both Netscape Communicator and Microsoft Internet Explorer have a long list of root certificates configured into the software. When using one of these Web browsers to access e-commerce sites, we have implicitly trusted Netscape or Microsoft to become the authority on distribution of the public keys of the various CAs.

7.2 Digital Certificate Formats

A *digital certificate* binds the identity of an entity and possibly its associated attributes to its public key. The authenticity of the information is guaranteed by the digital signature of the issuing CA. Three questions can be asked about the digital certificate:

- What kind of information should be contained in the digital certificate?
- How is the information arranged in the certificate?
- How is the signature bound to the information contained in the certificate?

It is crucial to develop standard methods to address the three questions. For example, without knowing the signature algorithm, it is not possible to verify the certificate. Several standards describe what information should be contained in the certificate, how the information should be arranged, and how to sign the certificate.[1]

7.2.1 X.509 Digital Certificate

As discussed in Section 6.2.2, the ITU-T Recommendation X.509 [ITU97] defines a framework for public key certificates, including a specification of the data objects—certificates—used to bind a name with a public key, and a specification of revocation notices for issued certificates that no longer should be trusted. The X.509 standard does not specify a PKI in its entirety—for example, it does not define policies. Instead, it provides a foundation on which a full PKI can be built.

X.509 defines the most widely used public key certificate format. The first version, X.509v1, was published in 1988 and provided the basic structure of the certificate. X.509v2, the second version, appeared in 1993, extending the certificate with two optional fields to provide additional uniqueness to the certificate

---

1. See the book *Digital Certificates: Applied Internet Security* by Jalal Feghhi, Jalil Feghhi, and Peter Williams, Addison-Wesley, 1999, for a comprehensive overview of various types of digital certificates and their uses.

issuer and subject. The third and current version, X.509v3, was published in 1997 with optional extensions (updated in 1999 [ITU99]) to help customize the certificate format for various applications.

An X.509 digital certificate is a signed document attesting to the binding of a name to a public key. The certificate, therefore, must contain at least the name and the public key. These and several other pieces of information are signed by a third party so that anyone trusting the signer's diligence in ensuring that the public key does in fact belong to the named entity will also trust this binding. The other pieces of information contained in an X.509 certificate are used to limit the scope of this binding.

In particular, two time values bracket the period of time the certificate can be considered valid, in the same way that a credit card has issuing and expiration dates.

The Abstract Syntax Notation One (ASN.1) syntax for an X.509v3 certificate is shown in Figure 7-2. ASN.1 [ISO8824] is the OSI's standard way to express abstract notions without implying an implementation strategy.[2] It is particularly useful for creating complex types from basic types, in much the same way that C or Pascal provides structures. The assignment operator "::=" is used to give complex types a name. In Figure 7-2, *Certificate* is assigned to a signed sequence of typed fields. The values in the square brackets, called *tags*, are used to distinguish component types within a structured type (they are included here for accuracy, but you can read right past them).

The X.509v3 format has ten fields; X.509v1 and X.509v2 are subsets of X.509v3. The *version* field contains an integer value that indicates which of the three evolved formats this certificate follows. The curly braces in the definition give the possible choices—v1, v2, and v3—as well as their values—0, 1, and 2, respectively. The default is value 0, indicating X.509v1.

X.509v1 certificates do not have the last three fields shown in the *Certificate* definition. X.509v2 added the *issuerUniqueID* and *subjectUniqueID* fields, and X.509v3 added the extensions field.

The value in the *serialNumber* field is used to distinguish among certificates issued by a CA and, therefore, must be unique among all serial numbers assigned by that CA. Some implementations use monotonically increasing values, either by

---

2. See [KALI93b] for an easy-to-understand guide to ASN.1.

```
Certificate ::= SIGNED {SEQUENCE {
        version             [0] Version DEFAULT v1 (0),
        serialNumber            CertificateSerialNumber,
        signature               AlgorithmIdentifier,
        issuer                  Name,
        validity                Validity,
        subject                 Name,
        subjectPublicKeyInfo    SubjectPublicKeyInfo,
        issuerUniqueID      [1] IMPLICIT UniqueIdentifier OPTIONAL,
        subjectUniqueID     [2] IMPLICIT UniqueIdentifier OPTIONAL,
        extensions          [3] Extensions OPTIONAL
}   }
Version ::= INTEGER { v1 (0), v2 (1), v3 (2) }
CertificateSerialNumber ::= INTEGER
AlgorithmIdentifier ::= SEQUENCE {
    algorithm           ALGORITHM.&id({SupportedAlgorithms}),
    parameters          ALGORITHM.&Type({SupportedAlgorithms}
                            {@algorithms}) OPTIONAL
}
Validity ::= SEQUENCE {
    notBefore           Time,
    notAfter            Time
}
Time ::= CHOICE {
    utcTime             UTCTIME,
    generalizedTime     GeneralizedTime
}
SubjectPublicKeyInfo ::= SEQUENCE {
    algorithm           AlgorithmIdentifier,
    subjectPublicKey    BITSTRING
}
UniqueIdentifier ::= BITSTRING
Extensions ::= SEQUENCE OF Extension
Extension ::= SEQUENCE {
    extnid              EXTENSION.&id({ExtensionSet}),,
    critical            BOOLEAN DEFAULT FALSE,
    entnValue           OCTETSTRING
}
ExtensionSet EXTENSION ::= {...}
```

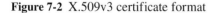

Figure 7-2 X.509v3 certificate format

incrementing a persistent counter for each certificate issued or by using a times-tamp. Even pseudo-random numbers can be used, as in the Microsoft CA.

The *signature* field specifies the identifier for the signature algorithms (a hash algorithm and a public key algorithm) used to sign the certificate, rather than the signature itself. The signature itself is external to the certificate and contains something similar to identify the algorithm used, so this field is somewhat redundant.

The *issuer* field identifies the entity that has signed the certificate. In the X.500 world (of which X.509 is a part), *Name* refers to a *distinguished name* (DN), which is a path through an X.500 directory information tree uniquely identifying the entity. A DN comprises a sequence of *relative distinguished names* (RDNs), which can be thought of as steps along the path.

The *validity* field specifies the time interval during which the certificate is valid. This means that the issuing CA warrants that it will maintain information about the certificate for at least this long. The validity period can be expressed in coordinated universal time (UTC), which uses two digits for the year and therefore makes assumptions about the century,[3] or in generalized time, which does not.

The *subject* field identifies the entity associated with the public key found in the *subjectPublicKeyInfo* field. As with the issuer field, *Name* refers to a distinguished name.

This *subjectPublicKeyInfo* field is used to carry the public key (and the algorithm with which the key is used) belonging to the entity described in the subject field.

The *issuerUniqueID* and *subjectUniqueID* fields were added in X.509v2 to uniquely identify an issuer and subject in case of name reuse. Although a *Name* is a distinguished name—and therefore completely identifies one entity from another within the X.500 directory information tree—the entities described by the distinguished name may come and go over time. If a *Name* is reused, it may be confused with the first use of the *Name*.

The *extensions* field allows the addition of new fields to the certificate structure without the need to modify the definition of the structure. This field is particularly useful when the certificate must carry additional information tailored to the

---

3. This is, technically, not Y2K-compliant, but because there is practically no certificate valid for 100 years, this is not a concern at this point.

```
This Certificate belongs to:
    Ruixi Yuan
    ryuan@bbn.com
    GTEI Users
    Burlington, MA, US

This Certificate was issued by:
    AWS Issuing CA
    VPN Advantage
    GTE Internetworking
    US


Serial Number: 00:A1
This Certificate is valid from Wed Aug 25, 1999 to Fri Aug 25, 2000
Certificate Fingerprint:
B4:43:20:82:09:99:69:34:E0:2D:2A:5D:18:4F:9C:E2
```

Figure 7-3 A browser's view of an X.509v3 certificate

context in which the PKI is deployed. A certificate can have one or more extension fields. An extension field consists of an extension identifier, a criticality flag, and an encoding of typed data associated with the extension. The criticality flag tells the application reading the certificate whether it is permitted to ignore the extension if it does not recognize the extension. There are three types of certificate extension fields: basic constraints, name constraints, and policy constraints.

Figure 7-3 shows a representation of an X.509v3 public key certificate in a Netscape browser. Note that not all of the X.509 attributes are given values because it is not necessary to populate every field.

In spite of the carefully specified format, there is still enough open to interpretation that interoperability is an issue [MOSK00]. Furthermore, certain target environments may wish to place limits on what can appear in various certificate types. Consequently, many groups have produced X.509 profiles that nail down many features otherwise left undefined or open to interpretation in the X.509 specification. The IETF PKIX profile [RFC2459] and the Federal PKI profile [FORD95] are two examples; many governments, including those of Germany and Finland, also have profiles. Peter Gutmann has written an X.509 style guide [GUTM00] to help reduce confusion and promote interoperability.

7.2.2 PGP Certificate

Another widely used certificate format is the Pretty Good Privacy [PGP99] certificate format. A PGP certificate includes (but is not limited to) the following information:

- **The PGP version number** This identifies which version of PGP was used to create the key associated with the certificate.
- **The certificate holder's public key and algorithm** This is the public portion of the key pair together with the algorithm of the key: RSA, DH (Diffie-Hellman), or DSA (Digital Signature Algorithm).
- **The certificate holder's information** This consists of identity information about the user, such as his or her name, user ID, photograph, and so on.
- **The digital signature of the certificate owner** This is also called a self-signature. It is the signature using the corresponding private key of the public key associated with the certificate.
- **The certificate's validity period** The certificate's start date and time and its expiration date and time indicate when the certificate became valid and will expire.
- **The preferred symmetric encryption algorithm for the key** This indicates the encryption algorithm to which the certificate owner prefers to have information encrypted. The supported algorithms are CAST, IDEA, and 3DES, among others.

A PGP certificate is constructed from a number of tagged records traditionally called *packets*. Figure 7-4 shows the ASCII armored version of a PGP certificate. An ASCII armor is an encoding of the binary certificate data into something that uses only the printable ASCII characters. The armored block is a useful way to send someone your PGP certificate or to get someone's certificate from a Web site. (The version shown in Figure 7-4 was generated by GnuPG [GPG], which, like all PGP version 5 implementations, adheres to the OpenPGP message format [RFC2440].)

A PGP implementation can read the armored key block and add the certificate to the key ring (see Section 6.2.3 for information about how the PGP trust model works). Figure 7-5 shows the key block's decoded contents. This PGP certificate consists of five packets: a public key packet, a user ID packet, a signature packet, a public subkey packet, and another signature packet. The first packet, the public

```
-----BEGIN PGP PUBLIC KEY BLOCK-----
Version: GnuPG v1.0.0 (FreeBSD)
Comment: For info see http://www.gnupg.org

mQGiBDiQgiIRBADd7G5Di5ibmr2I03cU+QsZ/J02cAVc9z8VX/gwj3nxm81hvOHP
1GZuHZB/guDPID7J6b0ZjOr+KQf71sMnXEdnMSnlpL1HYvvYeCeaV+XjPkmHmYpI
8bWx85XO5XyqfWK0yhh51FToE8UNboKTaKK8vsHXlbgZrQHPKIdG3zHzJwCg/2RV
iDPMuVQ4f+qnbTkX6cvn++cEAL8g41lr5Dx6fKehxccMiuntdealWFov8Cxj3UXm
101asg/bpdWVfu27oSZPRcSqXlZCSTRpjmXL15Tt7CiFJrz1hdrSE+yz95nRFD+0
jVSM3eh48xp2Q8rCq4OwrdpAIUs9FhOweOjU/pU0WCOV8MdHMw+LxdjQPV3ZfzDM
JuJAA/9zEy+7b+uxayTP0zdPYdiSqQYzvmZCs+f1EaKOcZg+JgL5mM3qUBgv+cOx
saNjXWJqtp11Y3TbYXcIL6y3bYFVKWZcAb7IxSsfec717dPggF0SfqA/c7LW95gm
B48tgiP1MbjYj0U74keR0iZN3YsVQAsLr/gvPKXtgUX4W7pbl7QdVGltIFN0cmF5
ZXIgPHN0cmF5ZXXJAYmJuLmNvbT6ITgQQEQIADgUCOJCCIgQLAwIBAhkBAAoJEDGc
ZNTSDkBa3CkAoLfJ8QeTn1I0WRBb3rqUJUxtA+m5AJwI0N49KvHjnRgsksSSMrqL
0izceLkCDQQ4kIIjEAgA9kJXtwh/CBdyorrWqULzBej5UxE5T7bxbrlLOCDaAadW
oxTpj0BV89AHxstDqZSt90xkhkn4DIO9ZekX1KHTUPj1WV/cdlJPPT2N286Z4VeS
Wc39uK50T8X8dryDxUcwYc58yWb/Ffm7/ZFexwGq01uejaClcjrUGvC/RgBYK+X0
iP1YTknbzSC0neSRBzZrM2w4DUUdD3yIsxx8Wy2O9vPJI8BD8KVbGI2Ou1WMuF04
0zT9fBdXQ6MdGGzeMyEstSr/POGxKUAYEY18hKcKctaGxAMZyAcpesqVDNmWn6vQ
ClCbAkbTCD1mpF1Bn5x8vYlLIhkmuquiXsNV6TILOwACAgf6A06n4wchIArv71x6
Bm01LmXX8/TD0auJTYgi7GHvaXi6CcUJmBxIfrJzkN4/8xVSmjduzudEpTMAan3g
IWLxF4xTZ0NCetRXxRhLuUIEwhAD1WESUW19Xo/iMue1byJUYdybOXNK/CT17Rtg
acQOn+ZUD7QJCdgvbEQpd5tIiS9DSrB8q8QkxqubwGupuqSqE1N2zOo0J39A3yQB
klqny+Vy6mC+DJuH3fpCo7p0omABrIJsmIUQv2firywEYiweEI14m78xlyFAcq0o
Nyctz8WjgzVgIoeF9NQilytfmxdVv478+KU3ZPMDZQDPvDz/f4iLIBV9530vIGbD
QzX95IhGBBgRAgAGBQI4kIIjAAoJEDGcZNTSDkBawMYAn3UyDIen1DqmaP/XTEbg
7y/yvyUYAKDhMIPywxWLSMTGS/ER1JDdJ/aa/Q==
=vTQH
-----END PGP PUBLIC KEY BLOCK-----
```

Figure 7-4 PGP public key block in ASCII armored encoding

key packet, starts the series of packets and includes the public key (the *pkey*) fields (the actual value of the public key is omitted in this figure). The *algo* field indicates that the key is a DSA (value 17), so the four *pkey* values are DSA parameters. The value following *created* is the creation time in UTC—the number of seconds since January 1, 1970. The value 0 for the *expires* field means that this certificate never expires and, therefore, must be revoked by the issuer (which happens to be the user).

The user ID packet simply contains the name and email address of the key holder. The signature packet binds the key from the public key packet to the identity from the user ID packet. The signature is generated using *algo* 17—DSA—using a key

```
                :public key packet:
                   version 4, algo 17, created 948994594, expires 0
                   pkey[0]: [1024 bits]
                   pkey[1]: [160 bits]
                   pkey[2]: [1024 bits]
                   pkey[3]: [1023 bits]
                :user ID packet: "Tim Strayer <strayer@bbn.com>"
                :signature packet: algo 17, keyid 319C64D4D20E405A
                   version 4, created 948994594, md5len 0, sigclass 10
                   digest algo 2, begin of digest dc 29
                   hashed subpkt 2 len 5 (sig created 2000-01-27)
                   hashed subpkt 11 len 4 (pref-sym-algos: 3 2 1)
                   hashed subpkt 25 len 2 (primary user ID)
                   subpkt 16 len 9 (issuer key ID 319C64D4D20E405A)
                   data: [160 bits]
                   data: [156 bits]
                :public sub key packet:
                   version 4, algo 16, created 948994595, expires 0
                   pkey[0]: [2048 bits]
                   pkey[1]: [2 bits]
                   pkey[2]: [2042 bits]
                :signature packet: algo 17, keyid 319C64D4D20E405A
                   version 4, created 948994595, md5len 0, sigclass 18
                   digest algo 2, begin of digest c0 c6
                   hashed subpkt 2 len 5 (sig created 2000-01-27)
                   subpkt 16 len 9 (issuer key ID 319C64D4D20E405A)
                   data: [159 bits]
                   data: [160 bits]
```

Figure 7-5 PGP certificate

whose key ID is the value following *keyid*. The key ID is a short way to refer to a key. The *md5len* value is 0 because the digest algorithm used—*digest algo 2*—is SHA-1 and not MD5. The *sigclass* 10 means that this is a generic certification of a user's ID, but the issuer has not verified the user's identity. That point is moot, however, because the key used to sign this certificate is the private key whose public key is in the public key packet. The certificate, therefore, is termed *self-signed*.

The signature packet consists of several subpackets. In Figure 7-5 there are four. The first one—*subpkt 2*—is the creation time (this time presented in a more readable way). The second subpacket, value 11, is the list of preferred symmetric algorithms to use for encryption. In this case, they are CAST, 3DES, and IDEA, in that order. The third subpacket, value 25, is a flag that states that this certificate's user ID packet is indeed the primary user of the key in the public key packet. The last subpacket, value 16, is the key ID once again.

Notice that the first three subpackets are marked as hashed, but the fourth is not. The signature is formed by taking the hash of the public key and user ID packets, plus the hash of the *hashed subpkts* from the signature packet, and signing the resulting hash value with the user's private key (whose key ID is given). The subpackets that are not hashed must be considered only advisory, but because proving the validity of the key ID is the same as validating the signature, omitting this subpacket has no implications.

The public subkey packet holds the keying material for the subkey. Generally, the top-level public key given in the public key packet is used for signatures, and any subkeys are used for encryption. This packet states that the algorithm used for encryption is ElGamal, and the *pkey* fields hold ElGamal's parameters. The final signature packet signs this subkey in the same way that the first signature packet signed the top-level key.

When other users sign a PGP certificate, they are stating that they vouch for the identity of the key holder. Each signature is then appended to and carried in the certificate in the form of a packet. This is how PGP forms the web of trust. Obviously, establishing the path of validation in this web of trust model is computationally quite complex compared with the X.509 model.

7.2.3 PKCS #6, Extended-Certificate Syntax Standard

RSA Laboratories has produced a series of specifications called the Public-Key Cryptography Standards (PKCS). These "standards" have benefited from the cooperation and participation of many people in the greater security community, but they are not to be confused with the documents issued by national or international standards bodies, where standards are subjected to votes. See Barton Kaliski's overview of PKCS [KALI93a] for information on the scope and charter of the PKCS series.

One such standard is PKCS #6, "Extended-Certificate Syntax Standard" [RSA93a]. PKCS #6 is a superset of the X.509 certificate, including optional additional attributes intended to extend the certification process past the basic binding of name to public key. Some of these attributes are explicitly listed in PKCS #9, "Selected Object Classes and Attribute Types."

7.2.4 X.509 Attribute Certificate

It is tempting to put a lot of extended information into the digital certificate because that information can be verified. However, there can be serious problems in putting too much information into the digital certificate. First, the information may be dynamic, and the more information that is included, the more likely it is that one or more fields in the certificate will become invalid over time. Because a certificate is valid only while all the information contained it is valid, any incorrect information will necessarily lead to the revocation of the certificate. Second, the digital certificate is a piece of public information, and putting too much information there will make some information public unnecessarily.

X.509 addresses these problems with an *attribute certificate*, default version 1. An attribute certificate is a separate structure from a X.509v3 public key certificate, and a user with one public key certificate can have multiple attribute certificates associated with it. Furthermore, the user can collect attribute certificates from CAs other than the one that issued the public key certificate. This allows CAs to specialize in certain types of attributes, such as authorizations, rather than requiring that all knowledge of all attributes, in addition to the public key certification, reside in the same place.

7.3 Certificate Management System

The collection of PKI components that manage the creation, renewal, maintenance, and revocation of digital certificates is called the *certificate management system*. These components include

- Certification authority
- Registration authority
- Certificate and CRL repository

Sometimes, all three components reside on the same computer.

7.3.1 Certification Authority

The CA is the entity that issues and revokes certificates. The functions implemented on a CA usually include the following:

- Creation and management of the CA's own public-private key pair
- Creation of the public-private key pairs for users when needed
- Creation of a certificate binding the user's public key to the user's identity
- Revocation of certificates
- Creation of the certificate revocation list
- Management of a secure information database that maintains the history of certificate issuance and revocation, and for key escrow
- Management of a comprehensive message log for audit purposes

The security of a CA's own private signing key is perhaps the most critical implementation issue for a CA. If the CA's signing key is compromised, every certificate issued by that CA must be considered untrustworthy. It is desirable, therefore, to minimize the exposure of the private signing key. One way to do this is to store the key in a separate hardware module that takes as input the data to be signed and outputs the signature. Of course, the security and reliability of the hardware module are paramount; Federal Information Processing Standard (FIPS) 140-1 [NIST94b] specifies the security requirements for such cryptographic modules. One example of a hardware module implementation is BBN's SafeKeyper signer [GARD93].

In most cases, the public-private key pair is created by the user, and only the public key is sent to the CA for certification. This helps maintain confidentiality because the user's private key does not have to be transmitted. Sometimes, however, the CA must create the public-private key pair for the user, especially if the private key is to be held in escrow. If the CA has a high volume of certification requests, it must be able to generate key pairs efficiently.

The CA creates a digital certificate by collecting the user's identification information and the user's public key and, to the extent provided by the CA's policies, verifying the identification information. These two pieces of data, along with perhaps other certification parameters such as the validity period, are signed by the CA.

The CA revokes a digital certificate by placing a reference to that certificate in the CRL. CRLs are generated and published periodically, either at regular intervals or when enough certificates are revoked. In the case of X.509, the CRLs always contain the next CRL update time.

A CA's role is not limited to simply signing certificates. It must manage the entire life cycle of all the certificates under its administration. To perform this duty, a secure database that contains all the information regarding all the digital certificates is required. Unlike the directory server that stores the CRL, this secure database is usually internal to the CA itself and is not intended for public access. This secure database should be backed up regularly so that a restoration can be performed in the case of CA failure.

It is critical that all significant transactions with the CA be recorded and the entire record be accessible for informational and auditing purposes. Regular auditing of the transactions can help to detect unauthorized usage and attacks against the CA.

A CA does not operate in a vacuum—it must serve its intended community. One way to ensure that a particular CA is appropriate for a particular use is to study the CA's *Certification Practice Statement* (CPS). Generally, a CPS includes statements that describe the following:

- *Verification procedures*, ensuring the identity of the user
- *Scope of certification*, establishing the set of users for whom the CA is authorized to issue certificates
- *Authorization*, specifying what the CA certifies (in addition to the key binding)
- *Certificate lifetimes*, limiting how long a certificate is valid
- *Cross-certification*, stating the agreements between this CA and others and conditions for accepting other CAs' certificates
- *Protection of keying material*, enumerating the steps taken by the CA to protect its own private key
- *Key escrow and archival*, if appropriate, describing how the CA makes the user's keys available to support access to user-encrypted data by someone other than the user

A CPS is a nice document, but it is of little consequence if the CA does not implement good security practices. Successful attacks against the CA can have more devastating effects on the whole PKI than attacks on almost any other component. Steve Kent [KENT98] outlines the many things that a CA must guard against.

7.3.2 Registration Authority

A CA is responsible for two things: verifying the user's information and issuing the certificate. Issuing a certificate requires access to the CA's private key so that the CA can sign the certificate. It is best to limit the number of places this private key is stored. Verification of user information, certificate request, key generation, and key archival, on the other hand, are aspects of the CA that do not require access to the CA's private key. One or more RAs are employed when it makes sense to separate these two functions.

A CA can have many RAs, strategically located to provide a high degree of availability. As the user population grows, more RAs can be added to maintain a stable level of service. One advantage of distributing RAs is that each RA may have its own CPS, allowing flexibility in serving the needs of the user community. The obvious disadvantage is that the distribution of functionality increases the complexity of maintaining security; each RA must be certified by the CA and must communicate with the CA and all other RAs concerning verification and revocation of certificates.

7.3.3 Certificate and CRL Repository

When a certificate is issued to a user, the CA may also publish a copy of the certificate to a repository. Similarly, when it is necessary to make a certificate invalid before its scheduled expiration, the CA must publicize the revocation through the publication of a CRL. It is convenient to publish the CRLs in the same repository as the certificates, creating a certificate and CRL repository.

The X.509v2 CRL format is shown in Figure 7-6. The *CertificateList* field is composed of three required fields: the *tbsCertList* field, the *signatureAlgorithm* field, and the *signatureValue* field. The *tbsCertList* field contains the name of the issuer, the issue date, the date of the next CRL issue (if there is one), the list of revoked certificates, and optional CRL extensions. The list of revoked certificates (the *revokedCertificates* field) contains the certificate's serial number, the time it was revoked, and optional CRL extensions. Interestingly, most PKI profiles use the X.509v3 certificate format and the X.509v2 CRL format.

A certificate cannot be deemed valid until it is checked against the CRL. Therefore, it is crucial for the CRL repository to be easily accessible. However, the ease

```
CertificateList ::= SEQUENCE {
    tbsCertList      TBSCertList,
    signatureAlgorithm AlgorithmIdentifier,
    signatureValue      BIT STRING
}

TBSCertList ::= SEQUENCE {
    version             Version OPTIONAL,
                            -- if present, version must be v2
    signatureAlgorithm AlgorithmIdentifier,
    issuer              Name,
    thisUpdate          Time,
    nextUpdate          Time OPTIONAL,
    revokedCertificatesSEQUENCE OF SEQUENCE  {
        userCertificate     CertificateSerialNumber,
        revocationDate      Time,
        crlEntryExtensions Extensions OPTIONAL
                        } OPTIONAL,
    crlExtensions       [0] EXPLICIT Extensions OPTIONAL
}

-- Version, Time, CertificateSerialNumber, AlgorithmIdentifier, and
-- Extensions are all as defined in X.509v3 certificate format
```

Figure 7-6 X.509v2 certificate revocation list format

of access also makes it vulnerable to various types of denial-of-service attacks. Proper security measures should be put in place to reduce such vulnerabilities and increase the robustness of the PKI. Sometimes it is helpful to have multiple redundant repositories.

7.4 Certificate Protocols

A user often needs to communicate with the CA or RA to send the public key and to retrieve the signed certificate. A validator must obtain the root certificate of a CA and contact the CRL repository to retrieve the current CRL. To operate in a networked environment, it is necessary for the entities to agree on a set of protocols and message formats.

The Public Key Infrastructure for the Internet (PKIX) working group of the IETF is the most important and active working group for using public key technologies over the Internet. A number of RFCs and Internet-Drafts[4] are focused on defining the operational protocols and message formats to enable a PKI to function in the Internet (see Table 7-1).

Table 7-1 PKIX operational protocols and formats documents

Document	Title
RFC 2510	Internet X.509 Public Key Infrastructure Certificate Management Protocols
RFC 2511	Internet X.509 Certificate Request Message Format
RFC 2559	Internet X.509 Public Key Infrastructure Operational Protocols — LDAPv2
RFC 2560	X.509 Internet Public Key Infrastructure Online Certificate Status Protocol — OCSP
RFC 2585	Internet X.509 Public Key Infrastructure Operational Protocols: FTP and HTTP
RFC 2587	Internet X.509 Public Key Infrastructure LDAPv2 Schema
RFC 2797	Certificate Management Messages over CMS
Internet-Draft	Using TCP as a Transport Protocol for CMP
Internet-Draft	OCSP Extensions
Internet-Draft	Limited Attribute Certificate Acquisition Protocol
Internet-Draft	Internet X.509 Public Key Infrastructure Certificate Management Protocols
Internet-Draft	Internet X.509 Public Key Infrastructure Data Validation and Certification Server Protocols
Internet-Draft	Simple Certificate Validation Protocol (SCVP)
Internet-Draft	Internet X.509 Public Key Infrastructure Time Stamp Protocols (TSP)

The PKCS is another source of protocols and formats. The most widely used operational protocol and format are shown in Table 7-2.

Table 7-2 PKCS operational syntax documents

Document	Title
PKCS #7	Cryptographic Message Syntax Standard
PKCS #10	Certification Request Syntax Standard

---

4. The list of RFCs and Internet-Drafts are available at http://www.ietf.org/html.charters/pkix-charter.html.

Perhaps the most important protocols in a PKI are the enrollment protocols that enable the request and retrieval of a digital certificate. Without the enrollment protocols, a user cannot obtain a certificate in the first place.

Verification is an important part of enrollment, but because of the complexity involved in the verification process and the variety of policies employed, it is not possible to standardize the verification process. What is generally standardized, however, are the message formats between the CA and the user or validator (e.g., PKCS #7 and #10, discussed next). Although several proprietary methods exist (e.g., SCEP, also discussed next), there is still no standardized way to communicate these messages to and from the CA and the user entities.

PKCS #7 and PKCS #10

PKCS #7, "Cryptographic Message Syntax Standard" [RSA93b, RFC2315, KALI97], defines the syntax for several kinds of cryptographically protected messages, including messages with digital signatures. PKCS #7 is derived from the Internet Privacy Enhanced Mail (PEM) standard [RFC1421], and supports PEM along with S/MIME [RFC2311] secure electronic mail applications. The general syntax allows the inclusion of arbitrary attributes that are authenticated along with the contents of the message, such as signing time and countersignatures. Figure 7-7 shows a certificate encoded in PKCS #7 format.

For the purposes of a PKI, the syntax provides a means for disseminating certificates and certificate revocation lists, which are, of course, digitally signed messages.

When a requestor uses a Web browser to obtain a certificate, the PKCS #7 encoded value can be copied from the browser and then sent to the appropriate software application, or it can be directly saved by the browser for later use.

One protocol used for certification requests is PKCS #10, "Certification Request Syntax Standard" [RSA00b]. PKCS #10 request messages consist of a distinguished name, the public key, and an optional set of attributes used either to give additional information about the requestor or as attributes to be included in the certificate. The message is signed and sent to the CA, where it is converted into an X.509 or extended certificate. PKCS #9 gives a nonexhaustive list of the attributes that can be included in a PKCS #10 message and subsequently placed into a PKCS #6 extended certificate, discussed in Section 7.2.3.

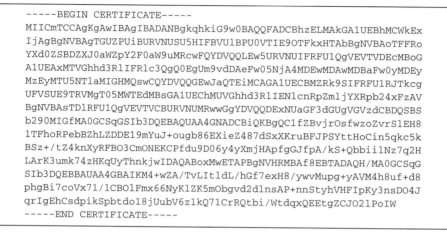

```
-----BEGIN CERTIFICATE-----
MIICmTCCAgKgAwIBAgIBADANBgkqhkiG9w0BAQQFADCBhzELMAkGA1UEBhMCWkEx
IjAgBgNVBAgTGUZPUiBURVNUU5HIFBVU1BPU0VTIE9OTFkxHTAbBgNVBAoTFFRo
YXd0ZSBDZXJ0aWZpY2F0aW9uMRcwFQYDVQQLEw5URVNUIFRFU1QgVEVTVDEcMBoG
A1UEAxMTVGhhd3RlIFRlc3QgQ0EgUm9vdDAeFw05NjA4MDEwMDAwMDBaFw0yMDEy
MzEyMTU5NTlaMIGHMQswCQYDVQQGEwJaQTEiMCAGA1UECBMZRk9SIFRFU1RJTkcg
UFVSUE9TRVMgT05MWTEdMBsGA1UEChMUVGhhd3RlIENlcnRpZmljYXRpb24xFzAV
BgNVBAsTDlRFU1QgVEVTVCBURVNUMRwwGgYDVQQDExNUaGF3dGUgVGVzdCBDQQSBS
b290MIGfMA0GCSqGSIb3DQEBAQUAA4GNADCBiQKBgQC1fZBvjrOsfwzoZvrSlEH8
1TFhoRPebBZhLZDDE19mYuJ+ougb86EXieZ487dSxXKruBFJPSYttHoCin5qkc5k
BSz+/tZ4knXyRFBO3CmONEKCPfdu9D06y4yXmjHApfgGJfpA/kS+QbbiilNz7q2H
LArK3umk74zHKqUyThnkjwIDAQABoxMwETAPBgNVHRMBAf8EBTADAQH/MA0GCSqG
SIb3DQEBBAUAA4GBAIKM4+wZA/TvLIt1dL/hGf7exH8/ywvMupg+yAVM4h8uf+d8
phgBi7coVx71/lCBOlFmx66NyKlZK5mObgvd2dlnsAP+nnStyhVHFIpKy3nsDO4J
qrIgEhCsdpikSpbtdo18jUubV6z1kQ71CrRQtbi/WtdqxQEEtgZCJO21PoIW
-----END CERTIFICATE-----
```

Figure 7-7 A certificate encoded in PKCS #7 format

Simple Certificate Enrollment Protocol

Although widely accepted, PKCS #7 and PKCS #10 do not define an automatic way to generate and deliver these encoded messages between the PKI entities. In fact, there are no government or industry standards to perform automatic certificate enrollment. Manual manipulation of the encoded messages is still required to request and retrieve a digital certificate, including the generation of key pairs, the encoding of the public key into a PKCS #10 message, and delivery of the message to a CA. Furthermore, these manual processes are not scalable. What is desirable is to have a more automated method for the certificate enrollment process. The Simple Certificate Enrollment Protocol (SCEP) [CISC98] is a joint effort by Cisco and VeriSign to support certificate enrollment in a scalable manner for VPN applications.

7.5 Certificate Use in VPNs

A public key infrastructure is designed to support a wide range of secure services, both in a networked environment and in situations without networks. VPNs, being secure network services, use digital certificates and PKIs in a variety of ways.

However, a VPN does not use all the capabilities of a PKI. For example because VPN traffic is encrypted only when it is in transit through the tunnel, there is no need to have key escrow to recover lost private keys.

In general, a VPN uses digital certificates and a PKI in three ways:

- **Authentication** Verification of the identities of the VPN devices
- **Key management** Authentication of the negotiation of encryption keys for secure communication between the VPN devices
- **Access control** Use of the information contained in the digital certificate for controlling access to the VPN

7.5.1 Authentication

VPN devices must authenticate themselves with each other before any secure communication can take place. Chapter 6 discusses various mechanisms of authentication; among them, digital certificates are perhaps the most scalable and secure. Therefore, VPN devices increasingly use digital certificates as the basis for authentication.

To use the digital certificates for authentication, VPN devices must implement the set of capabilities that enables generation of the public-private key pairs, request and retrieval of certificates, request and retrieval of CRLs, and performance of various public key cryptography algorithms.

7.5.2 Key Management

As we have previously discussed, using public key cryptography for encryption can be slow compared with many of the symmetric encryption algorithms. Therefore, in VPN applications, public-private key pairs are generally used to facilitate the secure negotiation of symmetric encryption keys. IKE defines the various methods for deriving keys securely from the Diffie-Hellman key exchange between the IKE peers. Because the Diffie-Hellman exchange is susceptible to man-in-the-middle attacks, digital signatures are employed to authenticate a Diffie-Hellman session.

7.5.3 Access Control

Digital certificates contain a rich set of information in addition to the public key of the user. This information (distinguished name, alternative name, etc.) and its related attribute certificate can be used for access control purposes in a VPN. We discuss access control in much more detail in Chapter 8.

8

Access Control

Fish cannot leave the water.
—LAO ZHI, THE BOOK OF TAO

Chapters 6 and 7 discuss how authentication confirms the identity of a user. Authentication does not, however, say anything about what that user is allowed to do; access control speaks to this issue.

Access control is the set of policies and mechanisms that permits authorized parties access to restricted resources. It also protects resources from being accessed, either maliciously or accidentally, by users not authorized to access them. It does not, however, protect against intentional misuse by authorized parties.

Figure 8-1 shows a client-server model for access control. We consider a *user* to be any entity—the actual person or an application working on behalf of a person—that desires access to a resource. The *resource* is any object that can be manipulated in some way, such as by reading, writing, or modifying, or caused to perform some action, such as running a program or sending a message. The client may be the user entity itself, may be collocated with the user entity, or may be an entity separate from the user. Similarly, the server may be the resource itself, may be collocated with the resource, or may be a separate entity acting on behalf of the resource.

A user has an *identity* and an associated set of *attributes*. The client sends the user's identity, attributes, and requested *operation* to the server. The server can authenticate the user's identity and then pass that on, along with the attributes and request, to the access control mechanisms. Policies are prescribed to the access

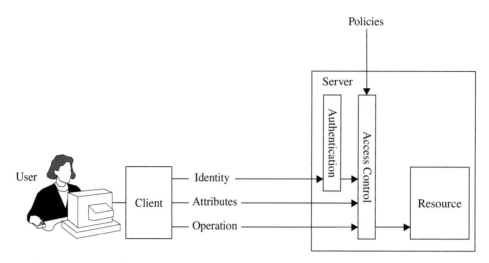

Figure 8-1 Access control in a client-server model

control mechanism; the user's information is compared to the policy rules to determine access rights to the resource.

Access control policies state the conditions under which access is granted. These conditions are based on a combination of the identity and attributes of the user, the identity and attributes of the target resources, environmental conditions, and the operation to be performed on the targeted resources. The policies are enforced by *access control mechanisms*; the access control for a system is adequate only if the mechanisms are sufficiently powerful to enforce the policies. *Access control policy management* includes the methods and procedures by which access control policies are created, expressed, and maintained.

Access control policies can be easily stated. It is often more difficult, however, to translate the policy statements into a format that can be easily enforced through the access control mechanisms. Managing and enforcing the access control policies in a distributed environment is even more challenging because there can be multiple policy enforcement points. Sometimes these multiple enforcement points must operate jointly to enforce a policy.

8.1 Access Control Policy

An access control policy is the set of rules that defines the protection of one or more resources. These rules are generally expressed in terms of the information about a user (user attributes) and the conditions for use of a resource (resource attributes and environmental factors).

In general, access control policies fall into one of two types: discretionary and mandatory. *Discretionary* access controls allow the owner of the resource to determine which access rights are granted and to whom. An example is the set of permissions placed on a file. Organizations specify *mandatory* access controls to reflect the sensitivity of the organization's resources. Military classification of resources according to the level of clearance is an example of this type of access control.

8.1.1 Attributes and Conditions

Whether discretionary or mandatory, the access control policies are sets of conditions based on the attributes of the user, the attributes of the resource, and the environmental conditions at the time of the request. These policies are expressed as rules to facilitate the access control mechanisms.

User Attributes

A user can have multiple attributes, the most obvious of which is the user's identity. After a user's identity is authenticated (perhaps by one of the methods described in Chapter 6), the identity may play an important part in determining access rights. On UNIX systems, for example, password authentication is required for the highly privileged user *root*; once authenticated, *root* can access configuration files whose access is denied to all others. Authentication is an implicit form of access control: If the user cannot prove identity, the user is denied access to the system.

Identity is not, of course, the only attribute of a user. In some cases, the user's identity is not even of concern, as long as the user exhibits certain other attributes. A ticket holder, for example, can access a sports facility without further identity checking. X.509 supports an attribute certificate framework called the Privilege Management Infrastructure (PMI) [ITU99], which is used to provide additional information about the user to support rule-based access control. Whether by X.509 attribute certificates or by some other means, it is necessary to bind attributes to a user before those attributes can be used for granting access. The list of required user attributes is dependent on what is appropriate for the resources in question.

In some circumstances, the user being authenticated is not the user wishing to gain access. The distinction between an *authentication identity* and an *authorization identity* is made in SASL, the Simple Authentication and Security Layer [RFC2222], a protocol that allows for one user to proxy for another.

Resource Attributes

The resource can also have attributes, such as its name and address. Unlike users, however, resources have a special type of attribute: the set of allowable operations that can be performed on them. For example, a file in the UNIX system can have read, write, and execute operations. The operation performed on the resource may change the attributes of the resource.

Another type of resource attribute is the requirements for accessing it. This attribute is often called the resource's *use conditions*, and access control systems have been constructed using special X.509 attribute certificates called *use-condition certificates* [JOHN98]. Use conditions include restrictions on users, such as which operations are permitted, and restrictions on environmental conditions, such as when the operations are permitted. For example, access to an electron microscope may require that the user have special training. The microscope may be turned on only when someone is on duty to monitor it. Another condition may be that the request for access to the microscope must come only from certain people. All three of these are use conditions on the microscope and are bound to the microscope as attributes.

Environmental Conditions

The user and the resource can be described in terms of their attributes. In addition, access control policies often take into account conditions outside the control of users or resources. These are called *environmental conditions*. If a use condition states that a resource has operational hours, the environmental condition is the time when access to the resource is permitted. When evaluating access control policies, the system must take into account the external conditions.

8.1.2 Access Control Rules

Access control policies represent the wishes of the stakeholders of a resource. *Stakeholders* are those entities that can claim some ownership or influence over the resource. In the abstract, the access control policies are rules that compare the user's information and environmental conditions with the resource's conditions for use. When the rules are expressed concretely, they become fodder for the access control mechanism.

In general, access control rules are expressed in terms of a set of matching conditions based on the user attributes, resource attributes, and environmental conditions. An access control rule can be expressed as follows:

```
rule := if {
   match({user attributes}, {required values}) and
   match({resource attributes}, {required values}) and
   match({environmental conditions}, {required values})
} then grant
  else deny
```

The *match* function compares the attributes and conditions with the values required to access the resource. For flexibility, this comparison handles ranges of values and conditional statements.

The act of translating policies—which can be informally specified to facilitate human understanding—into formal rules that can be readily understood by computers is an important and sometimes difficult task. A human may say that a file is restricted to read and write access by the owner and is inaccessible by all others, whereas a UNIX machine would rather see that as file permission "600." (Each octal digit, when represented in binary, represents a permission that is turned on; we will visit a UNIX file permissions example again soon.) For access control in an IP networking environment, the Security Policy Specification Language (SPSL) [COND00] is the first IETF effort that attempts to specify a language with syntax and semantics to express IPsec, IKE, and packet filtering formally, with the intent of machine-independent enforcement.

Organization of Rules

An access control policy can be expressed as a single complex rule, but more frequently it is organized as a set of rules. Each rule covers a specific case:

```
Policy := {rule1, rule2, ... rule n}
```

Often there is one general rule, called the *default* rule, that follows the set of more specific rules:

```
Policy := {rule1, rule2, ... rule n, default rule}
```

A common default rule is to deny access to everyone; then the other rules state the specific exceptions.

If the rules are completely disjoint, the order of the rules does not matter with respect to enforcement. More often, however, rules overlap, so stating the rules as an ordered set gives precedence to the rules, providing the tiebreaker if two or more rules apply to a particular access request. A good way to order rules is from most specific to most general. A fortunate consequence of this practice is that the access control mechanism can stop processing rules when an applicable rule is found.

Aggregation of Rules

Another way to simplify the set of rules is by exploiting any equivalence classes that may exist among the users and resources. A rule is written to cover users related by some set of attributes; any users with those attributes fall into the class. The class, then, is granted access. Any user with special training, as in the earlier microscope example, is granted access; the equivalence class ignores the user's identity and forms only around the training attribute. The concept of a *group* in the UNIX file system's permissions scheme is another example of an equivalence class.

8.2 Access Control Mechanisms

Whereas access control policies are abstractions representing the wishes of the resource stakeholders, access control mechanisms are the concrete ways the rules are expressed and enforced. *Access control lists* and *capabilities lists* are two common ways to specify these conditions. The enforcement of the expressed rules is then left to the specific implementation.

8.2.1 Access Control Lists

An access control list (ACL) associates each resource with an ordered list of which users may access it and, for each user, how that user may access it. This method is resource-centric; given a resource, a user, the user's attributes, and the operation, the access control mechanism can search the ACL for the resource and determine whether the user can perform the operation. When it is necessary to add new users or change old users' access rights, the ACL is easily modified. As we have seen in the preceding section, users are often placed into groups, or equivalence classes, in which everyone in the group has the same rights. This practice helps give ACLs good scaling properties as the number of users in the system grows.

The UNIX file system uses a form of access control lists to govern which operations can be done on files. There are three basic operations: read, write, and execute. Each file has associated with it three sets of permissions: one for the owner of the file, one for anyone belonging to the same group as the file, and one for everyone else. Each permission set consists of three rights: read ("r"), write ("w"), and execute ("x"); any right that is not granted is filled in with a hyphen. These three sets of three rights form a nine-letter string of permissions (rwxrwxrwx).[1] This string is a visual representation of the bitmapped binary permissions field. In this case, it is the output of the UNIX *ls* command, listing several files and showing their permissions and ownerships:

```
-rw-------  1 steve  staff     383 Mar 13 23:32 history
-rw-rw-r--  1 steve  staff     584 Mar 13 18:17 profile
-rwxr-x---  1 steve  project   164 Mar 13 18:17 useful*
```

Each line has eight fields: a string of permissions (called the *file mode*), the number of links to the file, the owner's name, the group's name, the file size, creation and modification information, and the file name. The file *history* has read and write permission granted only for the owner *steve*. In addition to the owner having read and write permissions, the second file, *profile*, grants the members of the

---

1. In directory listings, there are actually ten spaces for letters; the first letter in the string indicates the type of file. A hyphen means it is a regular file.

group *staff* the ability to read and write the file, and grants everyone else the ability to read it. The third file, *useful*, is a program (hence the asterisk) that *steve* and the members of the *project* group can read and execute but only *steve* can modify.

Access control in a network firewall device is another example of how ACLs are used. A firewall sits on the border between an intranet and the Internet (or some other external network). The firewall, therefore, has (at least) two interfaces: one addressed with an external, or outside, IP address, and the other addressed with an internal, sometimes private, IP address. The resource in this instance is the intranet, and the firewall implements an access control policy intended to protect the intranet from malicious access. Sophisticated firewall rules can maintain state information for network traffic and apply ACLs according to the state.

Assume that the variable *out_ip* has been set to the firewall's outside IP address, that is, known to the Internet. The following firewall rules are for use with *ipfw* [FREEBSD96], an IP firewall-controlling utility for FreeBSD, and are only a subset of the rules used to secure an intranet:

```
# Allow TCP through if setup succeeded
pass tcp from any to any established

# Allow setup of incoming email
pass tcp from any to ${out_ip} 25 setup

# Allow access to our DNS
pass tcp from any to ${out_ip} 53 setup

# Allow access to our WWW
pass tcp from any to ${out_ip} 80 setup

# Default rule
deny all from any to any
```

The directive *pass* tells the firewall to allow IP packets with certain properties to pass through. For example, the first rule states that any TCP connection already established can continue to have its packets traverse the firewall. The next three rules then state exactly which TCP connections can ever get into the established state: those supporting email (port 25), Domain Name System (DNS, port 53), and Web traffic (port 80). The last rule is the catch-all default, denying packets from anywhere to anywhere. If this rule were first and not last, it would make the firewall impenetrable; the default follows all the special cases.

8.2.2 Capabilities Lists

Capabilities lists (C-lists) are functionally equivalent to ACLs but are user-centric rather than resource-centric. Each user has a list of resources the user can access and, for each resource, the operations that can be performed on the resource.

C-lists are useful if resources can be grouped into equivalence classes, as is done with military security classification. A document—the resource—is labeled either unclassified, secret, or top secret. Personnel—the users—are cleared to one of those levels. A person's C-list is formed according to the level of clearance and the documents that person needs to see; unless a person has the appropriate clearance and the need to know, access is denied.

The major drawback to using C-lists is that it is difficult to determine all the users who have the access rights to a particular resource because the access rights are distributed among all the users rather than stored with the resource. Consequently, revoking or modifying the access rights on a resource may require visiting every user that has that resource in its C-list.

8.3 Access Control Policy Management

Access control policies are usually not static; they must be updated as old policies become no longer applicable and new situations arise. In a networked environment, access control policies may need to be distributed to many access control enforcement points. The process of creating, maintaining, and distributing the access control policies is called *access control policy management*.

A *policy administrator* is the entity that has ultimate control over the access control policies in a given system. The *policy manager* is a service responsible for providing policy administrators with an easy-to-use interface to define, install, modify, and view policies. The policy manager also translates the policies from the abstract language of the policy administrator to expressions that are useful for the access control mechanisms.

When multiple access control points exist in a network environment, policy management can be done in either a distributed or a centralized manner.

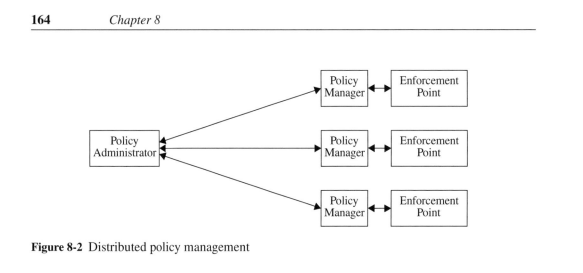

Figure 8-2 Distributed policy management

8.3.1 Distributed Policy Management

Distributed policy management is shown in Figure 8-2. The policy administrator uses policy managers that reside at or near the enforcement points. When policies must be created, updated, or deleted, the policy administrator contacts the appropriate policy managers. These managers store the policies internally. When an access control decision must be made, the enforcement point asks the policy manager to supply the policy. The policy manager is usually very close to—if not located with—the enforcement point. The manager retrieves its internally stored policies and then gives them to the access control mechanisms.

Distributed policy management allows the access control decision to be made more quickly because the policy manager is close to the enforcement point. Because the policies are not sent across the network for every decision, they are less susceptible to network-based attacks such as introducing false or altered policies.

The drawback to this approach centers on consistency. Because the policy administrator must create and maintain policies separately for each enforcement point, a lot of redundant policy information is communicated when multiple enforcement points must operate in concert. If any of this information is lost or altered, the global access control system is compromised.

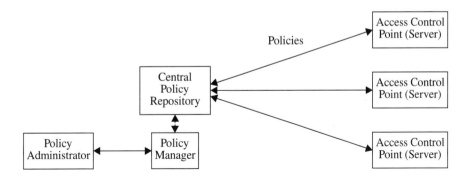

Figure 8-3 Centralized policy management

8.3.2 Centralized Policy Management

Whereas distributed policy management uses multiple policy managers, centralized policy management (shown in Figure 8-3) has only one, usually at or near the central policy repository. When the policy administrator must create, update, or delete a policy, it contacts the one policy manager, which in turn stores the policies in the central policy repository. The central policy repository is either close to or located with the policy manager. Each enforcement point obtains its access control policies from the central policy repository through standardized or proprietary policy exchange protocols.

An advantage to this approach is the ease of use for the policy administrator because there is only one point of contact. It is also easy to maintain consistency among the enforcement points because all enforcement points get the same master copy of the policy from the central policy repository.

The disadvantages have to do with the communication of the policies to the enforcement points. A certain amount of latency is incurred during the transfer of policies from the repository to enforcement points. Caching the policies at the enforcement points alleviates the latency problem, but it creates potential inconsistency. Also, these communications are subject to attack. The central policy repository is a single point of failure and the obvious place to direct an attack.

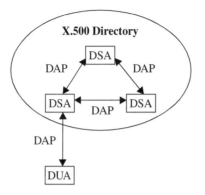

Figure 8-4 Relationships in an X.500 directory

8.3.3 Policy Repository

A policy repository is simply a database where policies are stored until needed. Often, the policies have already been translated into something the access control mechanisms can use. In a distributed environment, it makes sense to store these policies in a directory server such as that specified by X.500.

X.500 [CCITT88] is the ITU standard for directories. (Recall that the X.509 certificate standard is part of the larger effort to standardize directory storage and retrieval.) Because the directory acts as the central repository for information about users or other objects, the directory is a good place to store attributes pertaining to access control.

As with many international standards, the data access model in X.500 involves a set of formal transactions between abstractions, all with three-letter acronyms. Users access an X.500 directory using a Directory User Agent (DUA). The DUA transfers the request to a Directory System Agent (DSA) via the Directory Access Protocol (DAP), as shown in Figure 8-4. Furthermore, X.500 in general and DAP in particular take full advantage of the layers of abstraction in the ISO OSI Reference Model. Although this approach is useful for formal protocol proofs and international standards acceptance, however, it does not necessarily produce a protocol for practical use. The OSI stack has not enjoyed wide employment, and DAP over the OSI protocol stack is resource-intensive. LDAP, the Lightweight Directory Access Protocol, was developed specifically to address the access issue.

LDAP was designed to provide access to an X.500 directory (and many other types of directories as well) while not incurring the heavy resource requirements of DAP. This protocol is specifically targeted at management applications and browser applications that provide simple interactive access to the directory; it is simpler than DAP and works over Internet protocols, specifically TCP.[2] The first specification for LDAP [RFC1487] was focused mainly on this simple access. Subsequent versions (LDAPv2 [RFC1777] and LDAPv3 [RFC2251]) have expanded the protocol's ability to support communications between servers, server replication, and strong security via X.509 certificates.

Although LDAP provides a means for pulling the access control factors for a user into the access control mechanism for a resource, LDAP itself does not have a mature model for controlling access to the directories. The policies and mechanisms are currently considered outside the scope of the protocol, but some work has been done to set forth requirements and recommendations for improving access security in LDAP [RFC2820, RFC2829].

8.4 Access Control in VPNs

Access control in a VPN dictates whether a protected network resource can be accessed by VPN users. A VPN without access control only protects the security of the data in transit by encryption, not the network resource itself. Rigorous access control protects the corporation's network resources from unauthorized users while enabling access to authorized users.

Rather than instrument access control on the network resource itself, VPN designers usually implement access control in VPNs by putting access control mechanisms on one or more gateways. The access control policy is consulted before secure tunnels are established for the users and resources. In many cases, the access control policy is continuously consulted after tunnel establishment and is applied to every packet within the tunnel, as is done in an IPsec SPD, for example).

---

2. A useful book covering the many aspects of LDAP is *Understanding and Deploying LDAP Directory Services*, by Timothy A. Howes, Mark C. Smith, and Gordon S. Good, Macmillan Technical Publishing, 1999.

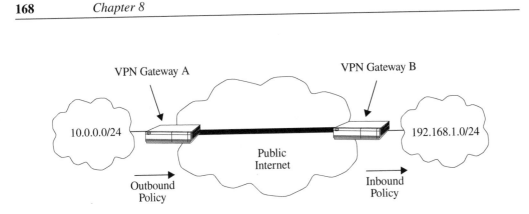

Figure 8-5 VPN access control rules example

Firewall access control policies are self-contained in the sense that the proper operation of a firewall does not depend on any other firewalls. A VPN gateway, in contrast, cannot operate in isolation from other VPN devices. A VPN gateway must cooperate with either another VPN gateway or a corresponding VPN client in order to accomplish secure communications. The VPN's access control policies can be managed in either a distributed or a centralized manner.

Inbound and Outbound Policies at the VPN Gateways

A VPN gateway must have two separate access control policies: an inbound access control policy and an outbound access control policy. The inbound access control policy is applied to inbound traffic, and the outbound policy is applied to outbound traffic. When two VPN gateways cooperate to establish secure tunnels between them, the outbound policy of one gateway will have direct correlation with the inbound policy of the other gateway. This is shown in the following example.

Suppose a secure tunnel is established between subnet 10.0.0.0/24 behind VPN gateway A and subnet 192.168.1.0/24 behind VPN gateway B, as shown in Figure 8-5. The inbound policy at gateway B will have an entry stating the following:

```
if {IP source address = 10.0.0.0/24} and
   {IP destination address = 192.168.1.0/24}
then apply IPsec
```

This rule accepts only traffic from the subnet behind gateway A destined for the subnet behind gateway B. This rule is absolutely necessary to protect the subnet behind gateway B. However, there is also an outbound rule at gateway A:

```
if {IP source address = 10.0.0.0/24} and
   {IP destination address = 192.168.1.0/24}
then apply IPsec
```

Because this outbound rule at gateway A is exactly the same at the inbound rule at gateway B, it seems redundant. However, if the outbound rule were missing, gateway A would not know how to process the traffic from 10.0.0.0/24 to 192.168.1.0/24. In addition, the outbound rule is useful to deny certain traffic—traffic that will not make it through gateway B anyway—*before* it goes into the tunnel. This practice saves bandwidth but, more importantly, also saves the encryption-decryption processing at both gateways.

Group-Based Access Control for VPN Clients

We have discussed how access control rules can be aggregated to simplify the policy expressions and the mechanisms used to enforce them. Aggregation is particularly useful for a remote access VPN scenario that has a potentially very large number of VPN client users and hence a large number of rule sets.

As an example, suppose a VPN has N users (u_1, u_2, ... u_N) and M rules (r_1, r_2, ... r_M). In theory, there can be $N{\times}M$ possible access control policy statements dictating whether a particular rule r_i is applicable to user u_j. As N and M grow, the number of policy statements can become too large to manage effectively.

To simplify the way access control policies are managed and implemented, the users are aggregated into user groups; users belonging to the same group share the same access control policy. Similarly, the rules can be aggregated into rule sets, which are then applied to the user groups. This situation is shown in Figure 8-6. First, the N users are separated into n user groups, where n is smaller than N. Next, the M rules are categorized into m rule sets, where another reduction is achieved. The mapping between individual users and the individual rules now becomes the mapping of the user groups to rule sets, which is usually much smaller than $N{\times}M$.

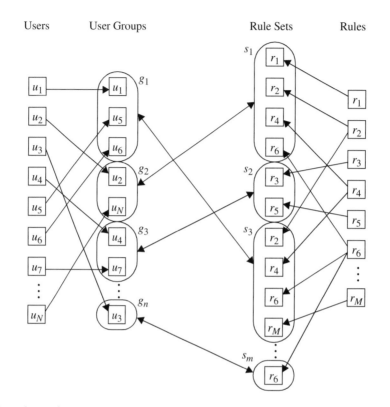

Figure 8-6 Groupings of users and rules

Users can be grouped in various ways. The preceding example is a mapping of many users to one group. In many-to-many mappings, a user may be in multiple groups at the same time. In another variation, groups are structured in a hierarchy of groups. Similarly, rule sets can be created in variations. In general, user-to-group mappings are typically many-to-one and rules-to-sets mappings are many-to-many. Group-to-rule sets mappings are one-to-one.

Attributes for VPN Access Control

Access control in a VPN is applied to the IP traffic being transported through the VPN's tunnels. As a result, all values in the packet's IP and higher-layer headers can be used as parameters for access control. These values include the source and destination IP addresses, source and destination ports, the protocol number, and any other header information that is accessible.

Sometimes it is not possible to base access control rules on a fixed port and protocol number. Such an arrangement is not flexible enough to accommodate many applications, especially those in which a server application listens on a well-known port. FTP, for example, listens on TCP port 21, but the client side often uses an arbitrary port number. The access control rules must be flexible enough to handle *stateful* situations such as this, adding rules only as needed and deleting them when the connections are released.

Separately, the user attributes obtained through authentication can also be used for access control purposes. For example, the username can be used to classify the user into an access control group. A digital certificate's distinguished name is a rich structure that holds much more information than just the user's name, such as organization name and perhaps email address. Any of this information can also be used for access control.

 # Part III

VPN Solutions

9

VPN Gateways

*One man defending a pass
can hold back ten thousand.*
—CHINESE PROVERB

VPN gateways are the clear points of separation between trusted private networks and untrusted public networks. As shown in Figure 9-1, these devices sit on the boundary between intranets and the Internet and act as endpoints for the tunnels carrying secured traffic through the public network.

A VPN gateway has two roles. First, the gateway enables the desired traffic to enter and leave the private network securely. Second, a VPN gateway keeps undesired traffic out of the private networks it protects and keeps private traffic from unintentionally leaving the private network.

Figure 9-2 is a block diagram showing how packets are processed in a VPN gateway. An outbound IP packet from the private network arriving on the private interface is passed through to the public interface, where it is examined according to the outbound policy rules to determine whether it should be tunneled, sent without modification, or dropped. An inbound IP packet from the Internet arriving on a public interface may be from an established tunnel. If so, it will be decapsulated and examined against the inbound policy rules. If the packet is not already part of a tunnel, it may pass through according to the inbound policy rules, or it may be requesting that a new tunnel be established (in which case a series of negotiations would ensue). The packets will be dropped if none of the policies applies.

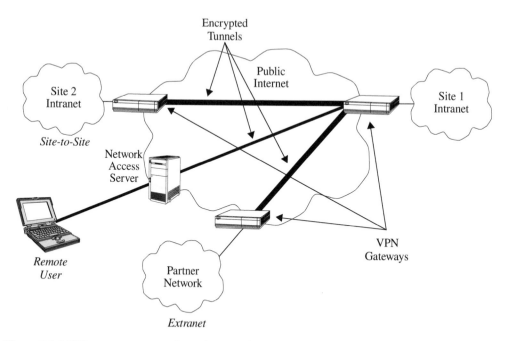

Figure 9-1 VPN gateways separating private and public networks

9.1 VPN Gateway Functions

VPN gateways implement four basic categories of VPN-related functions:

- Tunneling
- Authentication
- Access control
- Data integrity and confidentiality

Many different technologies can perform these functions, each using a different approach to achieve the same basic goal. In tunneling, for example, the choices include PPTP, L2F, L2TP, and IPsec; for encryption, DES, 3DES, CAST, RC4, and IDEA are among the algorithms available. It is difficult and generally unnecessary to implement all the technologies within a single category, but for a VPN gateway to be useful, it must implement at least one technology within each cate-

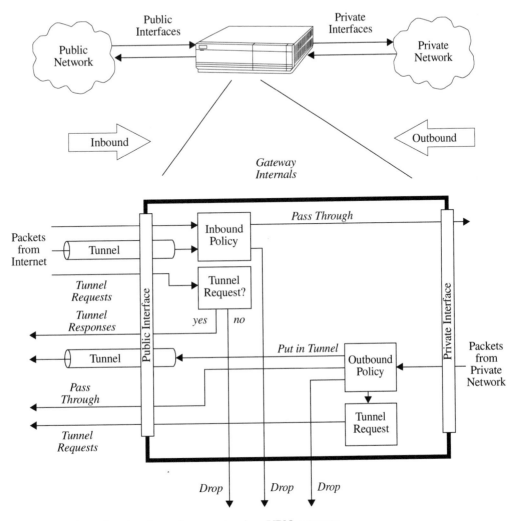

Figure 9-2 Inbound and outbound processing in a VPN gateway

gory. The task for the VPN gateway designer, therefore, is to choose a subset of the available technologies that best fits the needs of the target environment and then implement them efficiently in hardware, software, or a combination of the two. Figure 9-3 shows this "alphabet soup recipe" approach.

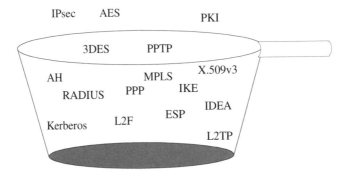

Figure 9-3 Alphabet soup recipe for designing a VPN gateway

In addition to these basic functions, a VPN gateway also needs to provide optional advanced features. For example, if quality of service of the network is important, VPN gateways should provide QoS support for network applications. VPN gateways should also provide redundant failover and load-balancing capabilities for mission-critical applications.

Recall from Chapter 3 that VPN architectures can be broken into three broad scenarios: site-to-site intranet VPNs, remote access VPNs, and extranet VPNs. Each of these scenarios has its own set of goals and constraints, and they help to shape the decisions about the specific technologies that are most appropriately applied to the VPN gateways to provide the desired service. We will look at each scenario in turn, posing a set of requirements and showing how those requirements drive decisions about VPN gateway functions.

9.1.1 Site-to-Site Intranet VPN Functions

Consider a site-to-site intranet VPN using two gateways residing in separate locations of the same company, as depicted in Figure 9-4. Each VPN gateway has two private subnets located behind it. Consider the following sample requirements:

1. All private traffic must be encrypted when transported across the Internet. The encryption algorithm should be 3DES, and the encryption key should be generated dynamically.

2. All the subnets can communicate with each other through the VPN.

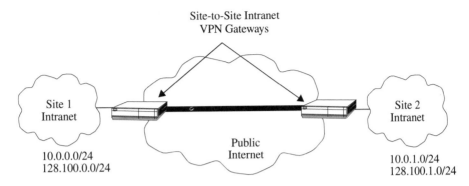

Figure 9-4 Site-to-site intranet VPN gateways

3. Digital certificates must be used for authentication between the two VPN gateways.

These requirements dictate which of the various functional choices should be implemented in the site-to-site VPN gateways. Let us examine the decisions in detail.

The first requirement specifies that a tunneling technology with strong encryption capability must be supported, and the encryption key must be generated dynamically. IPsec and IKE offer a standards-based solution for providing encrypted channels with these characteristics.

The second requirement mandates the need for fully encapsulating the intrasite private IP packets into publicly addressed packets so that the original net 10 source and destination addresses are preserved. Addresses in the net 10 address space (that is, the first of the four numbers in the dotted IP address is 10) are designated as private addresses, and consequently they cannot be routed through the Internet. IPsec's ESP in tunnel mode will satisfy this requirement.

Note that site 1 and site 2 also have addresses that start with "128.100." These addresses are routable through the Internet, and packets from site 1 addressed to 128.100.1.0/24 addresses[1] do not need the full encapsulation. However, address

---

1. This address notation is called CIDR, for Classless Inter-Domain Routing [RFC1519]. CIDR is a replacement for the old classes of IP address. The number following the slash is the number of bits in the address prefix identifying a network; the remaining bits after the prefix designate hosts. A "slash 24" address has 256 hosts.

hiding is only one of the reasons that packets are fully encapsulated. Although it is not stated here as a requirement, packets from site 1 to site 2 and vice versa may need to be either hidden from traffic analyzers or simply aggregated with the traffic addressed to net 10 destinations. Either way, IPsec ESP in tunnel mode also works well here. If the publicly routable intrasite packets do not require the full encapsulation of tunnel mode, ESP in transport mode can be used.

The third requirement subtly states two things: that the VPN gateway must offer PKI support and that the set of digital certificate support functions in IKE (as chosen for the first requirement) must be implemented. Here the VPN gateway designer has some flexibility on how to perform certificate enrollment, certificate revocation, certificate renewal, and CRL processing. Each possibility will have to be carefully studied by the engineers who actually implement it.

Of course, it is possible for a suite of proprietary technologies to satisfy all the requirements, and that approach may even offer advantages. Interoperability is certainly not among them.

9.1.2 Remote Access VPN Functions

The second scenario is the remote access VPN in which the VPN gateway is used as a remote access server; an example is shown in Figure 9-5. In this example—a VPN gateway with three private subnets located behind it—the VPN is expected to serve a large number of remote access clients.

The remote VPN clients do not have fixed IP addresses assigned to them because the ISPs use a variety of methods to distribute the addresses—some by static assignment, and others dynamically. Because these addresses are not under the control of the VPN gateways, a remote access user's ISP-assigned IP address will likely be different every time the remote access user requests connectivity. To facilitate the VPN, it is important for the remote access user also to have an IP address that is different from its address assigned by its ISP, one that can be appropriately routed within the corporate intranet. Otherwise, the routers and hosts would have to create host-based routing entries dynamically every time a VPN communication is needed.

Therefore, in addition to its other functions, the VPN gateway must implement address allocation and assignment in order to perform its duties as a remote access server. The address assignment must be under the control of the VPN gateway,

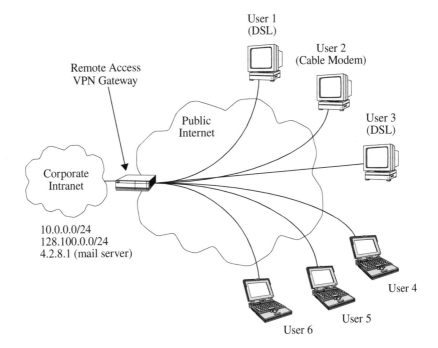

Figure 9-5 Remote access VPN gateway

whether the address is allocated by static or dynamic methods. If allocation is dynamic, DHCP (Dynamic Host Configuration Protocol) is a typical standard solution.

For the remote access client to function, merely acquiring an address in the corporate private network is not sufficient. Additional information about the corporate private network is needed. For example, the DNS server and the Windows Internet Service (WINS) server information should be passed from the VPN gateway to the remote access client. Without the address of these servers, the client cannot gain access to their services.

Consider the following sample requirements for the remote access scenario shown in the figure:

1. All private traffic must be encrypted when transported across the Internet. The encryption algorithm should be 3DES, and the encryption key should be dynamically generated.

2. Users 1, 2, and 3 can access all the subnets at the corporate site. Users 4, 5, and 6 can access only the mail server whose address is 4.2.8.1.

3. All users must be able to access the corporate intranet and the public Internet at the same time. The traffic destined to the Internet must not be tunneled back to the corporate site.

4. Remote access users can use either RADIUS or digital certificates to authenticate between the users and the VPN gateway.

Again, these requirements dictate which functions must be implemented on the VPN gateway as well as which functions must be implemented on the VPN remote access clients. The client functions are discussed in Chapter 10.

The first requirement is the same as in the site-to-site VPN scenario, and ESP tunnel mode and IKE offer an appropriate solution. The second requirement suggests that certain users be grouped so that access control rules can be applied to each group. However, the requirement does not prescribe specific ways to group the users. Can one user belong to two groups, or should separate user groups be created for those users? One possible solution is for the access control rules to be applied to individual users. The grouping decision is up to the VPN gateway designer.

The third requirement insists that access be permitted to both the public Internet and the private intranet. Having access to both networks means that the remote access client can become an involuntary conduit for network-based attacks. Particular care must be taken to keep unauthorized traffic away from the private network. Precautions should be taken both on the VPN gateway and at the client.

The fourth requirement states that the VPN gateway must support multiple authentication mechanisms: digital certificates (as in the site-to-site intranet scenario) and RADIUS. In the latter case, the VPN gateway can be the RADIUS server itself, or it can act as a proxy that simply passes the RADIUS authentication information to a corporate RADIUS server.

9.1.3 Extranet VPN Functions

Recall that the extranet VPN establishes business communication channels between companies. A typical example of an extranet VPN is shown in Figure 9-6. Consider the following requirements for this example:

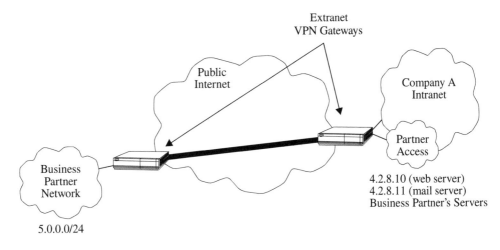

Figure 9-6 Extranet VPN gateways

1. All business partner traffic must be encrypted when transported across the Internet. The encryption algorithm should be 3DES, and the encryption key should be generated dynamically.

2. The business partner can access the servers only at 4.2.8.10 and 4.2.8.11. The only applications the business partner can access are the Web server on the host 4.2.8.10 and the mail server on the host 4.2.8.11.

3. Digital certificates will be used for authentication between the two VPN gateways.

There are many similarities between the two sets of sample intranet requirements and this set of sample extranet requirements because all of them are trying to establish secure communication channels between network entities. The major difference is that two companies, and not just one, are involved in the VPN configuration and policies. The trust extended to a business partner is certainly not the same as the trust extended within the company. In general, the access control of an extranet VPN is more complex and can require more sophisticated rule sets.

As with the earlier cases, ESP and IKE are appropriate for satisfying the first requirement. The second and third requirements demand that the gateway provide fine-grain access control on the VPN traffic. For example, a restriction can be established at the level of specific applications on a specific host.

It is possible that two separate VPN tunnels can be established between the business partner network (5.0.0.0/24) and the two hosts of company A that communicate with it (that is, 5.0.0.0/24 ⇔ 4.2.8.10 and 5.0.0.0/24 ⇔ 4.2.8.11). Alternatively, a single VPN tunnel can be established between the two sites, and the access control can be implemented using additional access filters before and after the traffic enters and exits the VPN tunnel. In the former approach, IPsec with the appropriate Security Policy Database (see Section 5.1.3) entries can provide this function. In the latter approach, a single pair of IPsec security associations can be used for all traffic between the two sites, leaving the access control and packet filtering mechanisms outside IPsec. In both cases, it is important to implement the appropriate rules at both gateways so that the traffic will not be processed and encrypted at one gateway only to be discarded at the other.

The fourth requirement is the same as the third requirement in the site-to-site intranet scenario: The VPN gateway must offer PKI support, and the set of digital certificate support functions in IKE must be implemented.

9.1.4 Forwarding, Routing, and Filtering Functions

In addition to the four basic categories of functionality, VPN gateways usually have basic packet routing and forwarding capabilities along with some basic firewall capabilities.

Because the routing protocols are still not necessarily secure,[2] many VPN gateways do not rely on routing protocol exchanges to create routes but rather rely on statically configured routes. For example, in the scenario discussed in Section 9.1.1, the subnets 10.0.0.0/24 and 128.100.0.0/24 are usually configured statically within the gateway rather than relying on the routing protocol to discover routes to them.

It is often desirable for the VPN gateway to exchange routing information with other network routers. Even if the gateway is not processing the routing information to populate its own routing tables, the gateway should be able to relay routing exchanges to its next hop routers. Because routing updates are usually handled

---

2. Two that are: OSPF with Digital Signatures [RFC2154] and Secure-BGP [KENT00].

through broadcast packets, the VPN gateway may be required to send certain broadcast packets through the secure tunnel.

Many VPN gateways also implement various firewall functions, network address translation (NAT) [RFC1631] being perhaps the most common. NAT is necessary because two privately addressed sites may in fact share the same private address space. Again, in the example in Section 9.1.1, if the subnets on both sides of the tunnel are both 10.0.0.0/24, it is possible that a host in each site is assigned the address 10.0.0.10 and that they will eventually try to send packets to each other. The VPN gateway, in this case, would employ NAT functions to replace the original source IP address in the IP header with a new, nonoverlapping IP address before it performs any IPsec tunneling. The gateway would also keep track of this mapping for packets sent back to the source.

Often, packet filtering is implemented on a VPN gateway to further restrict the traffic going into and coming out of the tunnel. In the case of L2TP, the protocol specifies only how to tunnel PPP traffic over the Internet (or ATM, in other cases). No per-packet security policy processing is present. In the case of IPsec, the Security Policy Database does specify per-packet policies, but they are closely associated with the security association. It is sometimes desirable to create a filtering capability that can be applied to multiple tunnels.

To illustrate this point, again consider the case in Section 9.1.1. This time, let us make the access control rules more strict: Subnets 10.0.0.0/24 and 10.0.1.0/24 can communicate with each other, and 128.100.0/24 and 128.100.1/24 can communicate with each other, but they cannot cross-communicate. In a strict IPsec implementation, four IPsec SAs can be established: one pair for 10.0.0/24 ⇔ 10.0.1.0/24, and one pair for 128.100.0.0/24 ⇔ 128.100.1.0/24.

Another approach for implementing this access restriction is to have a single SA pair established for {10.0.0.0/24, 128.100.0.0/24} ⇔ {10.0.1.0/24, 128.100.1.0/24}, an arrangement that permits the cross communication between the subnets. Packet filtering is then applied before and after the tunneling to prohibit the cross communication. This approach can simplify the complexity of the IPsec processing.

9.1.5 Advanced Functions

A VPN gateway can also support a number of advanced functions. These functions include quality of service support, failover and load balancing, and hardware acceleration.

QoS Considerations

One of the major criticisms of the shared public Internet is its lack of quality of service capabilities. Certain applications, however, require that network performance meet specific quality metrics in order to function properly. For example, a voice over IP application may require strict latency and jitter control so that the quality of the voice signal is acceptable.

QoS is a networkwide consideration—that is, for a VPN tunnel to have QoS, every hop and link along the tunnel path must have QoS support. For a VPN gateway to support QoS, it should have both the capability of classifying and marking the offered traffic based on the type of service quality the traffic should receive, and the capability of performing QoS negotiation with the network routers in the Internet infrastructure.

Sometimes having QoS support merely at the two tunnel endpoints can also be helpful. Suppose that two types of traffic are offered from a private network to a VPN tunnel: One is an email with a large file attachment, and the other is an interactive telnet session. If the VPN gateway at the tunnel endpoints can give the interactive telnet traffic higher priority, it can significantly improve the response of the telnet session without sacrificing the email performance.

Redundant Failover and Load Balance

When mission-critical applications are running over a VPN, it is imperative that the VPN gateway have redundant failover capabilities. This means that if a VPN gateway fails due to software or hardware failure, another gateway should be able to assume the role of the stricken gateway. Or, even better, two or more VPN gateways share the load of the VPN traffic simultaneously. If one gateway fails, the remaining gateways assume its load and only the absolute performance is affected. The network maintains operation.

There are several ways to provide redundant failover and load-balancing capabilities. Some VPN vendors (e.g., Alcatel) use clustering technologies to make multiple VPN gateways appear as a single "virtual" gateway. The Virtual Router Redundancy Protocol (VRRP) [RFC2338] was developed specifically to facilitate clustering. Other VPN vendors (e.g., Nortel Networks) take the approach that a single gateway acts as the primary active gateway, and another gateway assumes the active role only when the primary gateway is no longer available. Hot swap methods include the Hot Standby Router Protocol (HSRP) [RFC2281] proposed by Cisco.

Redundant failover schemes share two common issues. First, a method should exist to determine whether or not a VPN gateway is still functioning. This usually requires a periodic communication mechanism between the VPN gateway (e.g., a "hello" protocol, as in OSPF). Second, after it is determined that a gateway has failed, an alternative gateway should take over the secure communication.

Secure communication requires that certain state information be maintained. If a new secure tunnel must be established because of a failure, a significant amount of time can elapse between the request and the establishment of the tunnel. If the failover of the communication must be seamless and completed within a very short period, the state information will have had to be communicated to the alternative gateway by the original gateway a priori. The way the state information is synchronized is critical in the design of the redundant failover and load-balancing scheme.

Although it is critical, there is no standard method for synchronizing state information between VPN devices. Several vendors (e.g., Check Point and NetScreen) have their own proprietary implementations. At this point, little effort is under way in the IETF toward any such standard.

Hardware Acceleration

The encryption operation of a VPN gateway is computationally intensive, yet it is also well defined and repetitive. It is therefore advantageous to implement these functions in hardware when possible to off-load the general-purpose processor.

Hardware encryption is necessary for network speeds of T3 (45 Mbps) and higher, especially when long keys are used. Fortunately, many commercial ASIC manufacturers have high-speed encryption chips specifically designed for the various cryptographic standards. Such chips are already integrated into some vendors' VPN gateways.

9.2 Gateway Configuration and Provisioning

No matter how many or what types of functions are implemented on a VPN gateway, the gateway is not useful if it is not properly configured. Network operations personnel, rather than the gateway designer or manufacturer, are responsible for properly configuring the device for deployment. This configuration process is also called *provisioning*.

VPN gateway configuration interfaces can come in several forms, such as command line interfaces and GUIs. In many cases, more than one configuration method is implemented because each method has its own advantages. It is also possible that some kind of API is specified to facilitate customizing gateway configuration applications.

It is difficult to describe how to configure a VPN gateway without using a specific product from a VPN device vendor as an example. On the other hand, vendor information can change quickly, and singling out a particular vendor may show bias against or toward that product. Without losing generality, we will describe the set of parameters that should be configured on a VPN gateway to make it a functional device in a virtual private network.

VPN gateway configurations can be loosely separated into the following components: gateway identity information, external device information, and security policy information. The *gateway identity information* includes the information needed by other network devices to communicate with the VPN gateway. The other devices can be other VPN gateways, routers, firewalls, or simply IP hosts.

The *external device information* includes the addresses and parameters needed by the VPN gateway to obtain services from these external devices. This includes both VPN-related and other functions. For example, a default router on the public network interface is essential so that the VPN gateway can forward IP traffic.

The *security policy information* is the set of internal configuration parameters that deals exclusively with the VPN functions.

9.2.1 Gateway Identity Information

A VPN gateway is first and foremost a network gateway device, complete with network interfaces and IP addresses. IP addresses are how IP devices—hosts, routers, firewalls, and other machines—are known. For VPN gateways in particular, some of the addresses are exposed to the public so that the gateway can be known to the Internet. Some of the addresses may be valid only within the private network.

Equally important are identities not directly related to the IP addresses. These include the full host name of the gateway, and the digital certificates and other secret information used for authentication.

It is also desirable for a single VPN gateway to have multiple identities, one for each of its functions. For example, an identity can be dedicated to management purposes—the management identity—to help facilitate management-specific functions (we discuss VPN gateway management in more detail in Section 9.3). Another example is in the area of multiple tunnels; here, a VPN gateway may use one certificate for its intranet tunnel and use another certificate for the extranet tunnel.

The following list is an example of the kinds of identity information that can be associated with a VPN gateway:

- Public interface: 4.2.8.132
- Private interface: 4.2.8.5
- Private interface 10.0.0.1
- Management identity: 4.2.8.131
- Name: gate1.mycorp.com
- Digital certificates: certificate A and certificate B

These identities are shown in Figure 9-7. The public and private interface addresses are the most obvious ways to identify the VPN gateway. In the figure, one of the public addresses is dedicated to management, so it is the way the gateway is identified to the management functions. Equally valid is the use of an address on the private network as the management address. The gateway usually has a full host name, such as gate1.mycorp.com, which is the way the gateway is known through DNS. The certificates identify the VPN gateway for authentication purposes.

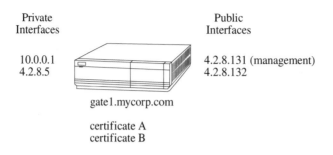

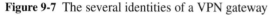

Private Interfaces

Public Interfaces

10.0.0.1
4.2.8.5

4.2.8.131 (management)
4.2.8.132

gate1.mycorp.com

certificate A
certificate B

Figure 9-7 The several identities of a VPN gateway

9.2.2 External Device Information

VPN gateways are not isolated devices; rather, they are nodes on a network that has many other such nodes with specialized functions. Because the VPN gateway has forwarding responsibilities, it must know about the availability of appropriate routers. It also performs authentication functions, so it must know where the authentication servers are. In fact, the VPN gateway must know about a long list of external devices, including the following:

- Router or routers connecting to each network interface
- Domain name server
- RADIUS authentication server and its shared secret password
- RADIUS accounting server and its shared secret password
- SNMP management station
- Policy management station
- Policy server
- One or more certification authorities
- X.500 directory server
- DHCP server for dynamic addressing
- WINS server for Microsoft networking

9.2.3 Security Policy Information

The primary responsibility of the VPN gateway is to extend the reach of a private network by establishing and maintaining secure tunnels. Consequently, the gateway must protect the resources on the private networks from unauthorized access.

This implies that the gateway should have full knowledge of the networks and resources it is tasked to protect. Furthermore, the VPN gateway must be configured with sets of security policies that spell out exactly how the protected resources can be accessed and by whom.

The network resources being protected by the VPN gateway are easily identified by their IP addresses and, to a finer granularity, the protocol and port numbers associated with the resources' application interfaces. The more difficult part is to precisely identify the allowable traffic from the public Internet.

It is usually helpful to separate the security policies into two parts: one addressing the site-to-site issues, and the other addressing remote access issues. Site-to-site situations are somewhat easier to handle because secure tunnels are established to other VPN gateways, which usually have their identity information defined (as discussed earlier) and thus are more readily identifiable. In the remote access situation, the IP address of the access device is usually assigned dynamically by the service provider. Therefore, other methods, such as digital certificates, are needed to identify those devices.

Site-to-Site Security Policies

The set of site-to-site security policies includes the policies related to the local VPN gateway—the starting point of the tunnel—and those related to the remote VPN gateway—the ending point of the tunnel. The attributes and policies related to the local tunnel endpoint include:

- The type of tunneling mechanism
- The public interface address of the local VPN gateway
- The local accessible addresses and subnets
- The local inbound access control filters
- The local outbound access control filters

Depending on the tunneling mechanism (IPsec, L2TP, etc.), other security parameters that must be specified. For example, in the case of IPsec, these parameters include a suitable encryption algorithm (e.g., 3DES), the pertinent message integrity algorithm (e.g., SHA-1), and the type of authentication method (digital certificate or shared secret).

Technically speaking, a VPN gateway can specify only those security policies that apply to itself. It is not possible for the local VPN gateway to specify the security policy for any other gateways. However, because a VPN tunnel has two end-points, it is necessary for the policy at least to identify the other endpoint of the tunnel, which is a public interface address of the remote VPN gateway. Furthermore, it is also necessary to identify the remote addresses and subnets for which this particular VPN tunnel will be used.

Because a VPN tunnel involves two VPN gateways, it is important for the security policies specified at both gateways to be consistent. For example, one VPN gateway may allow certain traffic, but if the corresponding gateway specifies otherwise, the tunnel cannot be established, or a tunnel could be established but no traffic would flow.

Remote Access Security Policies

As mentioned earlier, remote access clients cannot be readily identified by their IP addresses because the addresses may be dynamically assigned from an externally controlled (i.e., ISP) address pool. The remote access clients can be identified only after authentication has been achieved. Instead of the address, a unique user-name is usually used to identify each remote access user.

It is important to separate the remote users into groups and apply security policies on a group-by-group basis because the number of users can be very large (sometimes in the tens of thousands). To specify a security policy for each user individually is not feasible and, fortunately, not necessary.

The security policies to be specified for a remote access user group include the following:

- The type of tunneling mechanism to be applied to the group and the related parameters
- The public interface address of the local VPN gateway, the locally accessible addresses and subnets.
- The local inbound and outbound access control filters
- The address or address pool to be used for address assignment for the remote access group
- The access control rules for the remote user group

9.3 Gateway Management

A VPN is not a static communications infrastructure. The job of network operations personnel is not finished when the VPN gateways have been installed and configured. VPN gateways must be continuously managed to ensure that the VPN is meeting the needs of the business it serves.

Although it is easy to configure the VPN gateways at a centralized, well-equipped provisioning laboratory before deployment, it is much more difficult to modify the configurations while the gateways are running as active components of a network. Unfortunately, accommodating change is also absolutely necessary. This is called *configuration management*.

Once deployed, VPN gateways must be monitored continuously to ensure that they are functioning properly, and, when faults are found, diagnosis and correction must be applied in a timely fashion. This is called *network monitoring*.

It is also important to collect information about how and by whom the VPN is being used. This *accounting information* is useful for both security and billing.

Each of these topics is addressed in the following subsections, although VPN gateway management issues are not strictly limited to these three.

9.3.1 Configuration Management

There are four primary methods for accessing the configuration settings of a VPN gateway for management purposes: command line interface, graphical user interface, configuration file manipulation, and application programming interface. Generally, a VPN gateway is implemented with more than one method because each method can be used at different times for different purposes.

Command Line Interface

One of the most commonly used methods for configuring a network gateway is the command line interface (CLI). CLI has the advantage of being concise, and usually several commands can be concatenated using a scripting language to form complex functions that are easily sent across the network and easily stored as a template for later use. These advantages, and the fact that a CLI script is also a good way to provide configuration automation, make CLI a preferred choice

```
crypto ipsec transform-set MyTransform esp-md5-hmac esp-3des mode tunnel

crypto map MyMap 1 ipsec-isakmp
    set transform-set MyTransform
    match address 101
    set peer 192.168.1.1
interface Serial0
    cryptomap MyMap
access-list 101 \
    permit tcp host 10.0.0.1 0.0.255.255 eq ftp 172.16.4.0 0.0.0.255
```

Figure 9-8 Command line interface example: Cisco's IOS IPsec command set

among experienced network administrators. However, the emphasis on brevity and power sometimes causes readability to suffer (see Figure 9-8). It usually takes time for a beginner to become familiar with a vendor's CLI, so it is important that the CLI be accompanied by a good online help facility.

Graphical User Interface

Many VPN gateway vendors have a built-in GUI-based configuration tool. If designed well, a GUI tool can be illustrative and intuitive. It can provide an environment that helps the novice user to quickly learn and navigate between functions. In particular, when the Web is used as the GUI, most users are immediately familiar with the mechanism of operation.

GUI tools do have drawbacks. It is difficult to write a script around a GUI, so it is difficult to automate. The performance of a GUI tool may suffer because of slow screen refreshes and slow server response.

Figure 9-9 shows an example of an IPsec setting in the GUI display in Nortel Networks' Contivity Extranet Switch.

Configuration File Manipulation

In the case of mass manufacturing of configurations, a more convenient tool is to directly manipulate configuration files. In essence, the configuration of the VPN gateway is stored in the gateway in special configuration files (although their formats can vary). Configuration files are created at the management station and

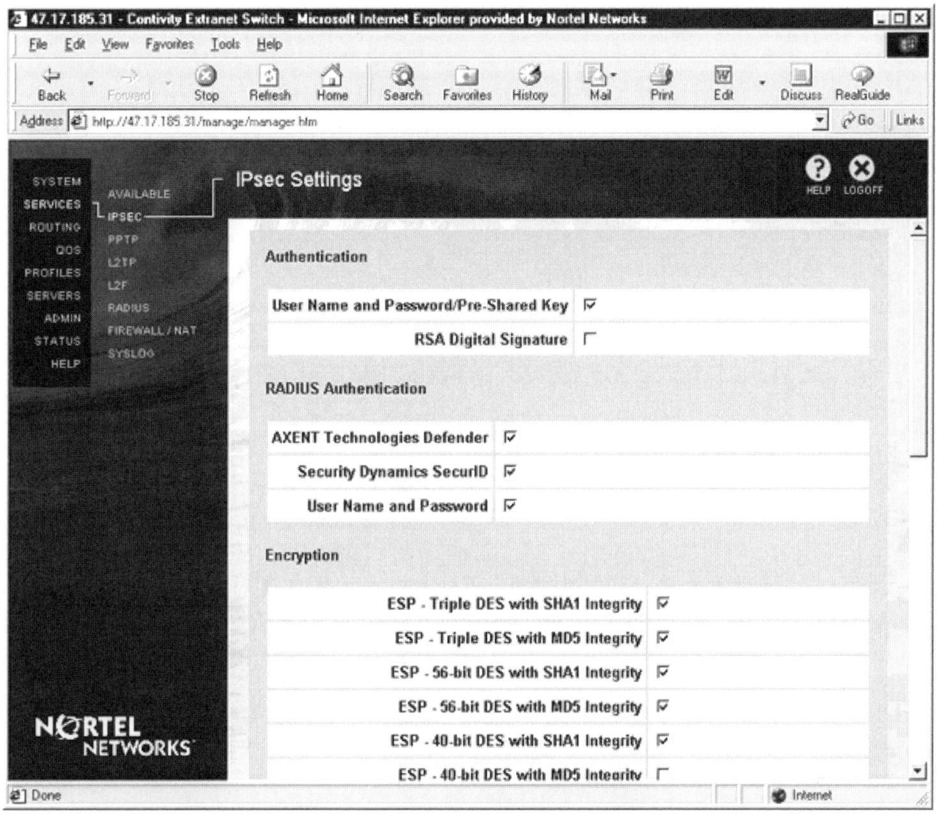

Figure 9-9 Web-based interface: Nortel Networks' Contivity Extranet Switch

uploaded to the VPN gateway when needed. This approach also lets you use revision control mechanisms to track changes and keep an archive of the VPN gateway's configurations. To make a change, you simply edit the existing file and upload it to the gateway. An example of an Alcatel Configuration file for IPsec settings is shown in Figure 9-10.

Application Programming Interface

Although it is not as common, some VPN gateways provide an application programming interface (API) for configuration management. An API enables various

```
begin security-descriptor
    Name "MySecurityDescriptor"
    IPsec "ESP 3DES HMAC MD5 MINUTES 360"
    ISAKMP "DES MD5 MINUTES 1440"
end
```

Figure 9-10 Alcatel/TimeStep configuration file for IPsec settings

custom configuration tools to be developed for the network provisioning system, and it gives third-party vendors of management software a clean way to access the gateways. A CLI can be considered as a crude type of API.

9.3.2 Network Monitoring

Continued monitoring of the network devices is needed in any network. The same holds true for VPN gateways. Monitoring ensures that a network device failure can be quickly found and corrective measures taken. Centrally located network operations personnel must have some means of finding out what is happening in the network, both to solve acute problems and to conduct long-term trend analysis.

There are several ways to monitor the health of the devices throughout the network. Some methods use request-response protocols for getting specific statistics and status notifications from the devices. Other methods—cruder but effective—include pinging and tracing routes using tricks enabled by the Internet Control Message Protocol (ICMP) [RFC792]. System logging is also an effective way to monitor when and where failures occur.

SNMP

The most widely used method for network management is the Simple Network Management Protocol (SNMP)[3] [RFC1157]. SNMP provides the mechanism for the management station to poll a managed device for desired status and statistical information stored in a database called the Management Information Base (MIB). SNMP also allows devices to voluntarily produce *traps* that cause notifications to

---

3. Marshall Rose [ROSE95] and Willam Stallings [STAL99] have good reference books for network management in general and SNMP in particular.

be sent back to the management station when certain important events happen on the device.

It is imperative for a network device to implement one or more standard MIBs. In addition to the standard MIBs such as TCP/IP MIB-II [RFC1213], several MIBs in RFC or Internet-Draft form are relevant to VPNs:

- IKE Monitoring MIB [JENK00b]
- IPsec Monitoring MIB [JENK00c]
- IP Tunnel MIB [RFC2667]

Also, VPN gateway vendors have developed private MIBs that are specific to the gateway products they offer.

Ping

A widely used monitoring technique is to use ICMP *ping* [BSD97] to provide live-ness and round-trip delay data and to give some indication of the congestion on the path to the target host. An ICMP Echo Request carrying a timestamp is sent to a destination IP address. If there is a host at that address, the host answers the Echo Request by placing the timestamp in an Echo Reply message. When the pinging host receives the Echo Reply message, it subtracts the timestamp from the current time to get the round-trip time. The echo packets also carry sequence numbers so that the pinging host can tell which and how many echo packets may have been lost.

As with all network devices, it is important that the VPN gateway support standard ICMP (it is, after all, an integral part of IP and therefore required). However, one should also be aware that pings can be used as a form of denial-of-service attack in which the VPN gateway spends too much time answering ICMP echo requests.

Traceroute

Another widely used monitoring mechanism is to use *traceroute* [JACO96]. Traceroute maps the path an IP packet takes from the sending host to the destination. Generally, traceroute provides latency information for each router along the path as well.

Traceroute uses a trick with the IP time to live (TTL) field. Each router along an IP packet's path decrements the TTL field value. When the TTL value reaches zero, the packet has exceeded the time it can live (more accurately, the number of hops it can traverse), and the packet is discarded. When this happens, IP implementations are supposed to send to the source address a Time Exceeded ICMP notification stating that the IP packet was dropped. Traceroute takes advantage of this by first sending a series of IP packets with TTL set to 1. The first router decrements the TTL and then is forced to drop the packets, but not before reporting the drop via the ICMP Time Exceeded messages. Traceroute then sends a series of packets with TTL set to 2, and so on, until the TTL is finally set large enough to allow the IP packet to reach the destination host.

Traceroute is extremely valuable for finding routing and reachability problems and discovering congestion.

Logging

Logging requires that the VPN gateway log events as they happen on the VPN gateway. In *syslog*, a popular logging facility, events fall into one of several categories [BSD93]: emergency (a panic condition), alert (a condition that should be corrected immediately), critical (critical conditions), error (error conditions), warning (warning messages), notice (conditions that are not errors but should possibly be handled specially), informational (conditions that are of interest), and debug (debugging information). A logging system within the VPN gateway can be configured to catch certain events and raise the appropriate notification.

When an event occurs, one of several actions are taken, from recording the event in an internal log file to sending log messages to a designated log collection server. In particular, events related to security should always be logged and special attention paid because maintaining security within a VPN gateway is essential to providing the VPN service. For example, any change of the VPN gateway configuration—or any management access on the VPN gateway, for that matter—should be logged.

9.3.3 Accounting Information

Much of a VPN gateway's status and statistical information can be used not only for network monitoring and management but also for billing purposes. When used for billing, the information is called *accounting information*. A VPN gateway should implement a mechanism to facilitate the collection of accounting information.

IP networks traditionally lack the support of such accounting mechanisms. Internet accounting was studied before the Internet became a commercial network, and concerns were raised that the availability of an accounting capability might be detrimental to the free spirit of the Internet [RFC1272]. However, the commercialization of the Internet and its use for business communication have changed all that. In particular, when a network service is provided by a service providers, an accounting mechanism is imperative so that the service provider can charge customers appropriately.

One important aspect of the collection of accounting information is the existence of an identifying parameter on which the status and statistics can be aggregated. For site-to-site intranet VPNs, a secure tunnel ID is an obvious identifying parameter. In remote access VPNs, a session ID is created whenever a user dials in to the ISP's network access server (NAS). All IP traffic statistics related to that session are collected using the session ID as the identifying parameter. All sessions belonging to the same user are then aggregated together. (RFC2139 defines an accounting standard for dial-up Internet service using RADIUS [RFC2139].)

RADIUS-like accounting can be used to obtain usage data for remote access users. The key is to create a concept of a *session* within the VPN's tunneling protocol and to aggregate all the IP traffic statistics onto that session. For example, if the tunneling protocol is IPsec, a session can refer either to an ISAKMP security association or to an IPsec security association. In the case of L2TP, a layer 2 tunnel can be treated as a session.

In general, the following accounting information should be captured for a remote user VPN session:

- Username
- Session start time
- Session stop time
- Remote user IP address
- VPN gateway IP address
- Input octet count
- Output octet count

- Input packet count
- Output packet count

9.4 Gateway Certification

With the inherent security concerns of Internet VPNs, it is important for the VPN gateways to adhere to the various standards. Merely claiming standards compliance is not sufficient; an "objective" third-party certification is usually necessary.

IPsec Certification from ICSA

International Computer Security Association (ICSA)[4] is a well-established organization that deals with computer and network security issues. To many equipment buyers, ICSA certification provides a level of assurance to customers that the VPN gateway meets a certain level of security and is to some degree interoperable with other products in the marketplace. ICSA charges a fee per product per year to certify IPsec compliance for VPN gateway vendors. Its certification process currently focuses on these areas:

- **Internet Key Exchange** Support for both IKE phase 1 and phase 2 is tested (refer to Section 5.4 for IKE phase details).
- **IPsec Encapsulation** The focus here is on the ESP implementation (see Section 5.3 for ESP details).
- **Cryptography** The focus is on the encryption algorithm and random number generation.
- **PKI** The focus is on the interaction with the certification authority and X.500 directory server (refer to Chapter 7 for PKI details).

FIPS 140-1 Certification

Because VPN gateways are security devices, they must also consider the aspect of physical security. There are two aspects to being physically secure: Access to the device is limited, and the device, if accessed, is tamper-resistant. The first aspect is a physical plant issue, and companies or VPN service providers must take measures to ensure controlled access to machine rooms. This is sometimes difficult to

---

4. http://www.icsa.net

do, especially when equipment must be placed on a customer's premises. As a result, tamper resistance is important. It should be difficult, for example, for someone to open the VPN gateway and read confidential information from the memory or steal the hard disk.

The Federal Information Processing Standard (FIPS) 140-1 publication developed by NIST [NIST94a] specifies several levels of physical security required for information security devices. In many cases, U.S. government organizations will not accept a security device that is not compliant with FIPS 140-1. NIST maintains a list of all vendors with validated FIPS 140-1 security devices.

9.5 Interaction with Firewalls

Another type of network security device is a *firewall*.[5] Firewalls examine all traffic going into and coming out of an intranet to make sure that unauthorized traffic is prohibited. There are several ways that a firewall prevents unauthorized traffic: through packet filtering, through stateful inspection, and using an application-level proxy. Almost all corporate private networks are protected by firewalls in one way or another.

Firewalls are concerned with preventing unauthorized traffic from coming into or getting out of the private network and are generally not concerned about the security of the traffic after it leaves the corporate private network. A VPN gateway, on the other hand, is more concerned about allowing legitimate traffic into the private network and ensuring that the traffic can still be secure after it leaves the private network.

VPN gateways and network firewalls are security devices, and their functions overlap in many ways, so much so that there is a trend to integrate VPN gateway functionality and firewall functionality in the same device. Here, we consider only the case when the two devices are separate but are both located at the corporate network boundary to protect the private network. The following subsections describe ways in which VPN gateways and firewalls can be arranged to complement each other.

---

5. The book *Firewalls and Internet Security: Repelling the Wily Hacker* by William R. Cheswick and Steven M. Bellovin [CHES94] is a good book on firewalls.

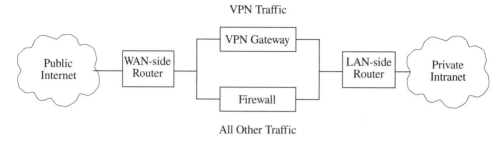

Figure 9-11 VPN gateway and firewall in parallel

9.5.1 VPN Gateway and Firewall in Parallel

One way to configure a VPN gateway and a firewall is to put them in parallel, as shown in Figure 9-11. In this configuration, traffic going through the VPN gateway and firewall are separated; VPN traffic goes through the VPN gateway and all other traffic goes through the firewall. The routers on both the WAN and the LAN sides should be configured to send VPN traffic to the VPN gateway.

It is relatively easy to configure the WAN-side router. Because all VPN traffic is tunneled and because all tunnels have an endpoint at the VPN gateway, the router simply needs to have a routing table entry for the VPN gateway only. The LAN-side router, however, is more difficult to configure because the traffic has yet to be tunneled. This router must separate the traffic destined to a VPN tunnel from all other traffic based on the destination addresses of the IP packets.

In the parallel configuration case, the VPN gateway and firewall configurations are separate; they do not interfere with each other.

9.5.2 VPN Gateway and Firewall in Series

Another arrangement of VPN gateway and firewall devices is to have them in series. As shown in Figure 9-12, there are two cases: The VPN gateway is on the LAN side and the firewall is on the WAN side, or the other way around.

In the serial configuration, the LAN-side and the WAN-side routers are easy to set up because they can merely point their default routes to the VPN gateway or fire-

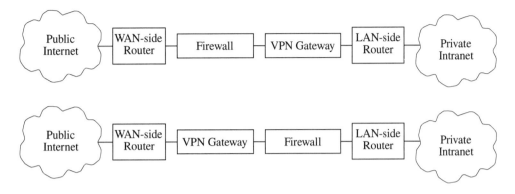

Figure 9-12 VPN Gateway and Firewall in Series

wall. The configuration of the VPN gateway and the firewall, on the other hand, is more difficult because they now depend on each other. Following are the two cases for the series configuration.

Firewall Near WAN Side

The top diagram in Figure 9-12 shows the firewall in front of the VPN gateway for traffic coming from the Internet. In this situation, specific rules must be installed in the firewall to allow VPN traffic to pass through. This arrangement is equivalent to opening a hole through the firewall; any tunneled traffic or tunnel creation messages destined for the VPN gateway must be permitted access. Opening the firewall to permit VPN-related traffic, although necessary, weakens the protection afforded by the firewall because the tunneled packets are opaque to the firewall and therefore are not subject to its rules.

Even if the firewall cannot screen the tunneled traffic, it can establish rules for which types of tunnels are legitimate. In the case of IPsec-based VPNs, special rules can be created to allow IPsec ESP and AH (protocol numbers 50 and 51, respectively), IKE (UDP port 500), and PKI (e.g., TCP ports 709 and 368 for Entrust-based PKI).

All the traffic that is permitted to pass through the firewall is then processed by the VPN gateway. Certainly the VPN gateway handles the encryption and decryption of traffic for which the gateway is a tunnel endpoint. In addition, the VPN gateway should satisfy the legitimate tunnel creation requests. All other traffic must be allowed to pass through to the intranet.

Because the firewall performs the filter on allowable traffic, the VPN gateway policies are no longer used for access control, but only for determining which traffic gets encrypted and which parameters are used for encryption. Furthermore, acting as a pass-through device for all non-VPN data still consumes some amount of the available processing capacity. For these reasons, this configuration is usually not recommended.

VPN Gateway Near WAN Side

The bottom diagram in Figure 9-12 shows the firewall and VPN gateway in the opposite order as shown in the top diagram; now the VPN gateway is in the front. As in the other case, the VPN gateway must handle the tunneled traffic and the tunnel requests. The VPN gateway can also perform some access control on the non-VPN traffic. The traffic allowed through the VPN gateway—including the decapsulated and decrypted VPN traffic—is then processed by the firewall. Because no tunnels penetrate past the gateway, all the traffic is in the clear and the firewall can apply policy rules. However, because the tunneled traffic should be allowed into the trusted network, it could require many special rules to grant the VPN access through the firewall.

This serial configuration is used more often than the firewall-first approach because the firewall can sometimes offer more sophisticated access control compared with a VPN gateway. The combined capability of the firewall and VPN gateway policies can provide highly desired traffic confidentiality and sophisticated access control.

9.5.3 Hybrid Configurations

In many situations, a simple parallel or serial configuration does not fully describe the complexity of a corporate network perimeter. The "three-legged" network firewall is one such case. In the traditional firewall configuration, a third leg—or connection—off of the firewall usually represents a separate policy control region, such as a *demilitarized zone* (DMZ) [CHES94].

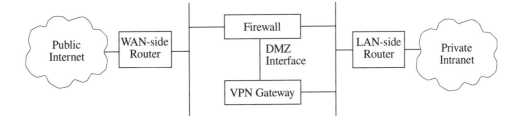

Figure 9-13 VPN gateway's public interface attached to firewall's DMZ interface

Figure 9-13 shows a VPN gateway attached to the third leg of a network firewall. Because the filters of the network firewall are usually applied to a specific interface, different set of filters can be used for the VPN tunnel traffic and the other firewall traffic. In this way, no holes are created in the filters for the general firewall rule set. The filters for the VPN gateway attached interface can be set up to allow only tunnel-related traffic to pass through.

Figure 9-14 shows a different way to attach a VPN gateway to the third leg of a network firewall. In this configuration, the decapsulated traffic leaving the VPN tunnel is the input to the firewall's third interface. Again, because the filters of the network firewall are interface-specific, different sets of filters can be used for the VPN tunnel traffic and the other firewall traffic. No holes are created in the rules for the traffic bypassing the VPN gateway.

Although it is possible to have a VPN gateway with three or more interfaces and have the network firewall attached to one of the private interfaces of the VPN gateway, this configuration offers no value.

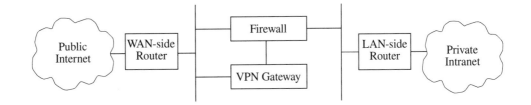

Figure 9-14 VPN gateway's private interface attached to firewall's third interface

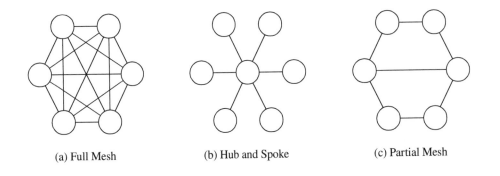

(a) Full Mesh   (b) Hub and Spoke   (c) Partial Mesh

Figure 9-15 Topology Choices in VPN Design.

9.6 VPN Design Issues

Certainly firewalls are not the only devices that interact with the VPN gateway at the network perimeter. Other devices include routers, address servers, and authentication servers. Furthermore, a VPN requires multiple devices at various locations working together to form the secure logical network.

In creating a wide-area VPN, network designers must choose among different alternatives by prioritizing the network requirements and making trade-offs using many criteria. In addition to central security considerations, the following major issues must also be considered in the design process.

Network Topology

Connecting more than two sites offers interesting topological choices. A full-mesh topology (Figure 9-15a) allows any two sites to directly communicate with each other. In a hub-and-spoke topology (Figure 9-15b), one of the sites must be the central hub, and the spoke sites are connected indirectly through the hub. In a partial mesh topology (Figure 9-15c), only selected sites are directly connected, and other sites are connected indirectly. A VPN designer must consider the traffic requirements between different sites and weigh the trade-offs between the different topologies. Although the full mesh arrangement offers efficient routing, it is complex and does not scale well. The hub-and-spoke approach is simpler to configure but has a single routing bottleneck.

Addressing and Routing

The IP address shortage has forced many private networks to use the RFC 1918 private IP addresses. It is important to hide these private IP addresses when the traffic is traversing the Internet. A registered IP address is required at the public interface of the VPN gateway so that encapsulated packets can be routed. When overlapping private IP address ranges are used at both ends of the VPN tunnel, network address translation (NAT) must also be employed to disambiguate the use of the addresses. If IPsec is the tunneling technology, address translation must be performed before the IPsec processing.

When VPN gateways are added to a network to build a VPN, the routing structure must be changed to accommodate the VPN devices. In particular, the router tables must be configured to forward encrypted and cleartext packets to the appropriate devices. Because many VPN gateways currently do not support dynamic routing, static routes are used on the VPN gateways and on the routers connected directly to the VPN gateways.

Quality of Service

Various types of traffic traverse a VPN, each type requiring a different quality of service. QoS on a shared connectionless network is a complex problem. When QoS is required, packets must be classified, marked, and processed according the QoS policies. Preserving that packet classification in the VPN tunnel is an issue requiring careful consideration.

For example, the IETF DiffServ working group is standardizing the use of the differentiated service code point (DSCP) in the IP header for identifying traffic with different class-of-service requirements. Many DiffServ-compliant routers reclassify the packet based on the congestion status of the network link. When the packet is decapsulated at the end of the tunnel, the VPN gateway can either copy the reclassified DSCP into the decapsulated packet, or keep the original classification.

Scalability

VPN implementations must scale with the increasing bandwidth demands of new users and network applications. In addition to the topological considerations, scalability includes load balancing, the number of concurrent secure tunnels, and rapid bandwidth provisioning. Scalability in site-to-site and remote access VPNs should be considered separately. In a site-to-site intranet VPN configuration, the amount of bandwidth is the primary concern in considering the load imposed on the VPN gateway. In the remote access scenario, both the amount of bandwidth and the number of simultaneous tunnels must be considered.

9.7 A VPN Solution Scenario

Consider a company having three corporate intranet sites. One site is at the corporate headquarters located in New York City. The other two sites are located in Los Angeles and Dallas. A site-to-site VPN must be established among all three sites. In addition, a business partner location in Atlanta needs access to a specific Web server located within the company's New York headquarters.

The company also has many remote access users, some of whom are traveling sales representatives needing access to the pricing and inventory information server on the corporate network. Other remote users are telecommuters using high-speed DSL or cable modem connections to perform work as if they are in their offices.

The following are the details of the internal networks and servers:

New York Headquarters
Internal Networks	10.0.1.0/24
	10.0.2.0/24
	10.0.3.0/24
Sales Network	4.0.4.0/24
Business Partner Server	4.0.5.10

Los Angeles Branch Office
Internal Network	10.0.4.0/24

Dallas Branch Office
Internal Network	10.0.5.0/24

Business Partner Office

Atlanta Network 170.1.0.0/24

Suppose you are developing a VPN solution to interconnect these separate network resources with the appropriate authentication and access control. Authentication between all gateways is to be performed via digital certificates, and authentication between the remote access users and the VPN gateway is to be performed via RADIUS authentication.

Let us look at two approaches to creating and managing a VPN solution for this situation. In the first one, the company creates and manages the VPN itself. In the second one, the company outsources the entire network service to a service provider.

Enterprise-Managed Solution

In this approach, the company decides to create and manage the VPN itself. Usually, the first step in creating an Internet-based VPN is to obtain connectivity from an ISP. Assume that the company did this and the connectivity for the four different sites is

- **New York Headquarters** T3 (45 Mbps) circuit
- **Los Angeles Branch Office** T1 (1.5 Mbps) circuit
- **Dallas Branch Office** T1 (1.5 Mbps) circuit
- **Atlanta Business Partner Office** 256 kbps frame relay circuit

In the second step, the company chooses a VPN gateway vendor with a suitable product and with whom the company is comfortable working. Currently, the VPN gateways from various vendors do not easily interoperate, so the choice of vendor is important. The company's information technology (IT) staff should obtain appropriate expertise of the vendor's product. In many cases, it is desirable for the company to conduct lab testing and field trials using the vendor's equipment and supporting service.

In the third step, the company determines how much traffic load will occur at each location and makes a series of design decisions based on the load. Among other things, these decisions should include the following:

1. Choosing the appropriate VPN gateway for each location from the vendor's models offered. The choice of model is based on the required performance

level, such as the bandwidth, throughput, and the number of remote users supported at each location.

2. Deciding the topology of the VPN, whether to establish full mesh, hub-and-spoke, or partial mesh connectivity among the locations.

3. Deciding whether to combine the site-to-site functions and the remote access functions (as discussed in Section 9.1) in the same VPN gateway for each location.

4. Determining where to locate the VPN gateway relative to the network firewall (as discussed in Section 9.5).

In this example, the company chooses three VPN gateway models. The high-end model will be used in the New York headquarters, the mid-range model will be used in the Los Angeles and Dallas branch offices, and the low-end model will be used at the business partner's office in Atlanta. The company also decides to combine site-to-site and remote access functions at headquarters in the same high-end device. A full mesh topology is chosen for all three corporate sites. The VPN gateway and the network firewall will be located in parallel with each other in all locations. No redundant failover gateways are used in any site.

After the VPN gateways and their locations within the overall network have been specified, the next step is to determine the configuration of the individual VPN gateways. Keep in mind that the configurations of the VPN gateways are not independent of each other, and care should be taken to make sure that the configurations are consistent. In addition, firewall and routers must be reconfigured to support the VPN.

The certification authority (CA), the certificate and CRL repository, and an X.500 directory server should be accessible by all the entities using digital certificates for authentication. In this case, the CA must be accessible by all four VPN gateways before the tunnel is established. Because RADIUS authentication will be used for the remote access users, the VPN gateway that serves the remote access users must be able to access the RADIUS server.

For our example, the configuration of each of the four VPN gateways should be as follows:

New York Gateway
Three site-to-site VPN tunnels:
- (10.0.1.0/24, 10.0.2.0/24, 10.0.3.0/24) ⇔ (10.0.4.0/24)
    serving all IP traffic
- (10.0.1.0/24, 10.0.2.0/24, 10.0.3.0/24) ⇔ (10.0.5.0/24)
    serving all IP traffic
- (4.0.5.10) ⇔ (170.1.0.0/24) serving Web traffic only

Two user groups:
- *Sales user group*: can access only subnet 4.0.4.0/24
- *Telecommuter user group*: can access all corporate networks

The addresses assigned to the sales group are from the subnet 192.168.1.0/24, and the addresses assigned to the telecommuters are from subnet 192.168.2.0/24. Note that the two user groups are assigned IP addresses from address pools, so care should be taken to ensure that the address pool is large enough to accommodate the maximum number of simultaneous users. It is important that the address pool used for remote access clients not overlap with any addresses within the corporate network. For example, although the sales user group is accessing the subnet 4.0.4.0/24, the address pool for the sales group is chosen to be 192.168.1.0/24 rather than 4.0.4.0/24. This approach avoids routing confusion.

LA Gateway
Two site-to-site VPN tunnels:
- (10.0.4.0/24) ⇔ (10.0.1.0/24, 10.0.2.0/24, 10.0.3.0/24)
    serving all IP traffic
- (10.0.4.0/24) ⇔ (10.0.5.0/24) serving all IP traffic

Dallas Gateway
Two site-to-site VPN tunnels:
- (10.0.5.0/24) ⇔ (10.0.1.0/24, 10.0.2.0/24, 10.0.3.0/24)
    serving all IP traffic
- (10.0.5.0/24) ⇔ (10.0.4.0/24) serving all IP traffic

Atlanta Gateway
One site-to-site VPN tunnel:
- (170.1.0.0/24) ⇔ (4.0.5.10) serving Web traffic only

After the configurations are applied to the VPN gateways, it is time to implement the VPN and verify that all the components are working as designed. The implemented network is shown in Figure 9-16.

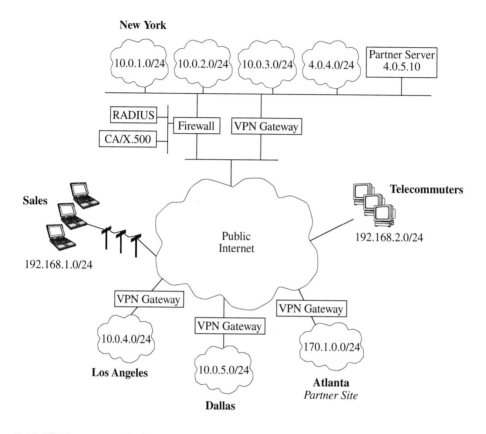

Figure 9-16 VPN gateway solution

The job is not complete even after the implementation of the VPN is verified. Continued monitoring and management of the constructed VPN is necessary to maintain its continued operation and to change its configuration as the business communication needs change. For example, if a new server is added for the business partner network, the configurations at both the New York headquarters and the Atlanta business partner office must be changed. Also, it is important to have the mechanisms in place for VPN gateway backup and redundant failover.

Service Provider–Managed Solution

Many of the same issues addressed in the enterprise-managed solution are also faced when an external service provider is employed to construct the VPN, and a similar configuration and implementation plan should be devised. However, there are differences. Some aspects to consider when outsourcing the VPN include the following:

- The service provider will have already chosen one or more VPN product vendors, conducted thorough evaluations, and obtained appropriate training on the vendors' hardware and software.
- The management and monitoring of the VPN are performed from the service provider's network operation center (NOC) with a team of security experts on a 24×7 basis.
- Service level agreements (SLAs) can be offered by the service provider to guarantee a certain level of availability and performance. The SLAs can cover both the security aspects and the underlying network infrastructure.
- The service provider must have access to and manage the VPN devices from networks external to the corporate network. As a result, the customer will lose some control over the security aspects of the VPN.
- The service provider should provide comprehensive information and reports regarding to the VPNs under its management—in particular, whether the SLAs are being met. If the SLAs are not being met, a refund or credit may be generated.

10

VPN Clients

Friends from faraway places are coming.
—CHINESE PROVERB

Chapter 9 describes how VPN gateways are used to protect and act on behalf of a wide range of network users and resources such as hosts, servers, and subnetworks. This chapter focuses on the VPN client, a much simplified implementation designed to work on behalf of just one computer to enable local applications secure access to the corporate network resources. The VPN client must therefore work in concert with the host's operating system and the local applications, as well as the VPN gateways, to provide secure communications through the network.

The term *client* implies that there is a server; the VPN client's corresponding server is the VPN gateway, as shown in Figure 10-1. (In certain special cases, two VPN clients can act as peers in establishing a secure communication channel between them, but this is rare.)

Implementing a secure communication service can be done at several layers of the ISO OSI protocol stack. Layer 2, the data link layer, is point-to-point, and consequently solutions at this layer require cooperation of all the hops along the path. Because each link must be a separate secure channel, the data is exposed as it is transferred from one link to the next. Solutions at layer 2 are generally intended for situations in which there is only one network hop, either physically or via a higher-layer tunnel. PPTP, L2F, and L2TP are layer 2 tunneling protocols that use higher layer encapsulation to provide end-to-end security.

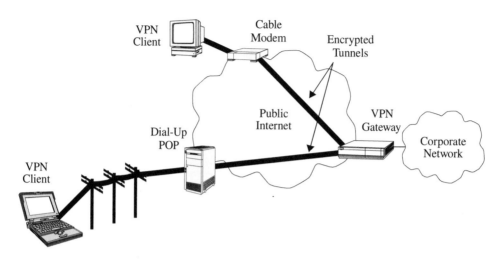

Figure 10-1 VPN clients enabling access to private network

Protocols at layers 3 and above are end-to-end. IPsec is an example of a layer 3 security protocol. Secure Shell (SSH) is a layer 4 security protocol that runs over TCP, a protocol that has no built-in security.

The application itself can also take responsibility for securing the data sent across the unprotected network, as is done with PGP for private email and with SSL (Secure Sockets Layer) and its effective equivalent TLS (Transport Layer Security) [HICK95, FRIE96, RFC2246, RESC01] for Web browsers and servers. We do not consider such application-specific security measures to be VPN clients because they do not carry general traffic. When SSL is session-specific, rather than application-specific, it can be considered a VPN client at layer 5.

10.1 VPN Client Functions

Like VPN gateways, VPN clients must implement functions from the four basic categories of VPN functions:

- Tunneling
- Authentication
- Access control
- Data integrity and confidentiality

However, VPN clients implement these functions from a different perspective than that of VPN gateways. Whereas VPN gateways support many different options within each functional category, VPN clients usually implement only a limited number of options within each category. This practice reduces the complexity of the VPN client, which should be simple to install and operate and should not consume too many resources on the user's computer.

Tunneling

A VPN client usually implements only one tunneling protocol and is classified by that protocol. For example, a client that implements IPsec is called an "IPsec client," and a client that implements PPTP is called "PPTP client." To implement multiple tunneling protocols on a single client would greatly increase the complexity of using and managing the client. Unlike VPN gateways, which are usually managed by dedicated IT professionals, VPN clients are generally operated by people simply using computers as tools for work. Because one protocol usually meets the requirements, there is little incentive to support multiple alternatives.

Authentication

Although one tunneling protocol is usually implemented, a VPN client often must implement multiple authentication options to accommodate user preferences or the configuration of the environment. The most frequently supported authentication options are

- Shared secret passwords
- RADIUS authentication
- Digital certificates

Although supporting several options certainly adds to the client's complexity, the added flexibility outweighs this concern for two important reasons. First, different organizations may use different authentication methods, and different authentication methods often exist even within the same organization. Second, implementing the client side of various authentication methods usually does not increase the complexity of the client software very much. RADIUS, for example, is just another variant of the shared secret password scheme. Although the RADIUS server side is complex, its client-side implementation and use are straightforward.

With digital certificates, however, a certain amount of complexity is inherent. To take advantage of a PKI in a VPN client, public key cryptographic functions and associated standards (as described in Chapter 7) must be implemented. This does add complexity to the VPN client software.

Currently, PKI services offered by operating systems are often too primitive and cumbersome for VPN use. Administrators want a seamless dial-up type of VPN experience for their users, and the OS certificate structure is geared toward Web browser use to authenticate a remote Web server. VPNs use certificates as an authentication mechanism for the client and for the secure gateway they will be interacting with. For this reason many VPN clients implement their own certificate management and retrieval interfaces using various toolkits other than the ones built into, say, Microsoft Windows.

Fortunately, as PKI products and services mature, the likelihood is increasing that a host computer will have general PKI functions integrated into the operating system. VPN clients targeted to hosts with such operating systems can certainly take advantage of the host's PKI implementation.

Access Control

Because the role of the VPN client is to enable the host computer to access resources rather than to restrict access of the host computer, the VPN client's access control role is somewhat limited. When in operation, the VPN client permits the user and the local applications access to the protected resources of the corporate network. This arrangement opens access into the corporate network through the client host, so it is important that the client host not become an ersatz gateway into the corporate network for unauthorized external users. Because the client host is connected to the Internet, such unauthorized access is a real possibility. In general, VPN client software should block access to the VPN tunnel from the Internet by outside hosts.

Often, the user on the client host will want to access the public Internet for other purposes at the same time. The client host has three routing choices. First, the client can route all traffic to the corporate network and let the VPN gateway separate the traffic for public Internet access from the traffic destined for the corporate network. This choice puts an additional burden on the VPN gateway. Second, the client can route the external traffic directly to the Internet. This puts additional burdens on the VPN client, such as installing and configuring a firewall on the client host to protect the VPN. The third approach is to treat the VPN client device as if it were located on the local system within the corporate network, subject to all traffic restrictions applied to that local system.

Data Integrity and Confidentiality

VPN client software must implement the same data integrity and confidentiality function as that of the VPN gateway; otherwise, the client could not interoperate with the gateway.

Other Functions

In addition to the basic VPN functions, VPN client software may also need to implement other complementary functions to improve the performance and ease of operation of the VPN client.

A VPN client needs a separate IP address that is routable within the corporate network. It obtains this new separate IP address when establishing the secure tunnel to the VPN gateway. During the tunnel establishment phase, the gateway assigns the IP address to the client. The client usually acts as a DHCP client, or as a client of any other assignment protocol that can achieve the same function.

A VPN client cannot be IPsec-based and also operate behind a firewall or router that performs dynamic network address translation (NAT) [RFC1631], in particular port address translation. Recall that IPsec performs an integrity check over the entire packet, including the IP addresses in the header. Consequently, any change in that address will destroy the checksum. To make the client functional behind a NAT device, it may be necessary to implement an extra layer of encapsulation on the IPsec packet.

In many cases, the client host computer obtains its Internet connectivity via a low speed dial-up connection. To make the best use of the available bandwidth, IP packet compression is used in the dial-up link. Unfortunately, packet encryption renders the compression useless because encryption converts the packet into the highest entropy form and no compression can be achieved. Therefore, it is desirable to compress the IP packet before encryption takes place.

VPN gateways often implement a timeout for idle clients. VPN clients can be idle for many reasons, including unexpected disconnections. The timeout in the VPN gateway catches lost connections to clients and reclaims the resources after a period of inactivity. To defeat this for normally working but occasionally idle VPN clients, the clients must implement some kind of keep-alive on the VPN tunnel.

10.2 Operating System Issues

VPN client software must work within the constraints of host computers' operating systems, whether the software is deeply integrated with the operating system or runs as an application. An overwhelming number of computers run the Microsoft Windows operating systems, but there are other widely used host operating systems of interest to VPN users. These include various UNIX[1] varieties and the Apple MacOS X.

Because networking is a major function of today's computers, almost all modern operating systems have built-in networking functionality. However, few have strong support for VPN capabilities integrated into the operating system. As a result, separate VPN client software must be written for those operating systems that lack the VPN functionality. Furthermore, the same VPN client software may need to be ported to different operating systems, even for the different release versions of the same operating system.

Because networking capabilities are usually built into the operating system, the VPN client software cannot avoid making changes to a computer's operating system. Such OS-level changes are usually difficult to make, and unless the software developer has the full knowledge of the internals of the OS, making these changes may inadvertently impact the other operating system functions.

Usually, a host computer's networking functions are relatively simple. The philosophy is that sophisticated network layer processing is best left to the network gateways. RFC 1122 specifies the communication layer requirements for an Internet host [RFC1122]. For outgoing IP packets, RFC 1122 requires that the host's IP layer do the following:

---

1. We use the term *UNIX* more loosely than perhaps we should. Strictly speaking, UNIX refers only to the timesharing operating system originally developed by AT&T; "BSD" is often used to indicate an operating system that is built on many of AT&T's concepts but enhanced by UC Berkeley. Linux is not a UNIX operating system; rather, it works like UNIX (really, like BSD). Nonetheless, we will use UNIX to refer to the group of operating systems characterized by AT&T's System V and BSD.

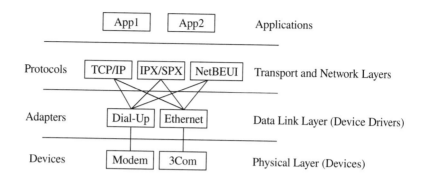

Figure 10-2 Windows network architecture

- Set any fields not set by the transport layer
- Select the correct first hop on the connected network (*routing*)
- Fragment the datagram if necessary or if intentional fragmentation is implemented
- Pass the packet(s) to the appropriate link layer driver

Clearly, these simple requirements are no longer adequate to satisfy the demand for VPN security.

However, to add VPN functionality to the IP or TCP/UDP layer adds substantial complexity to the networking stack of a computer host. Furthermore, to achieve all this within the constraints of an existing host operating system is more demanding.

10.2.1 Microsoft Windows

The Windows networking architecture is layered, as shown in Figure 10-2. Physical devices, such as Ethernet cards and modems, are controlled by device drivers. The device drivers are implemented according to Microsoft's Network Driver Interface Specification (NDIS). Each device driver is responsible for accepting a network layer protocol packet and then delivering it to the network interface device it controls. The following parameters are associated with each device driver:

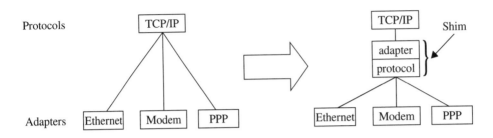

Figure 10-3 Adding a shim between TCP/IP and the adapters

- Adapter hardware MAC address
- Adapter IP address and netmask
- Default gateway associated with this adapter
- Windows Internet Service (WINS) servers
- DNS server (this is usually a global variable for the host but can be obtained through the adapter at configuration time)
- DHCP servers (if any)

Above the network adapters are the protocol-specific modules, such as TCP/IP or NetBEUI. Protocol modules bind with adapters according to the specified configuration at setup time.

To provide VPN functions for the Windows operating system, two approaches can be adopted. First, a software module can be inserted between the protocol layer and the network adapters. This is usually called a *shim* or *intercept driver* (see Figure 10-3). In this way, the existing binding between the TCP/IP protocol and the existing adapters is broken, and the TCP/IP module now binds with the shim module, which presents itself as a network adapter for the TCP/IP protocol. The shim module then creates a new series of bindings with the real network adapters and presents itself as a new network protocol (not TCP/IP).

In breaking all the original bindings between TCP/IP and the real adapters, the shim-based approach forces all traffic to be routed through the VPN software. This means that no traffic can bypass the VPN client software, and no change to the host computer's routing table is necessary. However, it requires that VPN client software be reinstalled every time a new adapter is created because, when a new adapter is created, it also creates a new binding between that adapter and the

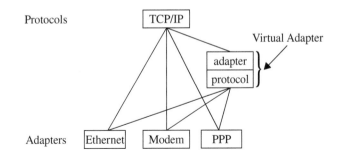

Protocols   TCP/IP

Virtual Adapter

adapter

protocol

Adapters   Ethernet   Modem   PPP

Figure 10-4 Adding a VPN virtual adapter between TCP/IP and the real adapters

TCP/IP protocol. This new binding must also be broken if the VPN client is to function correctly.[2]

A variant of the first approach is to not create a new adapter in the shim layer. Instead, the shim works within an existing adapter driver chosen at configuration time. The appropriate properties of the chosen adapter are modified when the VPN software is in operation. Because the shim is not expected to change the IP address of the existing adapter, separate address translation operations must be carried out.

The second approach is to create a new virtual adapter, as shown in Figure 10-4. Instead of breaking the existing protocol and adapter bindings, it allows all the original binding to remain intact. This approach avoids the problem of having to reinstall the software each time a new adapter is created. However, for the VPN client to function properly, it must change the routing table so that all traffic is routed to the new VPN adapter. This approach also allows the traffic to bypass the VPN adapter if necessary, but in other cases, it creates a security vulnerability.

Creating a shim above the TCP/IP layer is problematic because applications generally require visibility of the TCP/IP protocol features. If a shim were placed above TCP/IP, the shim would have to be an entirely new TCP/IP implementation within the Windows OS.

2. Windows NT does provide a mechanism for the intermediate driver to reexamine the protocol-adapter binding when new driver is installed. However, implementing this feature has proven to be difficult for many VPN vendors. Therefore, reinstallation of the VPN software is still preferred.

10.2.2 Other Operating Systems

The layered networking architecture is also implemented in other operating systems. UNIX-based operating systems have long had networking capability built into the system's kernel. In fact, UNIX included TCP/IP in the kernel more than 10 years earlier than did Windows.

As with Windows, UNIX supports two options for providing VPN functionality. The first way entails adding new functionality to the kernel itself, such as adding IPsec. This generally means that you must change networking source code and recompile the kernel. For UNIX variants for which the source code is readily available—FreeBSD, NetBSD, OpenBSD, and Linux—this method may be daunting but doable. For proprietary UNIX operating system implementations, adding VPN functionality may require waiting until the vendor adds the underlying kernel capabilities.

The other option involves installing a new separate device driver for the VPN functionality. The device driver module can be implemented to work directly underneath the IP layer without change to the original kernel networking source code. Most UNIX variants, including both free and propriety, permit recompiling the kernel to include device drivers even if the networking code is distributed only in binary form. Another popular way to add new modules is via a mechanism called *loadable kernel module*, in which no recompilation of the kernel is necessary.

Note that the UNIX networking functionality is much more exposed to applications than on a Windows platform. For example, user-level system calls can be used to change a number of parameters associated with a network interface. This allows the user to have a lot of control over the ways networking is conducted. The side effect is that users may need to be more savvy about the operation of their VPN client software.

Apple's MacOS can be viewed as a UNIX variant, with MacOS's networking implementation based on the UNIX System V STREAMS environment. STREAMS allows loadable modules to be inserted into the networking protocol stack dynamically at runtime. VPN implementations under MacOS can choose either to insert a *standard autopush driver* on top of each link layer device driver of interest or attach a module that gets pushed beneath the IP module.[3]

---

3. See http://devworld.apple.com/macos/OTAdvancedClientProg for more details.

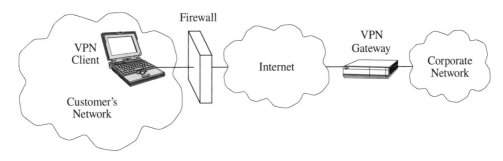

Figure 10-5 VPN client operating through a firewall

10.3 Operational Issues

VPN client users expect the experience of accessing resources through the VPN to be similar to that of accessing resources through a regular cleartext session. The vast majority of VPN users cannot be expected to troubleshoot the networking software. Therefore, the client software should be robust and easy to operate and should not produce a lot of overhead for the communication session.

However, the security added by using a VPN client does not come without cost. The encryption and encapsulation certainly increase the packet overhead, especially when the original IP packet is small. The consideration of security within the overall corporate network, and the client interactions with the DNS and WINS servers, also affects the operation of the VPN client software. The following are some commonly encountered operational issues.

10.3.1 Working with the Corporate Firewall

Chapter 9 discusses the relative positioning of a VPN gateway with respect to the corporate firewall. Here, we describe a different scenario, in which a VPN client must operate behind a corporate firewall, as shown in Figure 10-5. This scenario is common when a consultant working on the customer's network must access the corporate network of the home company. Obviously, the network of the customer's company is protected by its own firewall, so the VPN client must be able to traverse the firewall.

An IPsec-based VPN client requires that the firewall open a clear path for IP packets with the protocol field value set to 50 (ESP) and 51 (AH) to pass through the firewall. This usually is a security risk for corporate resources, and network administrators are not eager to provide such holes in the firewall.

For an IPsec-based VPN client to function without the holes, the VPN traffic is subjected to extra encapsulation using protocols the firewall can understand. For example, Cisco/Altiga's VPN client uses an extra UDP encapsulation to bypass the firewall restrictions. The IETF is considering standardizing the approach [HUTT00].

10.3.2 Working with Network Address Translation

Like VPN gateways, VPN clients may also encounter network address translation of private IP addresses when used in the corporate network. For IPsec in AH mode, the authentication value is calculated across the entire packet, including the source and destination IP addresses in the header. Any modification of the IP addresses—as by a NAT process—will result in the failure of the authentication value check. Therefore, it is important to perform NAT before IPsec processing. In ESP mode, authentication is not calculated across the outer IP header, so a one-to-one NAT performed after the IPsec processing is allowed.

Dynamic many-to-one NAT (usually referred as *port address translation*, or PAT) uses the same IP address but different TCP or UDP ports to conserve IP address space. Traditionally, these NAT devices expect a TCP or UDP header immediately following the IP header. However, after the IPsec processing, these expectations can no longer be met. In addition, ESP tunnel mode encrypts the TCP or UDP header in the packet, thus making it unusable for PAT. Therefore, in general, NAT should be performed before the IPsec processing.

There are other known incompatibilities between NAT and IPsec, and efforts are under way in the IETF to address these issues [ABOD00].

10.3.3 Fragmentation and MTU Issues

Although it is unavoidable for IPsec to add extra overhead to the IP packet, it is important to minimize the likelihood of packet fragmentation due to the added overhead. An IP packet is fragmented when it is larger than the maximum transmission unit (MTU) of the data link. The oversized IP packet is fragmented into two or more separate IP packets, and each is transmitted across the data link. The fragmented IP packets eventually are combined at the destination node. However, such fragmentation forces each intermediate network node and destination node to incur much more processing because most IP processing is the effort to process the header.

The fragmentation issue is especially acute in dial-up networking, in which the MTU setting of the dial-up link is usually set as optimal to maximize the link capacity. IPsec adds between 20 and 56 bytes of overhead to the original IP packet. Therefore, when the original packet size is already close to the MTU, every new packet will be fragmented. This can add significant delays to the packet processing and thus reduce throughput substantially. Also, fragmentation can cause the TCP flow control window to open more slowly, further reducing throughput.

The fragmentation problem can be alleviated by limiting IP packet size to less than the MTU minus any possible encapsulation overhead.

10.3.4 Private and Public Domain Name Servers

Most private networks have DNS servers that differ from the public network DNS servers in that they have different IP addresses and contain differing name resolution data. For example, the name resolution for hosts in the private network may not be available from the public DNS servers, and vice versa.

When a VPN client first obtains network connectivity but before the operation of the VPN client software, the remote host relies on the public DNS servers in the network for name resolution. This is shown in Figure 10-6a. When the VPN client software is operating, access to networks other than the private network is either blocked or rerouted, so access to the public DNS may have to go through the VPN tunnel and then be rerouted back out, as shown in Figure 10-6b.

If, after the VPN client software is launched, the DNS entries for the client host computer are still configured with the public DNS servers, any applications relying on DNS resolution (this includes Web browsers) will be affected. If public Internet access is completely blocked, those applications can no longer function. Even if access to the public DNS server is still available, the desired private DNS entries may not be available from the public DNS server.

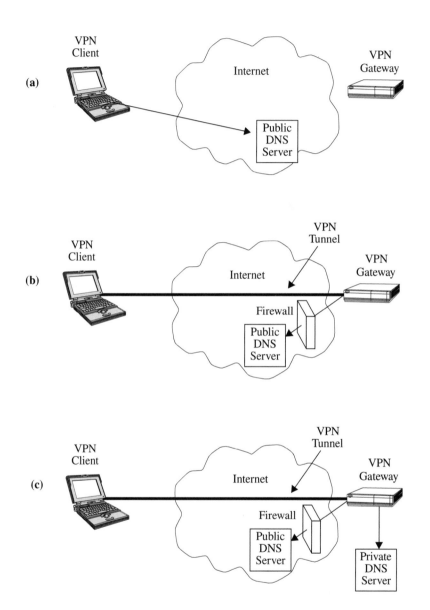

Figure 10-6 Public and private DNS servers

Therefore, it is crucial for the VPN client software to operate and be configured appropriately to make the private DNS servers available for name resolution, as shown in Figure 10-6c. When the VPN client software is no longer in operation, it should return to using the public DNS server.

10.3.5 WINS Server Issues

Similar to DNS servers, WINS maps the NetBIOS Microsoft Networking names to IP addresses for Windows platforms. DNS servers can be configured either as global parameters that are effective across all the networking adapters, or as local parameters associated with each individual adapter. WINS servers, on the other hand, are configured only as local parameters.

Therefore, the VPN client software, when in operation, should obtain the appropriate WINS server entries for the virtual adapters created by the VPN software. If the VPN client is expected to access corporate sites where different WINS servers exist, the client software should rely on the VPN gateways to relay the WINS information to the client.

In VPN implementations where no separate adapter is created, the VPN client software should be able to change the WINS servers associated with an existing adapter.

10.4 VPN Clients for Windows

Roughly 90 percent of the personal computers in the world run the Microsoft Windows operating system. Consequently, most VPN client software is designed specifically for Windows, including VPN software built into the Windows operating system by Microsoft.

10.4.1 Layer 2 Clients

PPTP is available on the Windows NT workstation as part of the remote access server (RAS), in Windows 98 as part of the dial-up networking (DUN), and also available on Windows 95 with versions of DUN 1.2 and higher. Microsoft's approach to PPTP is to create another virtual adapter (as in Figure 10-4) without breaking the protocol bindings with the existing adapters. In the Windows 2000 environment, the PPTP protocol is implemented as an NDIS WAN intermediate driver.

L2TP implementations are similar to PPTP; the difference is that the encapsulation protocol is applied to the PPP frame. Nonetheless, both PPTP and L2TP clients use the standard authentication mechanisms for PPP, such as CHAP or MS-CHAP.

L2F solutions do not have clients per se because L2F is used only for gateway-to-gateway connectivity.

10.4.2 IPsec Clients

IPsec client software is perhaps the most widely used VPN client software. VPN vendors are focusing on it because of the lack of a built-in IPsec client in Windows and because IPsec is increasingly becoming the standard for providing security for IP.

Although there are general approaches to implementing VPN clients within the Windows operating system—such as using a shim or a virtual adapter—there are still many differences from vendor to vendor in the actual implementations of VPN client software. The following aspects of implementation details may vary for IPsec clients:

- **Encapsulation modes** These are any combination of the four encapsulation modes for IPsec (ESP tunnel, ESP transport, AH tunnel, and AH transport). Sometimes, additional UDP or TCP encapsulation is used to facilitate traversal of firewalls because firewalls in general do not have policies to allow native IPsec traffic to pass.
- **Encryption options** These are the types of encryption algorithms available for the user. Examples include DES, 3DES, RC4, RC5, and AES.
- **Authentication options** These are the ranges of authentication options available for the client user. Examples include RADIUS and digital certificates.
- **Address assignment mechanisms** These are the ways new IP addresses are assigned to the IPsec client when the client is launched. For example, DHCP or proprietary protocols can be used for address assignment.

- **Compression capabilities** These determine whether IP compression is implemented in the client. Meaningful compression is not possible after encryption is applied.
- **Idle timeout mechanisms** These mechanisms implement a timeout in the VPN tunnel between the client and the gateway. Because IPsec is a connectionless protocol, it is not possible for the protocol itself to detect the loss of connectivity. Therefore, it is necessary to provide additional mechanisms to detect whether the connection is alive, perhaps by using a keep-alive protocol between the VPN client and the VPN gateway or by monitoring the traffic flow within a security association through a timeout mechanism. Such detection catches obsolete security associations and reclaims unused resources.

Table 10-1 compares of the implementation details of some of the IPsec client vendors for Windows at the time of this writing.

Table 10-1 Vendor comparisons for IPsec clients

IPsec Client Vendor	Encapsulation Modes	Encryption	Authentication	Address Assignment	Compression	Keep-alive/ Idle Timeout
Alcatel/ TimeStep	ESP and AH Tunnel and Transport	DES, 3DES, CAST, Blow-fish, RC4	RADIUS, PKI, Xauth	Proprietary, Static	LZS	Timeout
Check Point	ESP and AH Tunnel	DES, 3DES, CAST	RADIUS, PKI, TACACS	None	None	Timeout
Cisco/Altiga	ESP Tunnel	DES, 3DES	RADIUS, PKI, TACACS	Proprietary and DHCP	LZS	Timeout
Indus River	ESP Tunnel and Transport	DES, 3DES, RC4	RADIUS	Proprietary	Microsoft MPPC	Keep-alive
Intel/Shiva	ESP and AH Tunnel, Shiva Proprietary	DES, 3DES	RADIUS, PKI	DHCP	None	None
Nortel Networks	ESP and AH Tunnel	DES, 3DES, RC4	RADIUS, PKI	DHCP and Static	LZS	Keep-alive
Redcreek	ESP Tunnel and Transport, Redcreek Proprietary	DES, 3DES	RADIUS, PKI	DHCP	None	Timeout

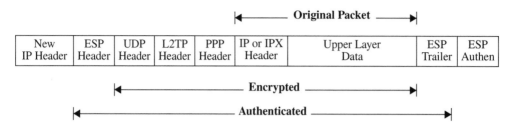

Figure 10-7 L2TP/IPsec packet format in Windows 2000

10.4.3 L2TP/IPsec Combination Clients

There is some interest in using L2TP with IPsec to provide tunnel authentication, privacy protection, integrity checking, and replay protection [PATE99]. Windows 2000, in fact, has a built-in L2TP/IPsec combination client. The encapsulation approach taken in Windows 2000 is shown in Figure 10-7.

The original packet header, shown with an IP or IPX header, carries the original source and destination addresses. The outer IP header, shown as New IP Header, contains the source and destination addresses of the tunnel endpoints. The L2TP header carries tunnel control information. The PPP header identifies the protocol of the original packet—for example, IP or IPX.

The IP (or IPX) packet first undergoes the L2TP encapsulation; then an additional IPsec encapsulation is wrapped around the resulting UDP packet. Both the L2TP control channel and the L2TP data channel are protected by the security mechanisms of IPsec, although the user authentication is not bound to the IPsec SA in this case, and the session-level information in the packet is rendered opaque to IPsec. L2TP's feature of retaining user session control and statistics is kept intact.

The L2TP/IPsec combination has a relatively large encapsulation overhead. Therefore, optional compression is performed at multiple stages of the encapsulation to reduce the overall overhead [VALE00].

User authentication is performed by the L2TP part of the process, when the same authentication mechanisms such as PAP, CHAP, MS-CHAP, and EAP are used (see Section 6.1.1). IPsec authentication and security association (SA) establishment are performed at the host-to-host level between the client computer and the server computer.

10.4.4 VPN Client Software Installation

Depending on the approaches taken by the implementation, the installation of the client software on Windows may create problems for networking operation. This is particularly true when multiple modules of networking software are to be installed.

Most VPN client software implementations require that Windows be of a certain release version (e.g., Windows 95 Release B) and have the appropriate operating system upgrades (e.g., DUN 1.2, as required by the Nortel Networks).

An important limitation of Windows 95 is that no more than four bindings exist between the TCP/IP protocol and the adapters. If four adapter bindings already exist, then you cannot create a new binding between the TCP/IP protocol and the virtual adapter for the VPN. A similar limitation also exists in later versions of Windows, but the number of permitted bindings is much larger and does not pose a practical problem.

The way VPN client software is implemented within Windows affects the order of installation between the VPN client and the other networking software (such as a new network adapter or virtual adapter). Generally, the VPN client software should be the last to be installed, especially in the shim-based implementation. When a new network adapter is installed, the adapter will create bindings between the various networking protocols and itself. Therefore, a new binding between TCP/IP and the new adapter will be created after the installation. This breaks the necessary operating condition of the shim-based VPN client, where TCP/IP cannot have direct linkage to the real adapters.

The order of software installation is not so crucial with adapter-based VPN client implementations because a direct binding between TCP/IP and any other real network adapter is permitted. However, it is still highly recommended that the user install the VPN client software last because the binding between the adapter and the VPN virtual protocol may not be created in some situations. Usually, the VPN virtual protocol is proprietary and specific to the client software vendor, so there is no assurance that the network adapter vendor has the necessary knowledge of such VPN virtual protocol to create the binding between the adapter and the protocol.

One particularly important issue is the PPP over Ethernet (PPPoE) problem in many DSL services. PPPoE, the variation of PPP used for DSL, has a number of advantages for DSL service, such as dynamic assignment of IP addresses, integration with RADIUS authentication, and the familiar interface similar to that of Microsoft dial-up networking. The problem, however, is that PPPoE implementations also create a new virtual adapter within Microsoft networking architecture. The PPPoE vendors are generally not aware of all the different VPN vendors. Therefore, a binding between the PPPoE adapter and the virtual protocol of the VPN client software may not always be created.

10.5 VPN Clients for Other Platforms

Aside from the set of Windows operating systems, few vendors sell VPN client products for other platforms. Nonetheless, a lot of work is being done to create VPNs for the open source UNIX environments. Because this work is largely noncommercial, often the end product is not very easy to install, configure, or use. But most of the software comes in source code form, so these solutions are an excellent way to become intimately familiar with the deep inner workings of networks in general and VPNs in particular.

A lot of good work is being done in the Linux community, where many programmers work on developing new code or perfecting old code. The same is happening in the free UNIX camps: FreeBSD, NetBSD, and OpenBSD. In the past, the efforts of any one group were largely incompatible with the other operating systems, but lately most of the code has been ported to the other free UNIX platforms and can run on them no matter the original target operating system. Because of the size of its user base, Linux is usually the original target.

Because Windows-based platforms dominate the market, there are few commercial IPsec clients for other platforms. Cisco/Compatible Systems offers VPN clients for the Apple MacOS, Sun Solaris, and Linux platforms. Alcatel/TimeStep has a VPN client for MacOS.

There are freely available implementations of PPTP and IPsec. These implementations alone do not, of course, constitute full VPN clients because a client must include all four categories of functions. Nonetheless, starting with a good tunneling protocol implementation is an important first step toward building a VPN client from freely available parts.

10.5.1 Layer 2 Implementations

One PPTP client implementation for Linux and other free UNIX operating systems is called PPTP-linux.[4] PPTP-linux permits a UNIX host to connect to a PPTP server. PPTP-linux sets up a PPTP call, after which the standard PPP daemon is invoked to set up a PPP link over that PPTP call. This PPTP client can access any PPTP-based VPNs.

10.5.2 IPsec Implementations

Many more projects are under way to provide free source code versions of the IPsec protocol suite for the open source UNIX operating systems. We list several here.

Linux FreeS/WAN

Linux FreeS/WAN[5] is a freely available implementation of IPsec and IKE for Linux. The idea behind this effort is to help spread the use of IPsec by providing source code that is freely available, runs on a range of machines including ubiquitous cheap PCs, and is not subject to U.S. or other nations' export restrictions. This project stems from the S/WAN initiative. S/WAN (secure wide area network) sought to promote the deployment of IPsec-based VPNs by agreeing on the details of implementation and through interoperability testing.

KAME

The KAME Project[6] is an effort to create a free reference implementation of IPv6 and IPsec for both IPv4 and IPv6 on several BSD UNIX variants, including FreeBSD, NetBSD, OpenBSD, and BSDI. KAME was started as a two-year project (April 1998 to March 2000) but has been extended until March 2002.

---

4. http://cag.lcs.mit.edu/~cananian/Projects/PPTP/
5. http://www.freeswan.org/
6. http://www.kame.net/

Cerberus

NIST Cerberus[7] is an IPsec reference implementation for Linux. It was developed based on the current ESP and AH specifications and several of the current algorithm drafts, including the AES draft, and it purports to provide host-to-host, host-to-router, and router-to-router IPsec services. The software is not subject to copyright protection and is freely distributed.

ipnsec

The ipnsec[8] software is an IPsec implementation based on merged code from Linux and OpenBSD.

10.6 Alternative VPN Clients

In the preceding sections, we discuss layer 2 and layer 3 VPN clients. These VPN clients secure lower-layer communication, so any TCP/IP application can work transparently without the knowledge of the presence of the VPN client software.

Some VPN client software approaches the secure communication problem from layer 4—the transport layer—or above. These approaches have their own advantages and disadvantages. We call these approaches "alternative VPN clients."

10.6.1 SSH as VPN Client

SSH, or Secure Shell, is a client-server application that permits remote login, remote execution, file transfer, and port forwarding over an authenticated and encrypted communications channel. SSH is intended to be a secure replacement for the "r" UNIX programs: *rlogin*, *rsh*, and *rcp*. SSH uses cryptographic authentication, automatic session encryption, and integrity protection of all transferred data. There are many freely available versions (OpenSSH for UNIX, several ports to Windows and Macs, and a Java port) and one commercial version of SSH (F-secure).

---

7. http://www.antd.nist.gov/cerberus
8. ftp://ftp.eunet.cz/icz/ipnsec

SSH defines a packet-based binary protocol used to provide the secure channels, and it is designed to work over any reliable stream protocol such as TCP. There are two major versions: SSH1 and SSH2. The old SSH1 version is being replaced by SSH2 to achieve improved flexibility, better scalability, and better security. The following discussion applies largely to both versions. SSH2 is currently described in several Internet-Drafts.

SSH performs both host and user authentication. Public-private key pairs are generated for both the user and the host. Sometime before use, the client host and server must have exchanged public keys, typically by hand or automatically when a client is asked to contact a new server. When a user is ready to employ SSH (through one of the "s" programs: *slogin*, *ssh*, or *scp*), the client host generates a random number to be used as a session key. It then chooses one of the supported symmetric encryption algorithms—usually Blowfish [SCHN94] or 3DES—encrypts the session key with both the client host's private key and the server's public key, and sends this to the server.

The server decrypts this package with its private key and the client host's public key, thereby authenticating the client host and recovering the session key. Now both the client and the server begin using the session key and the symmetric algorithm for encrypting all subsequent data exchanges.

After the client is authenticated to the server, the user must also be authenticated. This is done either by a traditional system password (transmitted over the encrypted channel) or by RSA authentication. For RSA authentication, the user must have placed its public key on the remote machine. The passphase chosen by the user at setup time is used to decrypt the private key on the local host so that it can be used for authentication.

SSH can be used in two ways to function as a VPN client. In the first technique, SSH provides the encrypted and authenticated channel through which PPP is tunneled, as shown in Figure 10-8. This model exploits SSH's remote execution capability. An SSH client opens a secure channel to the SSH server and tells the server to execute a PPP daemon process.[9] After the PPP daemon process is started, the user on the client machine opens a PPP connection. IP traffic is then

---

9. A *daemon process* is a UNIX term, although Windows has an equivalent; the process runs in the background listening for certain events that trigger it to act. The PPP daemon process is listening for a PPP setup call.

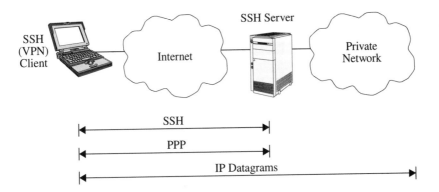

Figure 10-8 VPN client implemented with SSH remote execution

tunneled through the PPP connection over the SSH secure channel. This approach is similar to that of L2TP, but TCP (instead of UDP) is used to encapsulate the PPP frame. The problem with this approach is the instability associated with interactions between the two TCP connections. Say a TCP connection is open over the PPP connection, which is tunneled through SSH, a protocol implemented on top of TCP. Experience has shown that the interactions of the flow control windows between the two TCP connections can cause the VPN to be somewhat unstable and hang, sometimes indefinitely.

The second way that SSH can be used to build a VPN client is through its port forwarding capability, as shown in Figure 10-9. The user specifies a local port (port X), a destination host (host A), and a destination port (port Y). The SSH client opens an encrypted and authenticated channel to the SSH server. When the user is authenticated, the SSH client listens on the specified local port. Any application that sends packets to that port on the client machine has its packets sent instead to the server machine via the SSH channel. Once the packets are on the server machine, they are forwarded to the destination host and destination port. The advantage of this approach is that no PPP tunnel is involved. There are several disadvantages. First, this method works only for TCP and not for UDP. Second, there must be a specific configuration for each port to forward (this is not so bad if the client wants strict control over the forwarded ports). Third, the configuration forces the local port to be bound to only one destination host and port. If an application wanted to connect to two or more servers—each on a different machine but all of them listening on the same port—the SSH client would have to

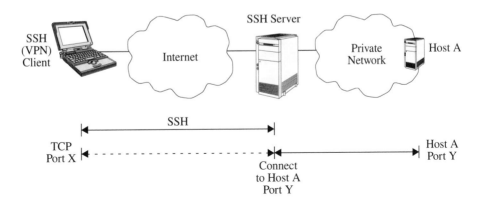

Figure 10-9 VPN client implemented with SSH port forwarding

set up a separate port forward for each destination, and for each one, the local port would have to be different to keep them distinct. Most applications cannot accommodate this arrangement.

10.6.2 SOCKS and SSL as VPN Client

Although most definitions of VPN consider tunnels to be an integral component, some people see firewall proxies—specifically, SOCKS version 5 [RFC1928]—as a way to create a private network through a public infrastructure. SOCKS v5 is a proxy protocol for client-server environments. A client application using SOCKS services connects to the SOCKS server, where the client is authorized and makes a request that is considered against access control rules. The SOCKS server, then forwards the request to the application server. Usually the client is outside a firewall and the server is inside, so SOCKS provides authenticated firewall traversal, as shown in Figure 10-10.

Advocates such as Aventail[10] see the SOCKS server as an ideal place for authentication and access control in an extranet VPN scenario. Because SOCKS operates at a level above the transport protocol—the session layer—the SOCKS server has a deeper understanding of the application's access control requirements. The SOCKS service port (the default is TCP port 1080) is the only "hole" necessary in

---

10. www.aventail.com

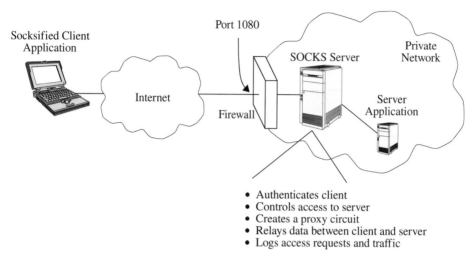

Figure 10-10 SOCKS v5 server

a firewall. Because all application service requests are made via the SOCKS server, and therefore through this one port, the firewall is more effective and the internal network structure is hidden from the external clients. In addition, the SOCKS server can do extensive traffic logging.

SOCKS provides authentication and access control but not data confidentiality. To make a VPN client, SOCKS is combined with SSL, the Secure Sockets Layer [FRIE96]. SSL constructs session-layer point-to-point authenticated (with X.509 certificates) and encrypted (with a choice of symmetric algorithms) connections for applications using TCP/IP. Like SOCKS, SSL supports client-server architectures, such as Web browsers and servers. Many e-commerce applications are using SSL to provide security for online transactions, exactly the environment that extranet VPNs strive to serve.

In a SOCKS/SSL extranet VPN, the client application data stream is intercepted by the SOCKSCAPS module before the socket function call. To support this, the client application must be "socksified"—that is, modified to include the SOCKS library socket calls. The data is then piped to the SOCKS server. User authentication and access control is then performed between the client and the SOCKS server. After the SSL encryption channel is set up, the SOCKS server acts as a proxy for the application. This is possible because the encrypted channel is established at the session layer; the TCP connections (one from the client to the proxy, and the other from the proxy to the application) simply carry an encrypted payload. This payload is transferred from one TCP connection to the other at the SOCKS server.

The major drawback of this approach is that two TCP connections are required to move requests and data between the client and server applications. This breaks the bidirectional model of TCP and adds latency as the payload is transferred between TCP connections. It also introduces a more complex dependency between the flow control of the client-server protocol and the flow control of TCP.

10.6.3 User-Level Daemon

Another approach is to have a user-level daemon provide the security functions. In the case of *vpnd,*[11] the virtual private network daemon, two networks are connected on the network level either via TCP/IP or a (virtual) leased line attached to a serial interface. The vpnd program acquires a pseudo terminal (a pty/tty device pair) and attaches SLIP (serial line IP) to it. This provides vpnd with its own network interface—the SLIP interface. All IP packets that are sent to this interface are read as a data stream by vpnd, encrypted, and sent through a TCP connection or over a serial line to the peer vpnd, where the data stream is decrypted and then written to the peer vpnd's pseudo terminal. All data transferred between the two networks is encrypted using the free Blowfish encryption algorithm.

10.7 A Remote Access VPN Scenario

Consider again the scenario described in Section 9.7, but now focus only on the remote access VPN. Suppose there is a third group of users, called consultants, shown in Figure 10-11. These users are technical consultants located within their clients' internal networks, and they need to access the subnet 10.0.1.0/24 to perform their work. In addition, digital certificates must be used to authenticate these users. VPN client software will be installed on all the consultants' computers, and digital certificates will be issued for all of them. The configuration of the Atlanta,

---

11. http://www.crosswinds.net/nuremberg/~anstein/unix/

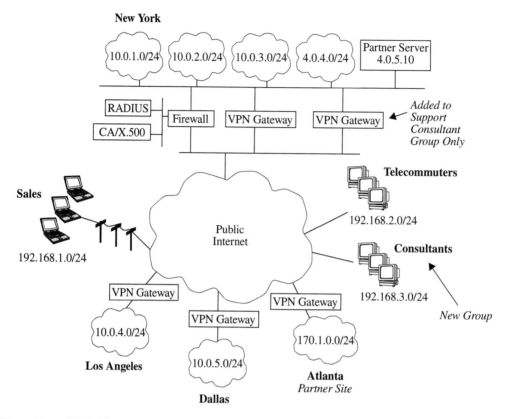

Figure 10-11 VPN Client Solution

Dallas, and Los Angeles gateways stays the same as in Section 9.7, but the New York site configuration is changed.

Several approaches can satisfy the requirements of this newly created user group. First, we can add a separate VPN gateway that is used to support the consultants group only, as noted in the figure. The new gateway will have no site-to-site VPN tunnels configured and will have only one user group:

Added New York Gateway

No site-to-site VPN tunnel

One user group:

- *Consultants user group*: can only access subnet 10.0.1.0/24, uses digital certificates for authentication

The second approach is to create a separate user group in the existing VPN gateway. In that case, the configuration of the VPN gateway will look like this:

New York Gateway

Three site-to-site VPN tunnels:

- (10.0.1.0/24, 10.0.2.0/24, 10.0.3.0/24) ⇔ (10.0.4.0/24) serving all IP traffic
- (10.0.1.0/24, 10.0.2.0/24, 10.0.3.0/24) ⇔ (10.0.5.0/24) serving all IP traffic
- (4.0.5.10/32) ⇔ (170.1.0.0/24) serving Web traffic only

Three user groups:

- *Sales user group*: can access only subnet 4.0.4.0/24, uses RADIUS for authentication
- *Telecommuter user group*: can access all corporate networks, uses RADIUS for authentication
- *Consultants user group*: can access only subnet 10.0.1.0/24, uses digital certificates for authentication

The configurations of the VPN gateways in other sites will remain the same.

11

VPN Network and Service Management

*Governing a big country is like
cooking a small delicacy.*
—LAO ZHI, THE BOOK OF TAO

A network requires monitoring and management to ensure that it remains in good working order and can satisfy the needs of the business. A *network management system* is key to gaining knowledge about the configuration, reliability, performance, and security of the network infrastructure. When problems occur, network administrators rely on the network management system to identify and isolate the fault, relay information to the appropriate personnel, and take corrective measures when possible.

An IP network comprises many types of physical components, including routers, bridges, switches, and servers. These devices are located throughout the network to connect subnetworks and network segments, and to provide services such as remote access and address allocation. Furthermore, each of the physical components uses functionality at several of the layers in the protocol stack. Managing an IP network, therefore, involves managing all these physical devices and, for each physical device, managing parameters across their functional layers. An ISP typically manages its part of the Internet. The company either manages its own network or outsources that task.

A VPN relies on the underlying network to function correctly, so VPN management must have a close relationship with the management of the underlying network, both inside and outside the company. In addition to managing the physical network, VPN management also includes managing the secure tunnels and any access control devices that constitute the virtual overlay network. Again, the company can either manage its VPN or outsource its management to a network service provider.

There are additional considerations when a service provider manages the VPN. First, the number of network devices to be managed is potentially large because a service provider will have a number of customers, each with its own VPN. Second, each VPN must remain securely separate from all others managed by the service provider, even if the service provider uses a common management system. Third, the service provider and the customer may enter into a service level agreement (SLA) that covers not only network-related aspects, such as bandwidth and latency guarantees, but also service-related aspects, such as the time it takes to satisfy a request.

One other aspect is critical, no matter who provides the VPN management. Because the VPN is a secure network service, the mechanisms used to manage it must themselves be secure. If the management mechanisms are not secure, it is not possible to secure the network being managed.

11.1 Network Management Standards

Network management standards formalize the interoperability of different vendors' equipment through common interfaces and message formats; these standards also make it easier to cross administrative domains. ISO developed a network management framework as Part 4 of the OSI Basic Reference Model [ISO7498-4]. The OSI model specifies a service definition—Common Management Information Service (CMIS) [ISO9595]—and a protocol—Common Management Information Protocol (CMIP) [ISO9596]—for controlling all parts of a computer network, including routers, queues, environmental sensors, accounts, security logs, installed software versions, clocks, and so on. The OSI network management standards are comprehensive and address all aspects of the seven layers of the OSI protocol stack. The OSI model is object-oriented, complete with object classes and inheritance rules. Consequently, it is complex and consumes a fair amount of the managed system's resources. Nonetheless, the OSI model is carefully organized, calling out five functional areas in network management (commonly referred as FCAPS):

- **Fault management** A fault is an abnormal condition and not an error. Fault management seeks to determine what the fault is, isolate its location, and reconfigure or repair the affected area.
- **Configuration and name management** These functions manage the configuration and naming of the individual components and logical subsystems in a network. These components and subsystems are called *managed objects*; the configuration and name management functions control, identify, collect data from, and provide data to these managed objects.
- **Accounting management** These functions track the use of network resources, looking for abuse, inefficiency, or signs that growth will need to be handled in the near future.
- **Performance management** These functions monitor and evaluate the behavior of the managed objects and the efficiency of the communication.
- **Security management** These functions facilitate managing information protection and access control, including generating, distributing, and storing encryption keys, passwords, and access control policies. Security management also ensures that resources are used appropriately.

The OSI network management specifications were published jointly by the ITU as the X.700 series; CMIS is X.710, and CMIP is X.711. The ITU also developed the Telecommunications Management Network (TMN), first published as the Blue Book Recommendation M.30 in 1988 [CCITT89]. TMN is based on the OSI model and is targeted to telecommunications networks and services.

At about the same time, the Internet Activities Board, the overseers of the Internet, recommended the Simple Network Management Protocol (SNMP, based on an earlier protocol called SGMP, the Simple Gateway Monitoring Protocol) as the basis for Internet network management [RFC1052]. The long-term goal was for SNMP to be closely aligned with CMIS/CMIP, but in the end it proved too difficult to both follow the international standards process and keep up with the needs of the quickly growing user and vendor communities [RFC1109]. The first version of the SNMP framework was stabilized with four RFCs defining the structure and identification of management information [RFC1155], the SNMP protocol definition [RFC1157], the concise MIB definitions [RFC1212], and the MIB for TCP/IP (MIB-II) [RFC1213]. As vendors and the IETF gained experience with SNMP, it became clear that it was too limited to meet all the critical needs of network management, so two major enhancements occurred: the addition of the RMON specification [RFC1757] for managing LANs, and the revision of SNMP to version 2 [RFC1905]. More recently, SNMP version 3 has been specified [RFC2571].

11.2 Network Management Architecture

The basic concept of network management is simple: A management application (the *manager)* residing on a network management station (NMS) accesses *variables* on *managed nodes* through an application on the managed node (an *agent*). The manager and the agent use a *network management protocol* to exchange monitoring and control information. A remotely located agent, called a *probe*, can collect and aggregate information and interact with the manager on behalf of a LAN segment and its hosts. In addition, management stations can also exchange information among themselves. This is shown in Figure 11-1.

11.2.1 Network Management Station

An NMS is a host running the network management protocol and one or more managers. The manager is responsible for gathering information about the managed nodes by communicating with the agents inside the managed nodes. The manager typically must process large amounts of data, react to events, and prepare relevant information for display. Many manager applications have a control console with a GUI interface, allowing the operator to view a graphical representation of the network, monitor and control managed nodes, and configure the manager itself.

Some managers can be programmed to react automatically to information collected from the agents based on a set of criteria established beforehand. For example, thresholds can be set to reconfigure certain parameters in the managed nodes. The manager also usually logs events and sends signals to console display so that the network operator can receive the information and react accordingly.

11.2.2 Managed Nodes

Managed nodes are devices with some sort of network capability. These include hosts, routers, firewalls, media-specific devices such as bridges and switches, and special-purpose servers such as NAS and DHCP servers. A network management agent is a process on the managed node and is responsible for providing informa-

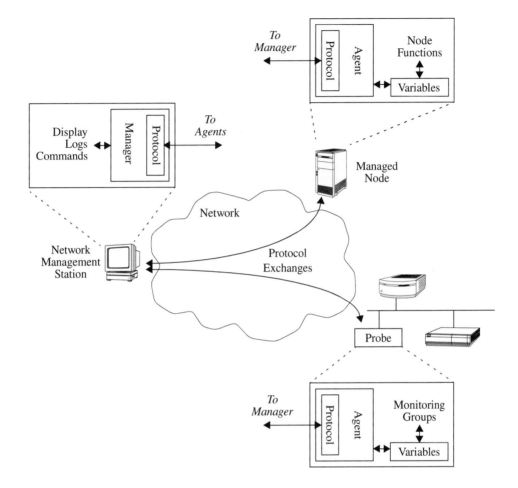

Figure 11-1 Network management model

tion about the managed node to the manager. Agents may also accept control information from the manager in order to control the managed node.

An agent interacts with the networking functions of the managed node via a structured set of management information called *management variables*. These variables keep track of the statistics gathered by the agent and are used to control various aspects of the node's functionality. For example, the managed node can watch a certain variable to determine when it should reboot.

11.2.3 Network Management Protocol

The network management protocol allows the management entities to exchange information. Each managed node has a set of variables representing the states of the functions being managed. There are four operations on these variables: reading, writing, traversing, and trapping. A manager can monitor a managed node simply by reading the values of the variables of interest. The manager can change the operation of the managed node by writing values to the variables and altering the functional parameters.

Traversing is useful when the manager does not know a priori which variables or how many of a certain type of variable are supported within a managed node. For example, a router has a number of interfaces—one or more for each network it serves—but the manager does not necessarily know how many interfaces each router has. The manager requests the agent to "walk" across each of the interface variables until there are no more interfaces.

Trapping is used to give the agents a more active role in managing their nodes. There are, in general, two ways to exchange information between the manager and the agents: polling and trapping. With polling, the manager is responsible for periodically asking the agents for information, and the managed nodes are completely passive. By using trap operations, the manager tells the agents which information is of interest and gives the agents value thresholds that trigger actions if crossed. The agents then actively monitor the values of interest and take action only when the values cross the thresholds.

11.2.4 Management Information

There must be some means of defining which management information can be exchanged. Management information has three important requirements:

1. The information has a common structure.

2. The structure is extensible.

3. Access to the information is controlled.

A unit of management information is called a *managed object*. In the OSI model, the managed objects are truly objects, but in the Internet model, they are simply scalar values. The *structure of management information* (SMI) defines the syntax and semantics of management information. A collection of related managed

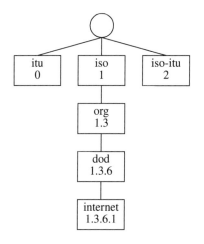

Figure 11-2 Management information tree

objects is called a *management information base* (MIB). A MIB standardizes the information available at each managed node supporting that MIB and also provides the structure of the objects. In this way, the network management protocols have a common means of accessing the same managed object in each managed node and a means for adding new objects as necessary. Many managed nodes adhere to one or more standard MIBs plus a set of proprietary MIBs, covering information that is common to all such devices as well as vendor-specific information.

Managed objects are uniquely defined by an encoding defined by the OSI model and used in the Internet model. The encoding is a tree structure called the *management information tree* (MIT). The prefix for Internet-related information is 1.3.6.1, as shown in Figure 11-2.

11.2.5 Probes

Remote monitoring probes are agents that are placed on data collection modules within a LAN segment. These probes collect statistics about the traffic going through the LAN, including interface statistics, traffic patterns, and packet traces. They also provide a means for setting alarm thresholds for asynchronous event notifications.

11.2.6 Other Means of Management

In theory, SNMP and CMIP can be used to exchange any kind of information between the management application and the management agent. In practice, however, there is so much information, and the formats are so widely varied and vendor-dependent that it is not always feasible to standardize the information and fit it into the protocol data unit (PDU) of SNMP and CMIP.

Although it is also possible to define a MIB for each and every managed object, either public or private, it is tedious and, in many cases, unnecessary. For example, there can be hundreds of exceptional conditions that may not be conducive to the probing or trapping approach of SNMP.

Transaction Language One (TL1) is an ASCII form management protocol defined by Bellcore (now called Telecordia) and widely deployed in telecommunication management. Much of the optical networking equipment in use today is managed via the TL1 standard.

Syslog [BSD93] is a utility that sends many system-related log messages to one or more facilities locally or across the network. Although Syslog can be very chatty, it is still one of the most effective means to find out what is happening with the device.

In many cases, it is more efficient and flexible to use traditional user interfaces and data transfer protocols to exchange management information between the management application and the management agent. For example, command line interface (CLI) is widely used to perform configuration management for network devices. The command requests and their responses are transported using the *telnet* protocol. Other vehicles for information exchange includes FTP (File Transfer Protocol) and TFTP (Trivial File Transfer Protocol), SSH (Secure Shell), HTTP (Hypertext Transfer Protocol), and, in many cases, vendor-specific mechanisms.

11.3 SNMP

The Simple Network Management Protocol provides a standard for monitoring and controlling IP-based networks. It is by far the most widely used network management protocol for data networking in IP environments because of its simplicity and the fact that IP-based networks are prevalent. SNMP allows the retrieval and alteration of networking information maintained by nodes associated with a network. A network administrator can use SNMP to monitor, diagnose, and correct network problems from network components.

As described Section 11.1, SNMPv1 was a stopgap measure, insufficient for complex networks and lacking adequate security facilities. SNMPv2 was issued in 1996 with many functional enhancements but, after contentious debate, without security enhancements. Issued in 1998, SNMPv3 was developed to meet the need for better security, and it goes further, providing a framework for all three versions and future developments of SNMP. Table 11-1 lists the documents that constitute the three versions of SNMP.

Management Information Base

A MIB is a virtual data store used to organize managed objects so that managers and agents can refer to specific managed objects efficiently and unambiguously. A MIB is a definition of a branch of a management information tree, where managed objects are the leaves of the tree. Related objects are grouped into *object groups* to facilitate the logical assignment of *object identifiers* (OIDs). Each object in a MIB has a unique OID defined by its position in the MIT as set forth by the OSI model. MIBs are defined using ASN.1.

MIB-II [RFC1213] is the second version of the MIB defined for Internet-related managed nodes. Its OID is 1.3.6.1.2.1. The first four numbers (1.3.6.1) are the `internet` prefix shown in Figure 11-2. The "2" is the `mgmt` object group holding all IETF defined objects. The "1" is the `mib-2` object group, defined by the MIB-II RFC. The word `internet` can be substituted for 1.3.6.1 in an OID, so `internet 2` refers to 1.3.6.1.2. Similarly, `mib-2` can be substituted for 1.3.6.1.2.1.

Figure 11-3 shows where MIB-II fits and shows the object groups under MIB-II. MIB-II is an example of an information structure intended to give the network management applications a standard way to access data collected by the managed nodes regardless of the vendor. A managed node may not collect all the information specified by a MIB because some of it may not be appropriate for that type of device. Each vendor, however, may wish to add objects that are specific to that vendor and not otherwise covered by a standard MIB. The `private` object group (`internet 4`) is used to provide vendors a space in the MIT for providing proprietary object definitions.

Table 11-1 SNMP RFC documents

SNMPv1

RFC 1155	Structure and Identification of Management Information for TCP/IP-based Internets
RFC 1157	A Simple Network Management Protocol (SNMP)
RFC 1212	Concise MIB Definitions
RFC 1213	Management Information Base for Network Management of TCP/IP-based Internets: MIB-II

SNMPv2c

RFC 1901	Introduction to Community-based SNMPv2
RFC 1902	Structure of Management Information for Version 2 of the Simple Network Management Protocol (SNMPv2)
RFC 1903	Textual Conventions for Version 2 of the Simple Network Management Protocol (SNMPv2)
RFC 1904	Conformance Statements for Version 2 of the Simple Network Management Protocol (SNMPv2)
RFC 1905	Protocol Operations for Version 2 of the Simple Network Management Protocol (SNMPv2)
RFC 1906	Transport Mappings for Version 2 of the Simple Network Management Protocol (SNMPv2)
RFC 1907	Management Information Base for Version 2 of the Simple Network Management Protocol (SNMPv2)
RFC 1908	Coexistence between Version 1 and Version 2 of the Internet-standard Network Management Framework

SNMPv3

RFC 2571	An Architecture for Describing SNMP Management Frameworks
RFC 2572	Message Processing and Dispatching for the Simple Network Management Protocol (SNMP)
RFC 2573	SNMPv3 Applications
RFC 2574	User-based Security Model (USM) for Version 3 of the Simple Network Management Protocol (SMNPv3)
RFC 2575	View-based Access Control Model (VACM) for the Simple Network Management Protocol (SNMP)

SNMP Operations

SNMP exchanges network information through messages called *protocol data units* between the network management station and the devices to be managed. All operations involve access to an object instance addressed using the object's OID.

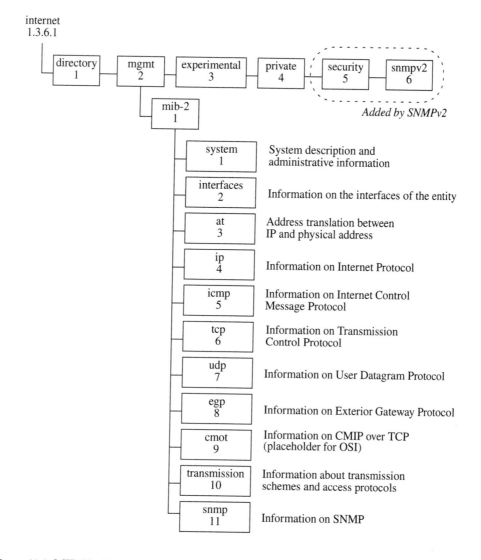

Figure 11-3 MIB-II object groups

Only leaf objects in the MIT may be accessed because SNMP's information model supports only scalar objects.

The following PDUs are defined in SNMPv2:

- **GetRequest** carries a list of object instances whose values are requested.
- **GetNextRequest** carries a list of object instances but retrieves the value of the object instance that is next in lexicographical order. By using a Get-Request and then a series of GetNextRequests, a network management application can walk the MIB across objects it is allowed to view.
- **GetBulkRequest** enables the manager to retrieve large blocks of data efficiently rather than specifying each individual object instance in a GetRequest.
- **SetRequest** is used to write a value to an object instance.
- **Response** carries a list of object instances whose values are requested.
- **Trap** is used to provide the management station with an asynchronous notification of some significant event. This can reduce the need to poll the managed nodes using GetRequests.
- **InformRequest** enables the exchange of information between management stations.

SNMP calls for using UDP as the transport protocol to carry these PDUs. UDP fits the SNMP model better than TCP for reasons of scalability and resource consumption. But UDP is, of course, a connectionless protocol with no guarantee of delivery. Consequently, network management applications that employ SNMP should take the appropriate measures to ensure that loss of a PDU can be dealt with. This is especially true for the Trap PDU because there is no acknowledgment that the trap has been set.

Communities

Although it is typical for a management station to be responsible for many managed nodes, from the managed node's point of view many management stations and other interested parties may be attempting to access its management information. Each managed node controls its own local MIB and must be able to control the use of that MIB by the managers.

An SNMP *community* is a relationship between a managed node's agent and a set of managers that defines authentication, access control, and proxy characteristics for those managers accessing the managed node's information. A unique community is established for each combination of these characteristics. Any number of communities—with overlapping management station memberships—can be defined at the managed node.

The community limits access to the managed node's local MIB to a selected set of management stations. A *MIB view* is the subset of all the MIB objects that a community is able to access. Access to the objects within a MIB view are further controlled by the access mode defined over that view's community: read-only or read-write. The community also helps support access policies for the proxy service, where an SNMP agent acts on behalf of other devices.

RMON

Remote Monitoring (RMON) is the IETF standard for monitoring and controlling remote local area networks. RMON defines the information and structure for exchanging statistics and control information between SNMP managers and the remote agents residing on the LANs. There can, of course, be multiple RMON agents in a managed network, usually one per LAN subnet.

As packets traverse the LAN, the RMON agent continuously collects and analyzes link layer data in real time and stores the data locally according to the RMON MIB specification.

There are two advantages to using RMON probes. First, the RMON agent monitors the LAN segment continuously, increasing the accuracy of the data used to control and provision the network. Second, because the monitoring is continuous, the RMON agent can determine when alarm conditions exist and can notify the management station asynchronously, thus reducing SNMP traffic.

The original RMON MIB was developed for Ethernet [RFC1757]. This specification monitors only the data link layer and defines nine groups.

- **Statistics group** records data measured on the network interfaces, such as packets sent, packets dropped, and CRC errors.
- **History group** manages and records the periodic statistical sampling from the LAN.
- **Host group** identifies hosts on the LAN by link address and records data on each host, such as host address and number of packets sent and received.
- **HostTopN group** ranks hosts according to statistic type.

- **Matrix group** stores statistics for packet exchanges between sets of two addresses.
- **Filter group** specifies a filter for capturing packets in the Capture group.
- **Capture group** enables the capture of a specified number of packets satisfying the filter.
- **Alarm group** sets alarm thresholds and sampling intervals to generate events for the Event group.
- **Event group** controls the generation and notification of events via SNMP traps when alarms occur.

A second RMON specification [RFC2021] addresses the parameters associated with the other layers in the protocol stack and adds many more groups.

Because of the complexity of RMON implementation, most equipment vendors have chosen to implement only four RMON groups: Statistics, History, Alarm, and Event.

Security

Traditionally, the security of the management infrastructure in an IP network has not been adequately addressed in the Internet community. The only security mechanism defined in SNMPv1—and still widely used—is the notion of an SNMP community. No authentication, access control, or encryption was built into the protocol.

Throughout the development of SNMP, security was recognized as a key component of the management framework. However, the complexity of security and the need to quickly establish a standard practice have rendered several previous efforts unsuccessful. At first, "SNMPsec" (RFCs 1351, 1352, and 1353) was introduced shortly after SNMPv1. Later, more elaborate security was designed into "SNMPv2p" (RFCs 1441 through 1452), where a *party-based* security model was introduced. It quickly became apparent that the model was too complicated and was not practical for implementation and operation. Then the concept of community was reintroduced, and the resulting standard is commonly referred to as "SNMPv2c." Even so, many of the security features were dropped. SNMPv2c, sometimes referred to as simply SNMPv2, is the default implementation on many devices today.

More attempts to address the SNMP security deficiency were made in the introduction of "SNMPv2u" and "SNMPv2*," in which a user-based security model was used. In 1997, the IETF established the SNMPv3 working group to address the security problem in SNMP and to integrate the approaches proposed previously. The result, SNMPv3, was issued in 1998 and became a draft standard in 1999, although it has yet to see wide implementation in the networking industry.

Because of the lack of security in SNMP, additional mechanisms are often used to restrict SNMP access on networking devices outside the SNMP scope. For example, to limit access to a router's MIB to only certain IP addresses, the router can restrict access to the TCP and UDP port 161, the assigned SNMP port. In many environments, the network administrators disable the SNMP SET operation so that only read access can be exercised.

Telnet, FTP, and other methods of management access also must be secured. Many device vendors are implementing SSH for in-band console access and file exchanges to and from the device.

A different approach is to establish a separate secure management network that has built-in authentication, access control, and encryption. Network management applications such as SNMP and other management access methods simply run over this secure management network without having to provide full security mechanisms themselves. We illustrate the concept of secure management tunnel in VPN in the next section.

11.4 VPN Management

Certainly, managing a VPN requires managing the underlying network infrastructure. Managing a VPN also requires additional considerations. Because a VPN is constructed of many secure tunnels crossing a shared IP infrastructure, VPN management also includes managing and monitoring the VPN gateways, ancillary servers that support the VPN, and all the security aspects related to the VPN tunnels.

Because a VPN is a secure network service, not only is it imperative that the VPN's security be carefully managed, but also the security of the management mechanisms themselves must be managed.

11.4.1 Managing Tunnels

Logically, a VPN can be viewed as a collection of secure tunnels established among the devices participating in the VPN. To manage the VPN tunnels, all aspects of the tunnel must be considered. These aspects include the following:

- The type of the tunnel (IPsec, MPLS, L2TP, etc.)
- The endpoints of the tunnel (VPN gateways, VPN clients and their network interfaces, etc.)
- The status of the tunnel (up or down, elapsed time, etc.)
- The traffic statistics of the tunnel (bytes, packet, etc.)
- The policies applied to the tunnel (authentication method, ACLs, etc.)

A good way to deal with VPN tunnels is to treat the endpoints of the tunnel as virtual interfaces. A *virtual interface* is a logical entity that is created, configured dynamically, and freed when it is no longer needed. The IP tunnel MIB specifies a generic way to represent tunnels in a standard MIB [RFC2667].

In many cases, more detailed tunnel information is needed for specific VPN tunnels. Therefore, attempts have also been made to create MIBs for each of the tunneling protocols. Current IETF efforts for three important VPN tunneling technologies (IPsec, MPLS, and L2TP) include the following:

- **For IPsec** IPsec Monitoring MIB [JENK00a], IKE Monitoring MIB [JENK00c], IPsec DOI Textual Conventions MIB [SHRI00], and ISAKMP DOI-Independent Monitoring MIB [JENK00b]
- **For MPLS** MPLS Traffic Engineering Management Information Base Using SMIv2 [SRIN00], and A MIB for MPLS Traffic Engineered LSPs [KOMP00]
- **For L2TP** Layer Two Tunneling Protocol "L2TP" Management Information Base [CAVE00]

Many of the variables defined in the various tunneling protocol MIBs are specific to the technology. For example, the IPsec-monitoring MIB defines an object for each security association and provides packet count for each SA. However, sometimes you need to aggregate statistics of multiple SAs into a single IKE SA entry for simplicity.

As mentioned earlier, not all information can be standardized in a MIB. Many of the policies for the tunnels are still stored in other formats. Usually, the policy information is stored as configuration files on the VPN devices, but sometimes policies are stored on a centralized LDAP or RADIUS server.

11.4.2 VPN Management in a Service Provider Environment

VPN management in a service provider environment is very different from that of the enterprise self-management environment in three areas: scalability, reliability, and security.

The number of devices in a service provider's infrastructure is much larger than in an enterprise's infrastructure because a service provider manages the devices for many enterprises. Therefore, the management operation should be much more automated. For example, manually typing commands through a CLI or clicking through a Web-based GUI may be acceptable in an enterprise environment, but in a service provider scenario, it is recommended that predesigned templates and scripts be used to speed configuration. A network management platform in a service provider must aggregate a huge amount of information and must correlate many events.

In the service provider environment, and sometimes in large enterprises, a dedicated network operations center (NOC) must be established to reliably monitor and manage the network infrastructure. The NOC is staffed for 24×7 operation so that the network's availability and performance are maintained.

In a VPN service, the NOC must monitor and manage multiple customers' secure network infrastructures. However, unlike an enterprise network in which the management station is within the trusted network of the enterprise, a NOC is inherently in a different domain of trust with respect to the customer's VPN. The NOC must manage multiple customers' VPN infrastructures securely without crossing into the trust domain of customers' VPNs.

11.4.3 Secure Management Tunnel in VPN

Because the overall security of a VPN is limited by its least secure aspect, it is critical that the management of the VPN be just as secure as the data carried by the VPN. This means that the management traffic should be sent through secure tunnels. In this way, the secure tunnels themselves can be viewed collectively as a virtual private network established exclusively for VPN management purposes.

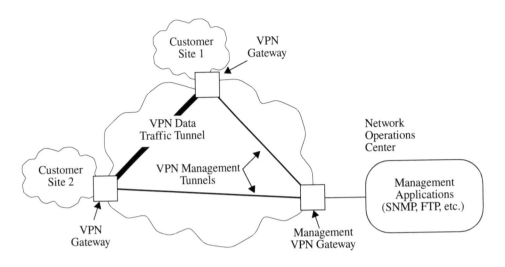

Figure 11-4 Management VPN

The concept of a secure management VPN is especially convenient in the service provider environment, as shown in Figure 11-4.

A secure management tunnel is a VPN tunnel that is established between a designated management entity and a managed VPN device. This management tunnel is different from a typical VPN tunnel because the VPN gateway is not acting as a proxy for other protected resources in the corporate network; instead, it acts on its own behalf. Access control filters are established for the tunnel so that only legitimate management traffic (e.g., SNMP, syslog, and FTP packets) is allowed to pass between the management application network and the VPN gateway. The VPN management tunnel negotiates separate encryption keys for the management traffic and may also use a different authentication mechanism from the one used by the data VPN tunnels.

In a service provider environment, the management VPN can consist of the set of VPN tunnels from the service provider's NOC to VPN gateways located at various customer premises. These tunnels form a separate secure management network because the management VPN is a special VPN that prevents management traffic from spilling over into the customer network. Similarly, the customer traffic is not allowed in the management tunnel because of the special access control rules established for the management traffic. By building an auditing and customer relationship management (CRM) infrastructure around the service provider's NOC, the VPN customers can be assured that management infrastructure is secure and is not mishandled.

11.4.4 Out-of-Band Access for Management

SNMP is designed to run over the IP infrastructure. In many cases, the IP infrastructure transporting the SNMP information is the very infrastructure it is managing. For most IP networks, this is fine, and the extra SNMP traffic is just added overhead.

However, when high availability (e.g., 99.99%) is required, it is not sufficient to rely solely on the same network for management. If the network becomes unavailable, management access is also unavailable. In this scenario, it is recommended that a physically separate management network be created. This separate management access is often referred as *out-of-band access*.

Out-of-band access means that the ability to access the managed devices is completely independent of the network the devices are supposed to create. In most cases, the access method of choice is the PSTN. Most network devices provide a console port that can be accessed either via a direct serial line attachment or remotely through a modem connection via a dial-up connection. In rare cases, a completely separate data network, usually of lower bandwidth, is employed to access the dedicated management Ethernet ports found on high-end network devices.

It is also important to secure the out-of-band access channel. Methods include using passwords, dial-back protected modems, terminal servers with various authentication options, or a modem with encryption capability.

11.5 Service Management

Increasingly, businesses are outsourcing their network infrastructure to dedicated service providers. This approach enables a corporation to concentrate its efforts on its core business rather than having to create a small networking company within the corporation. Network service providers, on the other hand, can leverage the economics of managing many corporations' networks to provide a great deal of expertise. The concern is that corporations lose a certain degree of control of the network management.

It is important for the service provider and its customers to reach an understanding about the exact nature of the service being purchased. In many situations, such an understanding is written in the form of an SLA.

11.5.1 Service Level Agreement

When you purchase network service, it should have a certain level of quality; how that quality is measured depends on the specific service provided. For example, the metrics for a dedicated network access service are the bandwidth of the access circuit and the network availability; for a dial-up network access service, the quality is measured in terms of the availability of modems when access is attempted, and the link speed after the connection is established.

For a VPN service, the important aspects are:

- The availability of the VPN tunnel (e.g., 99.99%)
- The bandwidth guaranteed through the VPN tunnel (e.g., 10 Mbps)
- The packet loss rate within the network
- The latency experienced through the VPN tunnel
- Modem pool availability

All these elements are dependent on the quality of the underlying IP network as well as the availability, correct configuration, and traffic load of the VPN devices under management.

Network service, of course, is not merely about the quality of the network. Many other important metrics affect the degree of customer satisfaction, such as the responsiveness of service provider to customer service requests, the timeliness of problem resolution, and even the courtesy of the service delivery personnel.

Many of these aspects can be too abstract to quantify or can be subjective. The goal of network service management is to provide as much visibility into the service as possible and to share control of the network with customers in an automated fashion. In this way, customers will feel more comfortable about the service purchased.

11.5.2 Network Operations Center

The NOC is the most critical piece of a service provider's management infrastructure. A NOC usually comprises a combination of organization structures, processes, staffing, technology products, and tools used by the service provider to operate the network services. Typically, a NOC has large screen consoles that display network topology and status maps. When a network fault occurs, visible changes on the display will alert the operational personnel.

A NOC's functions include the usual OSI FCAPS management as well as customer relationship management. The three most important aspects of building an effective NOC are as follows:

- **People** Experienced and motivated operations staff must perform the routine daily tasks as well as constantly update their technology expertise. Personnel must also interact with customers professionally.
- **Technology** Effective tools are needed to help the operations staff monitor network status, quickly isolate faults, and take appropriate corrective measures. Various FCAPS management tools must be integrated and must be customized to management solutions pertinent to the specific service provider network environment.
- **Process** Effective processes should be put in place to distribute and hand-off tasks between people and functional groups within the corporation. Proper escalation procedures must be established so that a problem that cannot be solved at a certain expertise level can be escalated into higher-tier support groups.

Because of the critical nature of the NOC, both its physical security and network security must be carefully considered. In many situations, geographically separated NOCs are established so that network operation can continue should one NOC become nonfunctional.

11.5.3 Customer Portal

Giving customers visibility into VPN services and the ability to control certain aspects of network configuration is another important aspect of VPN management in a service provider environment. Keeping customers informed on the network status and statistics increases customer satisfaction. Giving customers the ability to control their own networks reduces the amount of manual interaction between customers and network operations personnel and increases the speed of network configuration.

Increasingly, customers are provided with the needed information and control capabilities through a *customer portal* server. The concept of a customer portal is derived from the popular Internet portal model (e.g., my Yahoo). A portal can provide the user with all kinds of information that can be customized at the user's discretion.

A customer portal can include features such as:

- Network status reporting
- Network configuration reporting
- Network configuration change
- VPN user administration
- Trouble ticket information
- Ability to place new service orders
- Online billing information and payment
- Marketing, promotion, advertisements
- General content (news, stock quotes, etc.)
- Other information related to the operation of the VPN

Figure 11-5 shows an example of a service portal architecture.

Because of the sensitive nature of the customer's VPN and because multiple customers will access the same customer portal server, it is imperative that only designated personnel (both from the customer and from the service provider) be able to access the portal server. This calls for stringent authentication and access control as well as data security for the portal server. These portal security features can be implemented through a VPN, or through SSL, or through both.

11.6 International Issues

Another important issue is the import and export of encryption technologies. Many countries have established laws to restrict the import and export of such technologies—some for technical reasons, and others for political reasons. The United States, for example, permits the export of 3DES encryption technology to most countries except those on the State Department's controlled list. France, on the other hand, does not permit strong encryption technology to be imported into

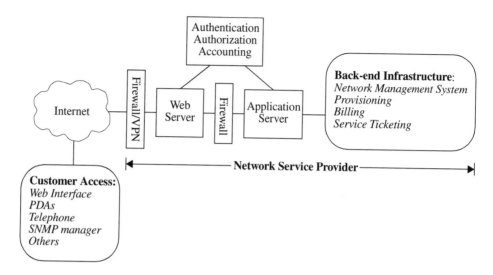

Figure 11-5 A customer portal example

the country. For parties wanting to establish VPNs with encryption across international boundaries, it is important to research the laws and regulations of each country—both import and export—thoroughly before undertaking such a venture.

12

VPN Directions:
Beyond Connectivity

If you want to look afar, please go to higher ground.
—WANG ZHI HUAN, TANG DYNASTY POET

The first 11 chapters of this book provide a tour of the basic VPN technologies and explain how they are used to build and manage VPN solutions. We have seen that building a VPN solution requires assembling an array of constituent technologies and ancillary services, some of which are more mature than others.

As the Internet continues to evolve from novelty to utility, customer expectations will also evolve from viewing the Internet as a simple connection service to seeing it as a set of feature-rich services whose underlying construction is transparent.

Certainly, VPN services are a prime example of value-added services on top of basic network connectivity. However, VPNs today are not transparent; the technology components are not seamlessly integrated, and performance often suffers. Until the four VPN technologies—tunneling, authentication, access control, and data integrity and confidentiality—are themselves integrated into the Internet infrastructure rather than assembled as add-on components with compatibility and interoperability issues, VPNs will be neither ubiquitous nor transparent.

Many factors will affect current and future developments of VPNs: The continued evolution of the underlying network infrastructure, and advances in the VPN-enabling technologies and the ways they are assembled and managed. In this chapter, we discuss several emerging trends—in the Internet infrastructure in general and in VPN technologies in particular—that give insight into the near- and mid-term directions of VPNs.

12.1 Evolutions in Network Infrastructure

Advances in networking technology now have more to do with the physics of optics than the physics of electronics. The use of silica fiber [KAO66] and lasers has increased the available communication bandwidth from the gigahertz range (the upper band of the microwave frequencies used for communication) to ranges in the hundreds of terahertz (the frequencies of the long-wavelength lasers used in the silica fiber). The result is increased transmission capacity and, with it, new networking capabilities that can transmit many terabits of data per second over a long-haul system—spanning, for example, the entire continental United States—without signal regeneration. New router technology can switch data packets at many terabits per second. The rapid deployment of fiber on long-haul, metropolitan area, and local area networks makes it easy to gain access to an optical transport. Improvements in last-mile access technology are enabling broadband access from nearly anywhere—home, office, or wireless mobile computers. Access bandwidth on the order of megabits to gigabits per second will be routinely available to all devices having Internet connectivity.

These advances in networking technology afford new opportunities for network service providers. Figure 12-1 shows a likely architecture for a large-scale IP network infrastructure. At the center of this network infrastructure is an all-optical core network. This optical core transports data packets at the ultra-high speeds of terabits to petabits per second (10^{12} to 10^{15} bps) using many strands of silica fiber. The optical switching path is established either through provisioning or by some kind of signaling protocol before the traffic is passed. It is unlikely that pure optical IP routing will be used within the core network until optical buffer and processing technologies become viable.

At the edge of this all-optical core are the *edge devices* that allow the network devices to connect to the core network via various broadband access technologies (e.g., copper or wireless). Edge devices also aggregate the packet traffic from access bandwidth rates in the 10^6 to 10^9 bps range to rates in the 10^{12} to 10^{15} bps range.

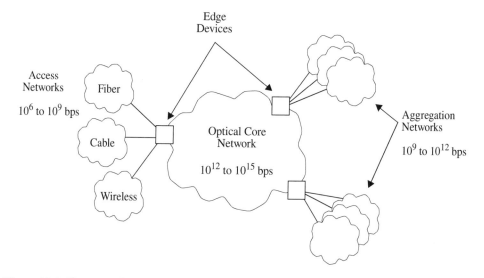

Figure 12-1 Conceptual architecture for a future network infrastructure

Another role of edge devices is to apply service policy to the traffic. It would be ideal if the traffic that came into the network from end devices (where network applications reside) were well behaved and already conforming to policy requirements. However, to manage every end device is a daunting task. Edge devices offer a more scalable solution because traffic has already been aggregated. Edge devices can examine the incoming packets, determine their policy requirements, and then act accordingly.

12.2 Evolutions in VPNs

VPN technologies will continue to evolve as the Internet infrastructure does, enabling more comprehensive, integrated, and transparent VPN solutions. Improvement in the Internet infrastructure, especially in its ability to provide quality of service and security guarantees, will make the distinction between *virtual* private networks and *physically separated* private networks increasingly less significant. For all practical purposes, a virtual private network will offer the same quality and security as a private network but with more flexibility.

Three major issues currently drive trends in VPN service offerings:

- **Where to put the tunnel endpoints** There is a trend to offer *network-based VPNs*, constructed so that the tunnel endpoints are at ISPs' POPs.
- **How to isolate the traffic within a VPN** There is considerable excitement about virtual private routed networks (VPRNs)—in particular, VPRNs based on MPLS technologies.
- **How to integrate VPNs with other services** There are advantages to incorporating VPN functions with firewall and other security technologies to create an all-purpose security device.

Network-Based VPNs

We introduce a VPN taxonomy in Chapter 3 that is based on the endpoints of the tunnels that make up the VPN. Although the End-to-LAN and LAN-to-LAN models have been the most widely adopted, indications are that the use of the other four models—in particular, POP-to-POP—will become as popular in the next several years.

The POP-to-POP model enables network service providers to manage policy at the service provider's infrastructure without touching the access devices at the customer's site, called *customer premises equipment* (CPE). A centralized policy can be applied at the POP device that aggregates customer traffic. A new class of POP devices, called *IP service platforms*, provides this capability. Figure 12-2 shows an example of how the IP service platform can be used in a service provider infrastructure.

The POP-based IP service platform offers several advantages for service providers:

- There is no need to install additional CPE devices for the VPN, thus saving the usually high operational cost of deploying and managing yet another piece of remote equipment.
- Aggregating traffic from different corporate sites to the same POP means that the traffic can be transported over a single VPN tunnel, thus reducing the number of VPN tunnels to be managed.
- Security and QoS policies can be applied once, where the traffic is aggregated—at the POP device.

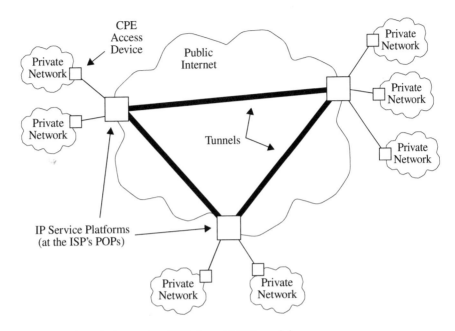

Figure 12-2 IP service platforms in a POP-based VPN model

The IP service platform also lets network service providers enable a wide range of value-added services to customers. For example, firewall rules on the IP service platform can be applied to traffic for network subscribers, eliminating the need to install firewalls for each customer.

Although a POP-to-POP VPN tunnel does not cover the traffic traversing the access link from the LAN device to the service provider's edge device at the POP, the access circuits are usually dedicated physical circuits, thus offering a degree of security through physical separation. Even so, customers may insist on an end-to-end VPN service. Fortunately, a network-based VPN solution does not preclude the composition of tunnels. Figure 12-3 shows an End-to-End tunnel between the application hosts within another POP-to-POP tunnel between the IP service platforms. This notion is supported in some of the VPN technologies: The IPsec specification defines nested security associations, called iterated tunneling (see Section 5.1.2), and the MPLS specification defines multiple label stacks for similar purposes.

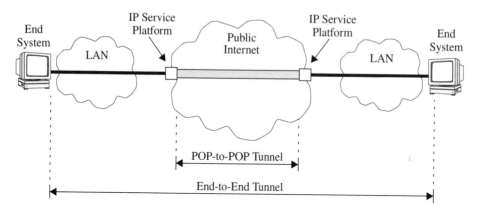

Figure 12-3 Nested tunnels in VPN

MPLS-Based VPNs

Although originally conceived to provide wire-speed switching for IP traffic, Multiprotocol Label Switching has now evolved into a set of technologies that enable QoS and traffic engineering (TE) capabilities for IP traffic over arbitrary link layer technologies. With wire-speed IP routing implemented using ASIC technology (for the 32-bit IP address space), attention has turned to using the MPLS label as a mechanism to instrument policy.

By itself, the source and destination address pair is usually not enough for a conventional IP router to identify which QoS or TE policy to apply to the packet because there may be many types of traffic between a given source and destination pair. (A unique flow identifier is included in the IPv6 header precisely for the this reason.) Therefore, for the intermediate devices (i.e., routers and switches) to apply policy to the traffic, it is often necessary to examine information from the higher-layer protocol headers, complicating the device's job and drastically reducing performance.

The MPLS label, on the other hand, is dynamically negotiated between the label-switching routers and carries only local significance. This arrangement decouples the policy instrumentation (forwarding is only one example of policy) from the information carried in the IP and higher-layer protocol headers. MPLS routers and switches can apply a unique label to all traffic subject to the same policy; such a

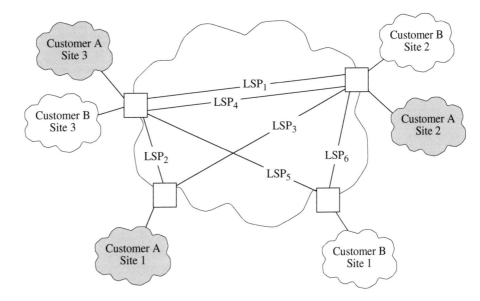

Figure 12-4 Example of an MPLS-based VPN

class of traffic forms a *policy equivalent class*. If the policy is for packet forwarding, the equivalency class formed is the *forwarding equivalent class*. MPLS also hides the IP address when the traffic traverses the MPLS cloud, thus reducing the need to have globally unique IP addresses.

MPLS can offer traffic isolation through the use of different label switched paths (LSPs) across the label-switching fabric. One can regard the LSP as an MPLS tunnel. Unlike IPsec tunnels, where the path traveled by the packet is left for the routers to decide, MPLS can control the traveling path during the LSP establishment phase.

Figure 12-4 shows an example of an MPLS-based VPN, where the tunnel endpoints reside in edge devices within the service provider's infrastructure. Two VPN communities are depicted in the figure. The first, for customer A, has three sites. Three LSPs (LSP_1, LSP_2, and LSP_3) are established to connect the edge devices. The second, for customer B, also has three sites and has three LSPs (LSP_4, LSP_5, and LSP_6) used to connect the three sites. LSPs can be established with specific QoS parameters and routing constraints.

Notice that site 2 for customer A and site 2 for customer B share a common edge device for the service provider. It is important that the routing tables for the two customer VPNs be maintained separately at this one physical device. If a single routing table is used, it is possible that traffic from the two separate VPNs might mix together. This can happen, for example, if the same private addresses are used for two different VPNs, because a single routing table cannot distinguish which address is from which VPN. Furthermore, for the VPN to be flexible, the edge device must exchange routing information with the customer's LAN devices. If a single routing table is used, it is possible for the edge router to receive wrong routing information—either by mistake or on purpose—causing the traffic to mix.

There are two ways to separate the routes between the two distinct MPLS-based VPNs. The first method is to maintain separate routing tables within a single routing process [ROSE00]. The second method is to create separate routing processes on the same physical devices, each instance having its own routing table [OULD00]. Both methods are under IETF working group consideration.

Integration of Firewall and VPN Devices

Recall that Chapter 9 describes how firewalls and VPN devices located at the corporate network perimeter can interact depending on their relative positions. Both firewalls and VPN gateways are security devices for private networks. When they are implemented as two separate devices, each device requires separate management, possibly leading to consistency problems. There are advantages to integrating the functions of a firewall and a VPN gateway into a single device so that it can take care of all the security needs of guarding the private networks. This approach is especially attractive in networks with a small-to-medium size traffic load, where performance requirements are moderate and a single device can satisfy the needs.

An added advantage of firewall and VPN device integration is that both NAT and IPsec can be processed at the same device. It is well known that IPsec and NAT have many incompatibilities [ABOD00]. If the operations are performed at the same point, the device can take precautions on how the operations are performed and can prevent the application of incompatible operations.

12.3 Internetworking Beyond Connectivity

The demand for wider connectivity and greater bandwidth has been the driving force behind the growth in the Internet infrastructure almost from the beginning. It is nearly inconceivable that the NSFNET backbone was once based on T1 lines when today cable modems and DSL bring almost that much bandwidth into private homes.

Although there will always be a demand for more bandwidth, it is increasingly clear that simple connectivity is becoming a commodity service. There will also be more demand for providing value-added services on top of the Internet connectivity. Therefore, we must look at the state of internetworking beyond the issue of connectivity.

Virtual private networking is perhaps the first major attempt to make the network more than just an interconnection medium. Security and service quality are essential for the network to satisfy the needs of business communication.

Placing these value-added functions in the end systems is the only choice when the network itself is a simple interconnect. However, this approach has drawbacks: Management of these systems is not scalable, and QoS requirements simply cannot be placed at the end system alone because the all the devices along the traffic path should work together to ensure QoS guarantees.

Increasingly, the trend is to shore up the infrastructure from the inside, adding functionality to provide or support security and service quality in the network. Certainly, better-equipped networks will make the deployment of services such as VPNs easier and more transparent.

12.3.1 Network Security

As soon as valuable information is stored on computers connected to a network, the information becomes vulnerable to inspection, modification, or deletion by malicious parties—hence the need for network security. We can separate network security issues into two broad categories: issues for public networks and issues for private networks.

Public Network Security

To function correctly, the public Internet depends on many systems. Often, these systems comprise servers distributed around the Internet; the servers exchange information with each other to provide a global view of the Internet. Because the services reside in the Internet and the information exchange is done over the Internet, they are subject to the vulnerabilities that VPNs try to guard against. Two systems in particular are critical for the operation of the Internet: the routing system and DNS.

The routing system in the Internet is composed of many routers grouped into management domains called *autonomous systems* (ASs). To forward packets appropriately, the routers exchange connectivity and other information among themselves. Within an AS, these exchanges are accomplished via interior routing protocols such as RIP (Routing Information Protocol), OSPF (Open Shortest Path First), and IGRP (Interior Gateway Routing Protocol). Routing information exchanges between ASs are handled via exterior gateway protocols such as BGP (Border Gateway Protocol).

It is imperative that the routing information be as accurate as possible so that the routers can forward packets correctly. Routers working from incorrect information will misroute IP packets, causing them to traverse other routers unnecessarily and wasting valuable resources. The integrity of the routing infrastructure relies on all the routers working collectively in a secure and scalable manner. It has been realized that the current Internet routing infrastructure is not secure; efforts such as securing OSPF [RFC2154] and BGP [KENT00] are under way.

DNS [RFC1035] is a distributed service that maps domain names (e.g., www.yahoo.com) into IP addresses (e.g., 216.32.74.53). DNS is organized in a hierarchical structure, with its root servers administrated by ICANN (the Internet Corporation for Assigned Names and Numbers). The dynamic nature of domain names means that mappings between the domain names and IP addresses are constantly changing and must be updated often. Clearly, both DNS system update messages and records inside the DNS servers should be secured against attacks. This is especially true for the top-level DNS root servers. DNS protocol extensions have been defined to authenticate the data in DNS and provide key distribution services [RFC2065], and DNS dynamic update operations have also been defined that use digital signatures to secure updates and restrict updates to those authorized to perform them [RFC2137].

Private Network Security

The security concerns of public networks also exist in private networks. However, because private networks often fall within a single administrative authority, it is usually easier to exert control over private network infrastructure. Consequently, the security issues surrounding private networks have to do mostly with preventing unauthorized access while facilitating authorized access to private data. A large portion of this book is devoted to these issues. The four basic VPN technologies—tunneling, authentication, access control, and data integrity and confidentiality—are essential to private network security, whether or not they are used to build a VPN.

A security attack can be mounted to gain unauthorized access to private data or to prevent legitimate access to data (both private and public). In the first type, the attacker intrudes into the private network. Intrusion detection systems (IDSs) are used to identify these situations.

The latter types of attacks are denial-of-service (DoS) attacks. Although DoS attacks can be launched against both private and public networks, it is more difficult to disrupt the entire public network infrastructure; it is much easier to attack a much smaller private network, which may contain single points of failure.

There are several ways to guard against a DoS attack. Redundant connectivity over geographically diverse routes adds reliability to the network. Firewalls drop packets from suspicious addresses and ports. Also, looking for certain attack signatures can help detect and, hopefully, thwart the attack. Content-smart switches that can analyze application behavior can also be used.

Compromised hosts not only leave data vulnerable, but can also be used to perform what is called a *distributed DoS* attack. In this attack, compromised computers become launching pads for other DoS attacks. Extensive logging can help detect such attacks, but not until some time after the fact.

12.3.2 Quality of Service

QoS in packet switched networks in general, and IP networks in particular, has been an important area of networking research over the past several decades. However, even though there have been rich research results in this area, relatively little has been put into practice in deployed networks. The IP header has 8 bits dedicated to the type of service (TOS) field, but the TOS field has not been used until recently, and even now, the use of TOS to indicate class of service is not common.

Queuing disciplines can also discriminate between service classes. Research has shown that packet delay can be bounded with a generalized processor sharing service discipline [PARE92], yet no network delay guarantee is based on the queuing arrangements along the packet transit path.

In general, QoS is needed when the demand for network resources outpaces the availability of resources. Therefore, policies are implemented to control whether a service request can proceed. If a request is allowed, efforts are made to ensure that the requested resources are available for it. The control mechanisms determining whether to admit the request, and the control mechanisms for subsequent policy instrumentation, are not free. If the cost of the control mechanisms outweighs the benefits derived from such control, there is no incentive to provide the control. The economics of the Internet service industry have not yet provided the incentives to move away from the current best-effort, flat-pricing service model.

Unlike security, which can be applied at the tunnel endpoints only, QoS must be applied at every hop a packet visits. If the QoS guarantee is not applied at any one of the intermediate hops, the effort to provide QoS by all other devices along the transit path becomes moot. The fact that an IP network is connectionless also poses a major problem for QoS. In an IP network, the intermediate routers along the packet transit path are not required to keep state information, including the parameters used to enforce the QoS guarantees.

MPLS—together with its signaling protocols, either RSVP-TE (Resource ReSerVation Protocol-Traffic Engineering) [AWDU00] or CR-LDP (Constraint-Based Routing using the LDP) [JAMO00]—is the important mechanism for enabling QoS in the Internet. The signaling mechanism establishes state information within the network. MPLS provides the traffic classification mechanism so that IP packets can be classified to correspond to the state established within the network. Various traffic shaping and queuing mechanisms (e.g., token bucket and weighted fair queuing) are then applied to the classified traffic according the state information, thus guaranteeing that the service provided is the service requested.

12.3.3 Intelligence in the Network

In his essay "The Rise of the Stupid Network," David Isenberg envisioned a dumb but ultrafast network whose only task is delivering a large amount of data from one place to another [ISEN97]. All intelligence resides on the computers attached to this network, and connectivity is the *only* service the network provides. This is the opposite of the PSTN model, where it is the network that is intelligent and the end devices (telephones) are dumb. One must subscribe to a three-way calling service from the telephone company to bridge two phone calls together. Imagine having to subscribe to a similar service in order to open two Web browsing sessions at the same time.

Although the stupid network paradigm serves a useful purpose, it is becoming increasing clear that mere connectivity is no longer the most important aspect of networking. Users are interested in increasingly sophisticated services that require the network—not just the end systems—to participate. The Internet is starting to resemble a utility, and users bring to it certain expectations, such as stability, availability, and protection from abuse and attack.

The computers connected to the Internet may have the appropriate software and enough processing power to guard against attack and abuse, but it is not always feasible to rely on users to properly configure their software and hardware resources for this task. If, on the other hand, the task of guarding against attacks and abuses is implemented within the network itself, the end system computer can focus on being a device used to access network services.

Internet access is quickly becoming the vehicle where all kinds of communication services are carried. Therefore, expectations are evolving far beyond that of simple connectivity. The development of virtual private networks is one step in that evolution.

Acronyms

3DES	Triple DES, an encryption algorithm using DES three times
AAA	Authentication, authorization, and accounting
ACL	Access control list
AES	Advanced Encryption Standard
AH	Authentication Header (from IPsec)
API	Application programming interface
ARPA	Advanced Research Projects Agency, also known as DARPA
AS	Authentication server, as in Kerberos, also
	Autonomous system
ASIC	Application-specific integrated circuit
ASN.1	Abstract Syntax Notation One
ATM	Asynchronous Transfer Mode
B2B	Business-to-business e-commerce
B2C	Business-to-consumer e-commerce
BGP	Border Gateway Protocol
BSD	Berkeley System Distribution, a UNIX operating system branch
CA	Certification authority, as in PKI
CAST	Symmetric encryption algorithm by C. Adams and S. Tavares
CCITT	Comite Consultatif Internationale de Telegraphie et Telephonie
CERN	Center for European Nuclear Research
CHAP	Challenge Handshake Authentication Protocol
CIDR	Classless Inter-Domain Routing
CIR	Committed information rate
CLI	Command line interface
C-list	Capabilities list
CMIP	Common Management Information Protocol
CMIS	Common Management Information Service
CPE	Customer premises equipment

CPS	Certification Practice Statement, as in PKI
CRL	Certificate revocation list, as in PKI
CR-LDP	Constraint-Based Routing using LDP, as in MPLS
CRM	Customer relationship management
DAP	Directory Access Protocol, as in X.500
DARPA	Defense Advanced Research Projects Agency
DDoS	Distributed denial of service
DES	Data Encryption Standard
DH	Diffie-Hellman
DHCP	Dynamic Host Configuration Protocol
DMZ	Demilitarized zone, as in firewalls
DN	Distinguished name, as in X.509
DNS	Domain Name System
DNSSEC	Secure DNS
DoD	U.S. Department of Defense
DoS	Denial of service
DSA	Digital Signature Algorithm, also Directory System Agent, as in X.500
DSCP	Differentiated service code point
DSL	Digital subscriber line
DUA	Directory User Agent, as in X.500
DUN	Dial-up networking, as in Windows
EAP	Extensible Authentication Protocol
EEPROM	Electrically Erasable Programmable Read-Only Memory
EGP	Exterior Gateway Protocol
ESP	Encapsulating Security Payload (from IPsec)
FCAPS	The initials for fault, configuration, accounting, performance, and security management, from the OSI management model
FIPS	Federal Information Processing Standards, as from NIST
FTP	File Transfer Protocol
GRE	Generic Routing Encapsulation
GUI	Graphical user interface
HMAC	Hashed message authentication code
HSRP	Hot Standby Router Protocol
HTTP	Hypertext Transfer Protocol
ICANN	Internet Corporation for Assigned Names and Numbers
ICMP	Internet Control Message Protocol
ICSA	International Computer Security Association

ICV   Integrity check value
IDEA   International Data Encryption Algorithm
IDS   Intrusion detection system
IETF   Internet Engineering Task Force
IGRP   Interior Gateway Routing Protocol, by Cisco
IKE   Internet Key Exchange
IMP   BBN's Interface Message Processor
IP   Internet Protocol
IPO   Initial public offering
IPsec   IP security protocol suite
IPv6   IP version 6
IPX   Novell's Internetwork Packet Exchange
ISAKMP   Internet Security Association and Key Management Protocol
ISDN   Integrated Service Digital Network
ISO   International Organization for Standardization
ISP   Internet service provider
IT   Information technology
ITU   International Telecommunication Union
kbps   Kilobits per second
KE   Key exchange (parameters), as in IKE
L2F   Layer Two Forwarding
L2TP   Layer Two Tunneling Protocol
LAC   L2TP Access Concentrator
LAN   Local area network
LCP   Link Control Protocol, as in PPP
LDAP   Lightweight Directory Access Protocol
LDP   Label Distribution Protocol, from MPLS
LNS   L2TP Network Server
LSP   Label switch path, from MPLS
LSR   Label switched router, from MPLS
MAC   Message authentication code, also Medium Access Control
MD4   Message Digest algorithm 4
MD5   Message Digest algorithm 5
MIB   Management information base
MIT   Massachusetts Institute of Technology, also
            Management information tree, as in OSI network management
MPLS   Multiprotocol Label Switching
MS-CHAP   Microsoft Challenge Handshake Protocol

MTU	Maximum transmission unit
NAS	Network access server
NAT	Network address translation
NBS	National Bureau of Standards, now NIST
NCP	Network Control Program, a TCP predecessor
NCSA	National Center for Supercomputer Applications
NDIS	Network Driver Interface Specification, as in Windows
NetBEUI	NetBIOS Extended User Interface, as in Windows
NIST	National Institute of Standards and Technology
NMS	Network management station, also
	Network management system
NOC	Network operations center
NSA	National Security Agency
NSF	National Science Foundation
OID	Object identifier, as in SNMP MIB
OSI	Open Systems Interconnection
OSPF	Open Shortest Path First routing algorithm
OTAR	Over the air rekeying
OTP	One-time password
PAC	PPTP Access Concentrator
PAP	Password Authentication Protocol
PAT	Port address translation
PDU	Protocol data unit
PEM	Privacy Enhanced Mail
PGP	Pretty Good Privacy
PKCS	Public-Key Cryptography Standards, from RSA Laboratories
PKI	Public key infrastructure
PKIX	Public Key Infrastructure for the Internet
PLI	Private Line Interface
PMI	Privilege Management Infrastructure
PNS	PPTP Network Server
POP	Point of presence
PPP	Point-to-Point Protocol
PPPoE	Point-to-Point Protocol over Ethernet
PPTP	Point-to-Point Tunneling Protocol
PSTN	Public switched telephone network
PVC	Permanent virtual circuit
QoS	Quality of service

RA   Registration authority, as in PKI
RADIUS   Remote Authentication Dial In User Service
RAS   Remote access server
RC4   "Ron's Cipher #4," a symmetric encryption algorithm
RC5   "Ron's Cipher #5," a symmetric encryption algorithm
RFC   Request for comments
RIP   Routing Information Protocol
RMON   Remote Monitoring
RSA   A public key encryption algorithm invented by Rivest, Shamir,
            and Adleman
RSVP   Resource ReSerVation Protocol
SA   Security association, as in IPsec
SAD   Security Association Database, as in IPsec
SASL   Simple Authentication and Security Layer
SCEP   Simple Certificate Enrollment Protocol, as in PKI
SCP   Secure Copy, from SSH
SGMP   Simple Gateway Monitoring Protocol
SHA-1   Secure Hash Algorithm 1, a one-way hash function
SKEME   Secure Key Exchange Mechanism
S/KEY   A one-time password system
SLA   Service level agreement
SLIP   Serial line IP
SMI   Structure of Management Information, as in OSI network
            management
S/MIME   Secure MIME
SNMP   Simple Network Management Protocol
SPD   Security Policy Database, as in IPsec
SPI   Security parameter index, as in IPsec
SPSL   Security Policy Specification Language
SSH   Secure Shell
SSL   Secure Sockets Layer
S/WAN   Secure wide area network, as an IPsec implementation for Linux
TCP   Transmission Control Protocol
TE   Traffic engineering
TFTP   Trivial File Transfer Protocol
TGS   Ticket-Granting Server, as in Kerberos
TGT   Ticket-Granting Ticket, as in Kerberos

TL1	Transaction Language One, management protocol defined by Bellcore
TLS	Transport Layer Security
TMN	Telecommunications Management Network, as in CCITT M.30
TOS	Type of service
TTL	Time to live
UDP	User Datagram Protocol
VPDN	Virtual private dial network
VPRN	Virtual private routed network
VPN	Virtual private network
VRRP	Virtual Router Redundancy Protocol
WAN	Wide area network
WINS	Windows Internet Service
WWW	World Wide Web
X.500	CCITT Directory Services
X.509	CCITT Public Key Certificate Specification

References

Many of the citations in this book are RFCs—Requests for Comments. An RFC is a note discussing networking protocols, procedures, programs, and concepts generally related to the Internet. RFCs are numbered sequentially starting from early documents in 1969.

Several Internet-Drafts are also cited. This is somewhat dicey because an Internet-Draft is *not* a means of publishing a specification. An Internet-Draft is a tentative document designed to stimulate discussion before the document is submitted for consideration as an RFC. Internet-Drafts have no formal status and are valid for only six months. RFC 2026, "The Internet Standards Process—Revision 3," states:

> Under no circumstances should an Internet-Draft be referenced by any paper, report, or Request-for-Proposal, nor should a vendor claim compliance with an Internet-Draft.

We have included a citation for an Internet-Draft here *only if* (1) it is the only documentation for a VPN protocol, or (2) it shows evidence of on-going work in an area. It is likely that an Internet-Draft cited in this book will have been replaced by a newer version, dropped, or promoted to an RFC.

See http://www.ietf.org for the latest versions of Internet-Drafts and RFCs. The RFC Editor (at http://www.rfc-editor.org) can help find Internet-Drafts and RFCs by keyword.

[ABOD00]   Aboda, B., "NAT and IPSEC," Internet-Draft (work in progress), July 2000.

[ADAM99]   Adams, A., and M. A. Sasse, "Users Are Not the Enemy," *Communications of the ACM*, Vol. 42, No. 12, December 1999.

[ARPA68]   Advance Research Projects Agency, "Resource Sharing Computer Networks," Program Plan Number 723, June 3, 1968.

[AWDU00]   Awduche, D. O., L. Berger, D.-H. Gan, T. Li, V. Srinivasan, and G. Swallow, "RSVP-TE: Extensions to RSVP for LSP Tunnels," Internet-Draft (work in progress), August 2000.

[BBN69]   Bolt Beranek and Newman, Inc., "Specifications for the Interconnection of a Host and an IMP," Technical Report 1822, April 1969.

[BBN75]   Bolt Beranek and Newman, Inc., "Interfacing a Host to a Private Line Interface," Appendix H, Technical Report 1822, September 1975.

[BERN89]   Berners-Lee, T., "Information Management: A Proposal," *Proposal to CERN Management*, March 1989, May 1990. http://www.w3.org/History/1989/proposal.html.

[BSD93]   4.2 Berkeley Distribution, SYSLOG(3), Unix Manual Page, June 1993.

[BSD97]   4.3 Berkeley Distribution, PING(8), Unix Manual Page, March 1997.

[CAVE00]   Caves, E., P. R. Calhoun, and R. Wheeler, "Layer Two Tunneling Protocol 'L2TP' Management Information Base," Internet-Draft (work in progress), March 2000.

[CCITT88]   CCITT Recommendation X.500, "The Directory: Overview of Concepts, Models and Service," 1988.

[CCITT89]   CCITT Blue Book: Recommendation M.30, "Principles for a Telecommunication Management Network" Volume IV, Geneva, 1989.

[CERF74]   Cerf, V., and R. Kahn, "A Protocol for Packet-Network Intercommunication," *IEEE Transactions on Communications*, May 1974.

[CHES94]   Cheswick, W. R., and S. M. Bellovin, *Firewalls and Internet Security: Repelling the Wily Hacker*, Addison-Wesley, 1994.

[CISC98]   Cisco Systems, Inc., "Cisco System's Simple Certificate Enrollment Protocol," White Paper, 1998.

[COND00]   Condell, M., C. Lynn, and J. Zao, "Security Policy Specification Language," Internet-Draft (work in progress), March 10, 2000.

[DAVI80]   Davies, D., and W. Price, "The Application of Digital Signatures Based on Public-Key Cryptosystems," *Proceedings of the Fifth International Computer Communications Conference*, October 1980.

[DIFF76]   Diffie, W, and M. Hellman, "New Directions in Cryptography," *IEEE Transactions on Information Theory*, vol. IT-22, no. 6, pp. 644–654, November 1976.

[ELGA85]   ElGamal, T., "A Public-Key Cryptosystem and a Signature Scheme Based on Discrete Logarithms," *Advances in Cryptography: Proceedings of CRYPTO'84*, Springer-Verlag, 1985.

[ELLI00]   Ellison, C., and Schneier, B, "Ten Risks of PKI: What You're Not Being Told about Public Key Infrastructure," *Computer Security Journal*, vol. XVI, no. 1, 2000.

[FELD90]   Feldmeier, D. C., and P. R. Karn, "UNIX Password Security—Ten Years Later," *Proceedings of Advances in Crytology—CRYPTO '89*, Springer-Verlag, 1990.

[FORD95]   Ford, W., "A Public Key Infrastructure for U.S. Government Unclassified but Sensitive Applications," FPKI Technical Working Group, September 1, 1995.

[FREEBSD96]   FreeBSD, IPFW(8), FreeBSD System Manager's Manual, July 1996.

[FRIE96]   Frier, A., P. Karlton, and P. Kocher, "The SSL 3.0 Protocol," Netscape Communications Corporation, November 18, 1996.

[GARD93]   Gardiner, C., "Distributed Public Key Certificate Management," *Proceedings of the Workshop on Network and Distributed System Security* (IEEE Press), February 1993.

[GPG]   Free Software Foundation, "The GNU Privacy Guard," http://www.gnupg.org.

[GUTM00]   Gutmann, P., "X.509 Style Guide," http://www.cs.auckland.ac.nz/~pgut001/pubs/x509guide.txt, October 2000.

[HICK95]   Hickman, K., "The SSL Protocol," Netscape Communications Corporation., February 9, 1995.

[HUTT00]   Huttunen, A. and J. Sierwald, "ESP Encapsulation in UDP Packets," Internet-Draft (work in progress), September 2000.

[ISEN97]   Isenberg, D., "Rise of the Stupid Network: Why the Intelligent Network Was Once a Good Idea, but Isn't Anymore. One Telephone Company Nerd's Odd Perspective on the Changing Value Proposition," *Computer Telephony*, August 1997. Revised version, "The Dawn of the Stupid Network," in *netWorker*, Vol. 2, No. 1, February-March 1998, pp. 24-31.

[ISO7498]   International Organization for Standardization, "Information Processing Systems—Open Systems Interconnection—Basic Reference Model," Draft International Standard 7498, October 1984.

[ISO7498-4]   International Organization for Standardization, "Information Processing Systems—Open Systems Interconnection—Basic Reference Model—Part 4: Management Framework," Draft International Standard 7498-4, October 1989.

[ISO7816]   International Organization for Standardization, "Identification Cards—Integrated Circuit(s) Cards with Contacts," Draft International Standard 7816, 1987-1995.

[ISO8824]   International Organization for Standardization, "Information Processing—Open System Interconnection—Specification of Abstract Syntax Notation One (ASN.1)," Draft International Standard 8824, February 1989.

[ISO9595]   International Organization for Standardization, "Information Processing Systems—Open Systems Interconnection—Common Management Information Service Specification," Draft International Standard 9595, November 1990.

[ISO9596]   International Organization for Standardization, "Information Processing Systems—Open Systems Interconnection—Common Management Information Protocol Specification," Draft International Standard 9596, 1991.

[ITU97]   International Telecommunication Union ITU-T Recommendation X.509 (1997 E), "Information Technology—Open Systems Interconnection—The Directory: Authentication Framework," June 1997.

[ITU99]   International Telecommunication Union FPDAM on Certificate Extensions, "Final Proposed Draft Amendment on Certificate Extensions," April 1999.

[Jaco96]   Jacobson, V., and S. Deering, TRACEROUTE(1), Unix Manual Page, September 1996.

[Jamo00]   Jamoussi, B., editor, "Constraint-Based LSP Setup using LDP," Internet-Draft (work in progress), July 2000.

[JENK00a] Jenkins, T., and J. Shriver, "IPsec Monitoring MIB," Internet-Draft (work in progress), July 2000.

[JENK00b] Jenkin, T., and J. Shriver, "ISAKMP DOI-Independent Monitoring MIB," Internet-Draft (work in progress), July 2000.

[JENK00c] Jenkins, T., and J. Shriver, "IKE Monitoring MIB," Internet-Draft (work in progress), July 2000.

[JOHN98] Johnston, W., S. Mudumbai, and M. Thompson, "Authorization and Attribute Certificates for Widely Distributed Access Control," *Proceedings of the IEEE 7th International Workshops on Enabling Technologies: Infrastructure for Collaborative Enterprises (WETICE'98)*, Stanford University, California, June 16-18, 1998.

[KALI93a] Kaliski, Jr., B. S., "An Overview of the PKCS Standards," RSA Laboratories Technical Note, November 1993.

[KALI93b] Kaliski, Jr., B. S., "A Layman's Guide to a Subset of ASN.1, BER, and DER," RSA Laboratories Technical Note, November 1993.

[KALI95] Kaliski, Jr., B. S., and M. Robshaw, "Message Authentication with MD5," *Cryptobytes*, vol. 1, no. 1, pp. 5–8, 1995.

[KALI97] Kaliski, Jr., B. S., and K. W. Kingdon, "Extensions and Revisions to PKCS #7," RSA Laboratories Technical Note, May 13, 1997.

[KAO66] Kao, K.C., and G. A. Hockham, "Dielectric-fibre Surface Waveguides for Optical Frequencies," *Proceedings of IEE*, vol. 113, no. 7, July 1966, pp. 1151–1158.

[KENT97] Kent, S., "How Many Certification Authorities Are Enough," *Proceedings of Milcom'97*, Monterey, California, November 2–5, 1997.

[KENT98] Kent, S., "Evaluating Certification Authority Security," *IEEE Aerospace Conference*, vol. 4, 1998.

[KENT00] Kent, S, C. Lynn, and K. Sao, "Secure Border Gateway Protocol (S-BGP)," *IEEE Journal on Selected Areas in Communications*, vol. 18, no. 4, April 2000.

[KLEI90] Klein, D. V., "'Foiling the Cracker': A Survey of, and Implications to, Password Security," *Proceedings of the USENIX UNIX Security Workshop*, August 1990.

[KOMP00]   Kompella, K., "A MIB for MPLS Traffic Engineered LSPs," Internet-Draft (work in progress), July 2000.

[KRAW96]   Krawczyk, H., "SKEME: A Versatile Secure Key Exchange Mechanism for Internet," *Proceedings of the Symposium of Network and Distributed System Security*, San Diego, February 22–23, 1996.

[LAI91]   Lai, X., and J. Massey, "A Proposal for a New Block Encryption Standard," *Advances in Cryptography—EUROCRYPT'90 Proceedings*, Springer-Verlag, pp. 389–404, 1991.

[MICR96]   Microsoft, "Microsoft Virtual Private Networking: Using Point-to-Point Tunneling Protocol for Low-Cost, Secure, Remote Access Across the Internet," Microsoft Windows NT Server White Paper, http://www.microsoft.com/ntserver/commserv/techdetails/prodarch/pptpwp.asp, 1996.

[MICR97]   Microsoft, "Understanding Point-to-Point Tunneling Protocol (PPTP)," Microsoft Windows NT Server White Paper, http://www.microsoft.com/NTServer/commserv/techdetails/prodarch/understanding_pptp.asp, 1997.

[MOSK00]   Moskowitz, R., "PKI at a Crossroads," *Network Computing*, May 1, 2000.

[MUTH00]   Muthukrishnan, K., and A. Malis, "Core MPLS IP VPN Architecture," Internet-Draft (work in progress), January 2000.

[NBS77]   National Bureau of Standards, "Data Encryption Standard," Federal Information Processing Standards (FIPS) Pub 46, January 1977.

[NIST85]   National Institute of Standards and Technology, "Password Usage," Federal Information Processing Standards (FIPS) Pub 112, May 1985.

[NIST93a]   National Institute of Standards and Technology, "Clipper Chip Technology," http://csrc.nist.gov/keyrecovery/clip.txt, 30 April 1993.

[NIST93b]   National Institutes of Standards and Technology, "Capstone Chip Technology," http://csrc.nist.gov/keyrecovery/cap.txt, 30 April 1993.

[NIST94a]   National Institutes of Standards and Technology, "Security Requirements for Cryptographic Modules," Federal Information Processing Standards (FIPS) Pub 140-1, January 1994.

[NIST94b]   National Institutes of Standards and Technology, "Digital Signature Standard," Federal Information Processing Standards (FIPS) Pub 186, May 1994.

[NIST95]   National Institutes of Standards and Technology, "Secure Hash Standard," Federal Information Processing Standards (FIPS) Pub 180-1, April 1995.

[NIST00]   National Institutes of Standards and Technology, "Commerce Department Announces Winner of Global Information Security Competition," Press Release, October 2, 2000. Also see http://www.nist.gov/aes.

[OULD00]   Ould-Brahim, H., B. Gleeson, G. Wright, T. Sloane, R. Bach, R. Bubenik, and A. Young, "Network Based IP VPN Architecture using Virtual Routers," Internet-Draft (work in progress), July 2000.

[PARE92]   Parekh, A. K. J., "A Generalized Processor Sharing Approach to Flow Control in Integrated Services Networks," MIT Laboratory for Information and Decision Systems, Report LIDS-TH-2089, February 1992.

[PATE99]   Patel, B., and B. Aboba, "Securing L2TP using IPsec," Internet-Draft (work in progress), February 1999.

[PERL99]   Perlman, R., "An Overview of PKI Trust Models," *IEEE Network*, November/December 1999.

[PGP99]   "PGP 6.5.1 User's Guide," Network Associates, 1999.

[RABI79]   Rabin, M., "Digital Signatures and Public-Key Functions as Intractable as Factorization," MIT Laboratory for Computer Science Technical Report MIT/LCS/TR-212, January 1979.

[RAWA00]   Rawat, V., R. Tio, S. Nanji, and R. Verma, "Layer Two Tunneling Protocol (L2TP) over Frame Relay," Internet-Draft (work in progress), November 2000.

[RESC01]   Rescorla, E., *SSL and TLS: Designing and Building Secure Systems*, Addison-Wesley, 2001.

[RFC714]   McKenzie, A., "A Host/Host Protocol for an ARPANET-type Network," Request for Comments 714, April 1976.

[RFC768]   Postel, J., "User Datagram Protocol," RFC 768, August 1980.

[RFC791]   Postel, J., editor, "Internet Protocol DARPA Internet Program Protocol Specification," Request for Comments 791, September 1981

[RFC792]   Postel, J., "Internet Control Message Protocol, DARPA Internet Program Protocol Specification," Request for Comments 792, September 1981.

[RFC793]   Postel, J., editor, "Transmission Control Protocol DARPA Internet Program Protocol Specification," Request for Comments 793, September 1981

[RFC801]   Postel, J., "NCP/TCP Transition Plan," Request for Comments 801, November 1981

[RFC927]   Anderson, B., "TACACS User Identification Telnet Option," Request for Comments 927, December 1984.

[RFC1035]   Mockapetris, P., "Domain names—Implementation and Specification," Request for Comments 1035, November 1987.

[RFC1052]   Cerf, V., "IAB Recommendations for the Development of Internet Network Management Standards," Request for Comments 1052, April 1988.

[RFC1055]   Romkey, J., "A Nonstandard for Transmission of IP Datagrams over Serial Lines (SLIP)," Request for Comments 1055, June 1988.

[RFC1109]   Cerf, V., "Report of the Second Ad Hoc Network Management Review Group," Request for Comments 1109, August 1989.

[RFC1122]   Braden, R., editor, "Requirements for Internet Hosts—Communication Layers," Request for Comments 1122, October 1989.

[RFC1155]   Rose, M., and K. McCloghrie, "Structure and Identification of Management Information for TCP/IP-based Internets," Request for Comments 1155, May 1990.

[RFC1157]   Case, J., M. Fedor, M. Schoffstall, and J. Davin, "A Simple Network Management Protocol (SNMP)," Request for Comments 1157, May 1990.

[RFC1212]   Rose, M., and K. McCloghrie, editors, "Concise MIB Definitions," Request for Comments 1212, March 1991.

[RFC1213]   McCloghrie, K., and M. Rose, "Management Information Base for Network Management of TCP/IP-based Internets: MIB-II," Request for Comments 1213, March 1991.

[RFC1272]   Mills, C., D. Hirsh, and G. Ruth, "Internet Accounting: Background," Request for Comments 1272, November 1991.

[RFC1305]   Mills, D. L., "Network Time Protocol (Version 3) Specification, Implementation and Analysis," Request for Comments 1305, March 1992.

[RFC1320]   Rivest, R., "The MD4 Message-Digest Algorithm," Request for Comments 1320, April 1992.

[RFC1321]   Rivest, R., "MD5 Digest Algorithm," Request for Comments 1321, April 1992.

[RFC1334]   Lloyd, B., and W. Simpson, "PPP Authentication Protocols," Request for Comments 1334, October 1992.

[RFC1421]   Linn, J., "Privacy Enhancement for Internet Electronic Mail: Part I: Message Encryption and Authentication Procedures," Request for Comments 1421, February 1993.

[RFC1422]   Kent, S., "Privacy Enhancement for Internet Electronic Mail: Part II: Certificate-Based Key Management," Request for Comments 1422, February 1993.

[RFC1487]   Yeong, W., T. Howes, and S. Kille, "X.500 Lightweight Directory Access Protocol," Request for Comments 1487, July 1993.

[RFC1492]   Finseth, C., "An Access Control Protocol, Sometimes Called TACACS," Request for Comments 1492, July 1993.

[RFC1510]   Kohl, J., and C. Neuman, "The Kerberos Network Authentication Service (V5)," Request for Comments 1510, September 1993.

[RFC1519]   Fuller, V., T. Li, J. Yu, and K. Varadhan, "Classless Inter-Domain Routing (CIDR): An Address Assignment and Aggregation Strategy," Standards Track Request for Comments 1519, September 1993.

[RFC1631]   Egevang, K., and P. Francis, "The IP Network Address Translator (NAT)," Informational Request for Comments 1631, May 1994.

[RFC1661]   Simpson, W., (ed.), "The Point-to-Point Protocol (PPP)," Standards Track Request for Comments 1661, July 1994.

[RFC1701]   Hanks, S., T. Li, D. Farinacci, and P. Traina, "Generic Routing Encapsulation (GRE)," Informational Request for Comments 1701, October 1994.

[RFC1757]   Waldbusser, S., "Remote Network Monitoring Management Information Base," Standards Track Request for Comments 1757, February 1995.

[RFC1760]   Haller, N., "The S/KEY On-Time Password System," Informational Request for Comments 1760, February 1995.

[RFC1777]   Yeong, W., T. Howes, and S. Kille, "Lightweight Directory Access Protocol," Standards Track Request for Comments 1777, March 1995.

[RFC1883]   Deering, S., and B. Hinden, "Internet Protocol version 6," Standards Track Request for Comments 1883, December 1995.

[RFC1905]   Case, J., K. McCloghrie, M. Rose, and S. Waldbusser, "Protocol Operations for Version 2 of the Simple Network Management Protocol (SNMPv2)," Standards Track Request for Comments 1905, January 1996.

[RFC1918]   Rekhter, Y., B. Moskowitz, D. Karrenberg, G. J. de Groot, and E. Lear, "Address Allocation for Private Internets," Best Current Practices Request for Comments 1918, February 1996.

[RFC1928]   Leech, M., M. Ganis, Y. Lee, R. Kuris, D. Koblas, and L. Jones, "SOCKS Protocol Version 5," Standards Track Request for Comments 1928, March 1996.

[RFC1938]   Haller, N., and C. Metz, "A One-Time Password System," Standards Track Request for Comments 1938, May 1996.

[RFC1994]   Simpson, W., "PPP Challenge Handshake Authentication Protocol (CHAP)," Standards Track Request for Comments 1994, August 1996.

[RFC2021]   Waldbusser, S., "Remote Network Monitoring Management Information Base Version 2 using SMIv2," Standards Track Request for Comments 2021, January 1997.

[RFC2065]   Eastlake, D., and C. Kaufman, "Domain Name System Security Extensions," Standards Track Request for Comments 2065, January 1997.

[RFC2104]   Krawczyk, H., M. Bellare, and R. Canetti, "HMAC: Keyed-Hashing for Message Authentication," Informational Request for Comments 2104, February 1997.

[RFC2137]   Eastlake 3rd, D., "Secure Domain Name System Dynamic Update," Standards Track Request for Comments 2137, April 1997.

[RFC2138]   Rigney, C., A. Rubens, W. Simpson, and S. Willens, "Remote Authentication Dial In User Service (RADIUS)," Standards Track Request for Comments 2138, April 1997.

[RFC2139]   Rigney, C., "RADIUS Accounting," Informational Request for Comments 2139, April 1997.

[RFC2154]   Murphy, S., M. Badger, and B. Wellington, "OSPF with Digital Signatures," Experimental Request for Comments 2154, June 1997.

[RFC2222]   Myers, J., "Simple Authentication and Security Layer (SASL)," Standards Track Request for Comments 2222, October 1997.

[RFC2246]   Dierks, T., and C. Allen, "The TLS Protocol, Version 1.0," Standards Track Request for Comments 2246, January 1999.

[RFC2251]   Wahl, M., T. Howes, and S. Kille, "Lightweight Directory Access Protocol (v3)," Standards Track Request for Comments 2251, December 1997.

[RFC2281]   Li, T., B. Cole, P. Morton, and D Li, "Cisco Hot Standby Router Protocol (HSRP)," Informational Request for Comments 2281, March 1998.

[RFC2284]   Blunk, L., and J. Vollbrecht, "PPP Extensible Authentication Protocol (EAP)," Standards Track Request for Comments 2284, March 1998.

[RFC2311]   Dusse, S., Hoffman, P., Ramsdell, B., Lundblade, L., and L. Repka, "S/MIME Version 2 Message Specification," Informational Request for Comments 2311, March 1998.

[RFC2315]   Kaliski, Jr., B. S., "PKCS #7: Cryptographic Message Syntax Version 1.5" Informational Request for Comments 2315, March 1998.

[RFC2338]   Knight, S., D. Weaver, D. Whipple, R. Hinden, D. Mitzel, P. Hunt, P. Higginson, M. Shand, and A. Lindem, "Virtual Router Redundancy Protocol," Standards Track Request for Comments 2338, April 1998.

[RFC2341]   Valencia, A., M. Littlewood, and T. Kolar, "Cisco Layer Two Forwarding (Protocol) 'L2F,'" Historic Request for Comments 2341, May 1998.

[RFC2401]   Kent, S., and R. Atkinson, "Security Architecture for the Internet Protocol," Standards Track Request for Comments 2401, November 1998.

[RFC2402]   Kent, S., and R. Atkinson, "IP Authentication Header," Standards Track Request for Comments 2402, November 1998.

[RFC2403]   Madson, C., and R. Glenn, "The Use of HMAC-MD5-96 within ESP and AH," Standards Track Request for Comments 2403, November 1998.

[RFC2404]   Madson, C., and R. Glenn, "The Use of HMAC-SHA-1-96 within ESP and AH," Standards Track Request for Comments 2404, November 1998.

[RFC2405]   Madson, C., and N. Doraswamy, "The ESP DES-CBC Cipher Algorithm With Explicit IV," Standards Track Request for Comments 2405, November 1998.

[RFC2406]   Kent, S., and R. Atkinson, "IP Encapsulation Security Payload (ESP)," Standards Track Request for Comments 2406, November 1998.

[RFC2408]   Maughan, D., M. Schertler, M. Schneider, and J. Turner, "Internet Security Association and Key Management Protocol (ISAKMP)," Standards Track Request for Comments 2408, November 1998.

[RFC2409]   Harkens, D., and D. Carrel, "The Internet Key Exchange (IKE)," Standards Track Request for Comments 2409, November 1998.

[RFC2410]   Glenn, R., and S. Kent, "The NULL Encryption Algorithm and Its Use with IPsec," Standards Track Request for Comments 2410, November 1998.

[RFC2411]   Thayer, R., N. Doraswamy, and R. Glenn, "IP Security Roadmap," Informational Request for Comments 2411, November 1998.

[RFC2412]   Orman, H., "The OAKLEY Key Determination Protocol," Informational Request for Comments 2412, November, 1997.

[RFC2433]   Zorn, G., and Cobb, S., "Microsoft PPP CHAP Extensions," Informational Request for Comments 2433, October 1998.

[RFC2440]   Callas, J., L. Donnerhacke, H. Finney, and R. Thayer, "OpenPGP Message Format," Standards Track Request for Comments 2440, November 1998.

[RFC2459]   Housley, R., W. Ford, W. Polk, and D. Solo, "Internet X.509 Public Key Infrastructure Certificate and CRL Profile," Standards Track Request for Comments 2459, January 1999.

[RFC2547]   Rosen, E., and Y. Rekhter, "BGP/MPLS VPNs," Informational Request for Comments 2547, March 1999.

[RFC2571]   Harrington, D., R. Presuhn B. Wijnen, "An Architecture for Describing SNMP Management Frameworks," Standards Track Request for Comments 2571, April 1999.

[RFC2637]   Hamzeh, K., G. Pall, W. Verthein, J. Taarud, W. A. Little, and G. Zorn, "Point-to-Point Tunneling Protocol (PPTP)," Informational Request for Comments 2637, July 1999.

[RFC2661]   Townsley, W., A. Valencia, A. Rubens, G. Pall, G. Zorn, and B. Palter, "Layer Two Tunneling Protocol 'L2TP,'" Standards Track Request for Comments 2661, August 1999.

[RFC2667]   Thaler, D., "IP Tunnel MIB," Standards Track Request for Comments 2667, August 1999.

[RFC2759]   Zorn, G., "Microsoft PPP CHAP Extensions, Version 2," Informational Request for Comments 2759, January 2000.

[RFC2764]   Gleeson, B., A. Lin, J. Heinanen, G. Armitage, and A. Malis, "A Framework for IP-Based Virtual Private Networks," Informational Request for Comments 2764, February 2000.

[RFC2820]   Stokes, E., D. Byrne, B. Blakley, and P. Behera, "Access Control Requirements for LDAP," Informational Request for Comments 2820, May 2000.

[RFC2829]   Wahl, M., H. Alvestrand, J. Hodges, and R. Morgan, "Authentication Methods for LDAP," Standards Track Request for Comments 2829, May 2000.

[RIVE78]   Rivest, R., A. Shamir, and L. Adelman, "A Method for Obtaining Digital Signatures and Public-Key Cryptosystems," *Communications of the ACM*, vol. 21, no. 2, pp. 120–126, February 1978.

[ROSE95]   Rose, M. T., *The Simple Book: An Introduction to Networking Management*, Revised Second Edition, Prentice Hall, 1995.

[ROSE99]   Rosen, E. C., A. Viswanathan, and R. Callon, "Multiprotocol Label Switching Architecture," Internet-Draft (work in progress), August 1999.

[ROSE00]   Rosen, E. C., Y. Rekhter, T. Bogovic, S. J. Brannon, R. Vaidyanathan, M. J. Morrow, M. Carugi, C. J. Chase, T. W. Chung, J. De Clercq, E. Dean, P. Hitchin, A. Smith, M. Leelanivas, D. Marshall, L. Martini, V. Srinivasan, and A. Vedrenne, "BGP/MPLS VPNs," Internet-Draft (work in progress), July 2000.

[RSA93a]   RSA Laboratories, "PKCS #6: Extended-Certificate Syntax Standard," Technical Note, Version 1.5, November 1993.

[RSA93b]   RSA Laboratories, "PKCS #7: Cryptographic Message Syntax Standard," Technical Note, Version 1.5, November 1, 1993.

[RSA00a]   RSA Laboratories, "PKCS #9 v2.0: Selected Object Classes and Attribute Types," February 25, 2000.

[RSA00b]   RSA Laboratories, "PKCS #10 v1.7: Certification Request Syntax Standard (Final Draft)," May 4, 2000.

[RSA00c]   RSA Security, "Frequently Asked Questions about Today's Cryptography," RSA Laboratories, Version 4.1, 2000. http://www.rsalabs.com/faq/index.html.

[SCHN94]   Schneier, B, "Description of a New Variable-Length Key, 64-Bit Block Cipher (Blowfish)," *Fast Software Encryption, Cambridge Security Workshop Proceedings*, Springer-Verlag, pp. 191–204, 1994.

[SCHN96]   Schneier, B., *Applied Cryptography*, 2nd Edition, John Wiley & Sons, New York, 1996.

[SCHN98]   Schneier, B., and Mudge, "Cryptoanalysis of Microsoft's Point-to-Point Tunneling Protocol (PPTP)," *Proceedings of the 5th ACM Conference on Computer and Communications Security*, ACM Press, pp. 132–141, 1998.

[SCHN99]   Schneier, B., Mudge, and D. Wagner, "Cryptoanalysis of Microsoft's PPTP Authentication Extensions (MS-CHAPv2)," White Paper, October 19, 1999. http://www.counterpane.com/pptp.html.

[SHRI00]   Shriver, J., "IPsec DOI Textual Conventions MIB," Internet-Draft (work in progress), June 2000.

[SPAF89]   Spafford, E. H., "The Internet Worm: Crisis and Aftermath," *Communications of the ACM*, Vol. 32, No. 6, June 1989.

[SRIN00]   Srinivasan, C, A. Viswanathan, and T. D. Nadeau, "MPLS Traffic Engineering Management Information Base Using SMIv2," Internet-Draft (work in progress), July 2000.

[STAL99]   Stallings, W., *SNMP, SNMPv2, SNMPv3, and RMON 1 and 2*, Third Edition, Addison-Wesley, 1999.

[TJOE00]   Yves T'Joens, Y., P. Crivellari, and B. Sales, "Layer Two Tunnelling Protocol: ATM Access Network Extensions," Internet-Draft (work in progress), July 2000.

[VALE00]   Valencia, A. J., "L2TP Header Compression ('L2TPHC')," Internet-Draft (work in progress), November 2000.

[ZIMM95]   Zimmermann, P. R., *The Official PGP User's Guide*, MIT Press, Boston, 1995.

Index

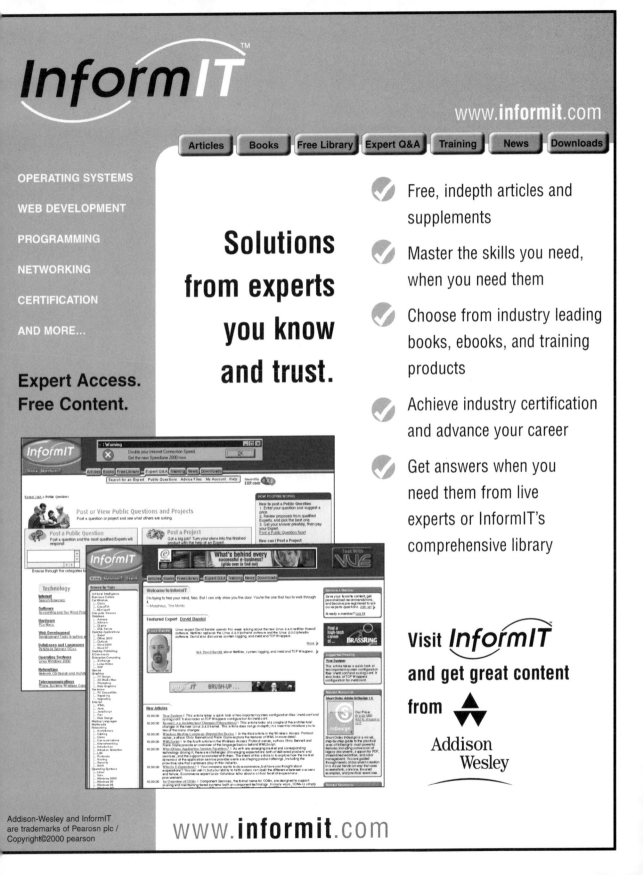

Register
Your Book

at www.aw.com/cseng/register

You may be eligible to receive:

- Advance notice of forthcoming editions of the book
- Related book recommendations
- Chapter excerpts and supplements of forthcoming titles
- Information about special contests and promotions throughout the year
- Notices and reminders about author appearances, tradeshows, and online chats with special guests

Contact us

If you are interested in writing a book or reviewing manuscripts prior to publication, please write to us at:

Editorial Department
Addison-Wesley Professional
75 Arlington Street, Suite 300
Boston, MA 02116 USA
Email: AWPro@aw.com

Addison-Wesley

Visit us on the Web: http://www.aw.com/cseng